THE FRENCH REVOLUTION
AND BRITISH CULTURE

THE
FRENCH
REVOLUTION
AND
BRITISH
CULTURE

EDITED BY
CERI CROSSLEY
AND
IAN SMALL

Oxford New York
OXFORD UNIVERSITY PRESS
1989

Oxford University Press, Walton Street, Oxford OX2 6DP
Oxford New York Toronto
Delhi Bombay Calcutta Madras Karachi
Petaling Jaya Singapore Hong Kong Tokyo
Nairobi Dar es Salaam Cape Town
Melbourne Auckland
and associated companies in
Berlin Ibadan

Oxford is a trade mark of Oxford University Press

Published in the United States
by Oxford University Press, New York

Introduction © Ian Small 1989
Essays © the individual authors 1989
This collection © Oxford University Press 1989

British Library Cataloguing in Publication Data
The French revolution and British culture.
1. British Culture, History. Influence on French
revolution 1789–1799
I. Small, Ian   II. Crossley, Ceri
941
ISBN 0–19–215893–7

Library of Congress Cataloging in Publication Data
The French Revolution and British culture/edited by Ceri Crossley
and Ian Small.
p.cm.
1. Great Britain—Civilization—18th century. 2. Great Britain—
Civilization—19th century. 3. Great Britain—Civilization—French
influences. 4. France—History—Revolution, 1789–1799—Influence.
5. France—Foreign relations—Great Britain. 6. Great Britain—
Foreign relations—France.   I. Crossley, Ceri.   II. Small, Ian.
DA520.F72   1989   941.07—dc20   89–31652
ISBN 0–19–215893–7

Typeset by Cambrian Typesetters, Frimley, Surrey
Printed in Great Britain by
Biddles Ltd, Guildford and King's Lynn

CONTENTS

ACKNOWLEDGEMENTS

THE editors would like to record their gratitude to Dr Ben Benedikz, Rare Books Librarian in the University of Birmingham.

INTRODUCTION

The French Revolution and British Culture

THE essays in this volume attempt to illustrate the complexity and diversity of the influence of the French Revolution upon British thought, and in so doing they controvert two widely held assumptions. The first, derived in part from the work of British social and cultural historians, is that the impact of the Revolution was slight—that among all European countries its influence was felt least in Britain.[1] The second view, this time derived principally from literary historians, is that the influence of the French Revolution was that of a controlling myth, making possible the forms of much of Britain's literary and artistic culture.[2] However much these two traditional views might seem to be in opposition to each other, their apparent contradiction stems to a large extent from the fairly unsophisticated concept of influence which they invoke as an explanation. That the French Revolution has been interpreted in so many different ways is, as much as anything else, simply an indication of the nature of the complexity of its influence.

This complexity, operating at the same time on many levels, becomes clear if the concept of influence between national cultures is defined a little more carefully. The first distinction to be made is that influence between national cultures occurs in both manifest and covert ways; the second is that, given this qualification, there are different degrees and different kinds of influence operating in quite unrelated disciplines of thought. Hence the nature of literary or artistic activity ensures that the influence of the ideology of the French Revolution for artists and writers will be quite different from its effects on the disciplines of history, sociology, or politics: such diversity of influence is only the product of the different disciplinary perspectives and preoccupations of those influenced.

None the less it is possible to categorize loosely the range of influence of the Revolution on British thought. In the first place there is manifest and positive influence: the clearest example here, and that most usually recognized and documented, is influence operating in the areas of statecraft and politics. This direct influence is best seen in the well-rehearsed view of British nineteenth-century social and political history, that British

gradualism, together with a belief in tradition and thus in ameliorative social legislation, opposed itself to the French idea of revolutionary change. Some of the contributors to this volume reassess
aspects of this influence; they describe the ways in which the experience of, and attitude towards, Revolutionary France were instrumental in forming elements of British political thought throughout
the nineteenth century. George Woodcock describes how British
reactions to the French Revolution were determined to a large
extent by the historiography of the Glorious Revolution of 1688.
John Harris discusses a hitherto neglected topic in the area of
influence, the effect of the Revolution on the transfer of technology
from Britain to France, and contrasts the *dirigiste* aspects of the
French economy, before and after the Revolution, with the *laissez-
faire* economy of Britain. Lord Beloff analyses the impact of
Revolution upon British statecraft and describes how experiences
of it were instrumental in determining British reactions to the
Russian Revolution. Some of the details of the assimilation of the
politics of the Revolution into the fabric of British political life are
rehearsed by Clive Emsley, who writes about the impact of the
Revolution on British radical thought; and by Brian Rigby, who
analyses the representation of the Revolution in one key British
periodical publication.

The other category of influence is broader and less easy to
identify immediately, for it is of a covert nature. Here it is
possible to detect two kinds of influence at work. The first may be
termed a *self-conscious* engagement with French Revolutionary
ideas: an attempt, that is, to assimilate them by adapting them to fit
British traditions. In a British context, the 'covert' thus begins to be
identifiable with subversiveness. A good example exists in the
reactions to the early English Romantic poets to Revolutionary
ideas. English Romantic poets began by rehearsing avant-garde
ideas derived from the Revolution, but only to disown them later—
in a way that is strikingly reminiscent of later British avant-garde
writers and artists. (The essay in this volume by Ian Small and
Josephine Guy examines the instrumentality of the Revolutionary
myth in shaping the avant-garde in British art and literature,
although at first glance the relationship between French Revolutionary ideals and the conservatism of nineteenth-century British
artists is not easy to see.) Indeed, this self-conscious use of influence
was recognized fairly soon after the event: in periodicals published

as early as the 1820s, for example, it is possible to find critics assessing the consequences of the French Revolution on English literature. Later in the century a critic as celebrated as Edward Dowden could describe the effects of the Revolution in a similar way: such effects were local and specific, but finally of no lasting use within a British context.[3]

The second kind of covert influence, though, is more pervasive, because it invariably involves the assimilation of what may be termed *subconscious*, and certainly unavoidable, ideas derived from the Revolution. This assimilation affected a whole variety of disciplines of thought. Immediate memories of the Revolution faded very quickly. One historian has estimated that by 1826 in France two-thirds of the citizenry were under 40 and that only one-ninth of the French population could remember the Ancien Régime.[4] But as memories of the Revolution faded, so it took on the status of a myth. One of the clearest and best-documented examples of the impact of this Revolutionary myth is upon language itself, particularly upon the creation of neologisms. Coinages such as 'sansculotte', 'terrorist', 'Jacobin', or 'le peuple'; or the semantic changes in political terms such as 'republic' or 'nation', all point to the linguistic significance of the Revolution, where ideological shifts resulted in the creation of a new language of politics, which in its turn made the articulation of changes in sensibility and civilization possible.[5] Hence in the post-Revolutionary world, in both France and Britain, certain terms, such as 'mass' or 'terror', became charged with new meanings. In a demonstration of how these specific changes took effect, another of the essayists in this volume, David Lodge, argues that the Revolution informed the way in which a whole generation of British novelists represented violence, particularly mob violence. By 1800, as Lennard J. Davis has pointed out the discourse of fiction had become autonomous, distinct, that is, from the discourses of journalism and of history, to which its origins had been intimately related.[6] The novel, by virtue of this new status as exclusively fiction, could thus examine and explore neologisms derived from journalism and history; and so in the first half of the nineteenth century, fiction could utilize certain subversive words or ideas which journalism could not. Hence the mob, with its incomprenhensible anger but equally incomprehensible potency, became virtually a 'character' in English literature in writers as diverse as Carlyle, Dickens, Gaskell, and Arnold.

There are many other examples of this type of covert influence: indeed, perhaps the most persistent was that which caused many forms of human activity to be seen for the first time in explicitly political terms. As the Revolution generated a new politics and a new political language, so it provided a means whereby complex political issues could be simplified, first by offering simplifications of the concepts themselves—such as liberty—and second by providing a simplified political rhetoric or polemic. In France the Revolution put liberty, equality, and fraternity, considered as political values, simply beyond question. It is well known that the French Revolution occasioned the central British texts of political philosophy of the eighteenth century—those of Burke and Paine. Indeed an essay by Roger Scruton in this volume maintains that the arguments of Burke in *Reflections on the Revolution in France* are strikingly relevant to contemporary national and international political debates. During the course of the nineteenth century, the French Revolution motivated a debate about the nature of political liberty and political equality. Here one of the important issues— articulated most famously perhaps by John Stuart Mill in his essays *On Liberty* and *On Representative Government*—was whether liberty and equality were in fact finally compatible. A consequence of this debate, particularly in the context of the agitation for franchise reform (an issue once more widely documented in a whole tradition of mid-century popular fiction) was that, if liberty and equality were indeed incompatible, then the liberty of the individual might be the more important value.

The same general impetus towards the politicization of explanations of human behaviour can be seen in the well-documented divergence in developments in historiography in Britain and France after 1800. (In this volume, John Clive continues this discussion, documenting the lessons derived from the Revolution in the work of one of its most famous British historians, Macaulay.) One of the crucial areas of debate in this respect lies in the historical representations of the Revolution itself, which, together with the decline of the Roman Empire, was perhaps the most systematically analysed historical subject in the nineteenth century. (The reasons for the conjunction, of course, are that both were perceived as different forms of decline; and the topic of decline had inescapably important lessons for Britain and her Empire.) In his *History and Historians in the Nineteenth Century*, G. P. Gooch has identified three kinds of early French histories of the Revolution: the first were those narrative historians, exemplified by Thierry and Michelet, whose interests were pro-revolutionary and who saw the 'mass' as the subject of history; the second group comprises those historians whose aim was to explain events rather than narrate them, historians such as Guizot and Mignet; and the third group were historians such as Thiers, whose object in undertaking a detailed narrative of events was political.[7] Such a categorization points to the most significant distinction between British and French history, for the main feature of the historiography of the Revolution in France was that the writing of history, from the work of Buchez through to that of Lamartine and Tocqueville, became increasingly political in its implications. The culmination of the process was perhaps the creation for Alphonse Aulard of a chair of the history of the French Revolution at the Sorbonne in 1885. For Aulard the processes of the past culminated in the Revolution; it was, as it were, the consummation of the past. Taking as his subject French historiography during the Restoration, Stanley Mellon has made precisely this point: that for a significant period in the nineteenth century—that of the Restoration—the writing of history was a function of politics: that history was popular precisely because it was the language of politics.[8] Every political issue was given a historical dimension and every historical issue was given a political dimension. Mellon went on to suggest reasons for this state of affairs: that, with the rapid succession of Ancien Régime, Revolution, and Empire, and a withered system of restoration and constitutional monarchy, French historians looked to the past for some precedents to support a future. More importantly, the liberal account of French history, propagandizing a view of the Revolution acquitted of its crimes, was an attempt to split the conservative coalition of monarchy, clergy, and aristocracy. The liberals' discovery from history was that such a coalition had not always been united, and hence that old antagonisms might be capable of being revived. The writing of history was thus inevitably involved in the practice of politics.

That the reactions of British historians to the French Revolution were profoundly different has been amply documented by Hedva Ben-Israel.[9] She has argued that, despite local differences of opinion, the Whig, Tory, and Radical views of the Revolution underwent remarkably little change throughout the course of the nineteenth century. She has claimed that it is impossible to categorize British histories of the Revolution along party lines: that is, the politics of historiography in Britain did not manifest itself as it had done in France. Historiography *was* political, of course, but its politics were not immediately apparent. Indeed, historians in Britain attributed the causes of the Revolution to the whims of individuals rather than to a set of abstract principles embodied—so their French counterparts claimed—by the Revolution. Moreover, British historians insisted upon treating the Revolution in terms of political and social rebellion. Ben-Israel has also argued that a consistent feature of much nineteenth-century European historiography was to interpret history in terms of the general ideas, forces, or processes which underlay particular historical events, an intellectual tendency which itself owed something to the view that the French Revolution seemed to follow a course determined by abstract notions. But British historians, on the other hand, were hostile to such arguments. Causation, in their minds, was always related to *human*, and invariably individual, agency. The concept of historiography which invoked collective explanations of historical events diminished the responsibility of individual human actants and thus threatened to dispense with morality. The course of the Revolution in British eyes was always determined by human agency and was thus invariably seen in terms of criminality or error. J. W. Burrow has described the course of such debates in Britain, charting the shift from Macaulay's dramatic, personal, and heroic history to William Stubbs's arguments for an archeological and constitutional history modelled on contemporary German scholarship. The model of German scholarship was amenable to the British because Germany too had evolved a reaction to the Revolution which was patriotic, populist, and traditionalist, asserting the primacy of practical reason above abstract systematizing, and asserting too the uniqueness of a nation's historic legal institutions.[10] A lecture by Stubbs to an Oxford audience in 1876 is particularly revealing: to teach the history of the French Revolution and the Great Revolution of 1688 was, for Stubbs, simply too dangerous.[11] Indeed the controversies over the teaching of certain periods of history and the introduction of certain sorts of historiography into the curriculum in British universities relate to the problems of the introduction of sociology into Britain. Both disciplines were entrusted to social élites which had powerful vested

interests in keeping to descriptive rather than analytic methodologies. Moreover British historiography was effectively immune
from radical change. When in 1857, in his *History of Civilization in
England*, the historian Henry Buckle challenged the hegemony of
these views, it was by invoking a concept of material causation. The
subsequent debate over the scientific status of history was also a
debate about a materialist determinism and the cherished Victorian
value of free-will. British historiography rejected Buckle's highly
abstract and systematized notions of universal laws and instead
followed the German model of specialization and archival research.[12]

The point of all this is that the French Revolution, and the
intellectual revolution it was instrumental in bringing about,
determined, albeit negatively, the direction of much British thought.
Revolutionary historiography developed concepts of collective
activity and impersonal social processes. British historiography, on
the other hand, retained concepts of tradition and of the primacy of
individual agency, but largely in reaction to those competing
Revolutionary explanations of human behaviour.

A similar pattern of 'negative' influence can be detected in other
areas of nineteenth-century intellectual controversy, particularly in
the formation of sociology as a discrete discipline. At the most
simple level, the disruptive and destructive function of the French
Revolution satisfied the primary precondition for sociological
thought, namely a fundamental doubt about the very premiss of
society. The Revolution made necessary some kind of theoretical
analysis of the very nature or structure of the new society which it
had brought about. In Britain, though, where historiography had
alienated the concept of revolution from British history, and
valorized instead constitutional continuity, there were no such
corresponding doubts. Indeed the impetus was in the opposite
direction: towards a complacency which took for granted one
single concept of society. Social ills were perceived only as social
problems requiring cosmetic changes, piecemeal reforms which did
not challenge the underlying structure of society. Thus British
society was immune from sociological inquiry in a way which
French society was not. The French Revolution, however, though
playing a central role in the history of social thought, was more
catalyst than agent of this intellectual controversy, for there were
far deeper ideological differences between the two cultures.

Geoffrey Hawthorn has described the differences between French and British post-enlightenment traditions of social thought.[13] What characterized the French intellectual tradition was its rationalist, deductive, and monist systems of thought rather than the empiricist and inductive methods operating in Britain. Moreover, in post-Revolutionary France, the monistic confidence of the rationalists prevailed, a confidence that there was one principle which, if established, would produce a society at once just, coherent, and enduring, in which the intellectual and institutional errors of the past would be swept away. Such confidence in its turn led to the foundation of classical sociology with its vision of revolution and reconstruction; and it was to allow the construction of systems as all-embracing and as comprehensive as the ecclesiastical and monarchic models which it attempted to challenge or supersede. On the other hand, British social thinking, in a manner similar to historiographical speculation, took as its model of authority the individual: there was no collective authority demanding submission, such as the church, the monarchy, or the state. Nor, correspondingly, was there a belief in an overarching principle, only in the notion of a variety of causes, effects, and futures, each changing according to circumstances. These conflicting ideologies necessarily gave rise to different sorts of social and sociological thought, and they also account for the failure of analytic sociology to become securely based in Britain. For sociology to emerge as a discrete and socially valued field of intellectual inquiry, existing intellectual patterns had to be overturned. Philip Abrams has argued that in Britain the intimate nature of the relationship between institutions and intellectual activity made such a rupture difficult, if not impossible.[14] The intellegentsia, then as now, was sponsored by a set of social institutions which guaranteed its conservative nature: British intellectual activity was intimately involved with the political, ecclesiastical, and social élites of the country, which ensured that British thinking about social concerns was always in a direction which openly discouraged the foundation of a tradition of analytic sociology. As a consequence, social science became reduced to matters of facts and figures—to the domain of the famous Victorian Blue Books: the governmental inquiries and statistical surveys which made those books possible were derived from (and in their turn strengthened the base of) those British traditions of empirical research. Hence, what sociology there was in Britain came about under a set of political restraints and grew out of statistical analyses, finally formalized in the creation of the National Association for the Promotion of Social Science in the 1850s. In the middle years of the nineteenth century, social problems presented themselves only as surface problems, in that they triggered no ideological crisis and could be met by ameliorative social reform. Indeed, all mid-century social research eschewed systems of analytic inquiry: *analytic* sociology was unlikely to occur in Britain precisely because of the fundamentally *descriptive* strategies of statistical analysis. J. W. Burrow has taken this argument even further and argued that the weakness of theoretical sociology in Britain derived from the fact that its evolutionary (rather than revolutionary) preoccupations led it all too easily away from the domain of structural analyses of society.[15] However, in the 1870s, for the first time in the century, social and economic conditions *did* result in a crisis in ideology, one of the consequences of which was a debate over the function and direction of the human and social sciences, a debate in which French analytic thought, represented by Auguste Comte's systematic sociology, was firmly rejected.[16]

French sociologists, on the other hand, could utilize recent French speculation in historiography in a manner effectively impossible for their British counterparts. If the effect of post-Revolutionary French historiography was to give a new importance to the political in history, it was also to assign significance to the historical in sociology. Post-Revolutionary French sociology was to emphasize the fact that societies were located in history, and were therefore susceptible of change *through* history; and thus the task of the new analytical French sociology was to explain the workings of *change* in societies.[17]

These, then, are the general directions in which the French Revolution exercised its influence upon British intellectual culture: in a variety of complex ways and in a variety of otherwise unrelated disciplines of thought. Thus the subject of this volume is twofold. It is a documentation of the extent of some of the most significant post-Revolutionary cultural exchanges; but more importantly it is an elucidation of the nature of those exchanges. As such, it might perhaps throw some light on the importance of the French Revolution in the creation of modern British cultural and social values, and on the continuing relevance of the issues of the Revolution for contemporary British political life.

IAN SMALL

NOTES

[1] This view has a long pedigree; the most recent example is a review by Theodore Zeldin of George Rudé, *The French Revolution* (London, 1988) in the *Sunday Times* (11 Sept. 1988).

[2] This view has an equally long tradition. For a recent example, see Carl Woodring, *Politics in English Romantic Poetry* (Massachusetts, 1970).

[3] See, for example, the anonymous 'The Influence of the French Revolution on English Literature', *Edinburgh Magazine* (Sept. 1824), pp. 305–10; and Edward Dowden, *The French Revolution and English Literature* (London, 1897).

[4] For estimates of the French population during these years, and speculation about the consequences of demographic patterns, see F. W. J. Hemmings, *Culture and Society in France* (Leicester, 1987).

[5] See J. M. Roberts, *The French Revolution* (Oxford, 1978), p. 76.

[6] See Lennard J. Davis, *Factual Fictions: The Origins of the English Novel* (New York, 1983).

[7] G. P. Gooch, *History and Historians* (London, 1913; rev. edn., London, 1952).

[8] Stanley Mellon, *The Political Uses of History: A Study of Historians in the French Restoration* (California, 1958).

[9] Hedva Ben-Israel, *English Historians on the French Revolution* (Cambridge, 1968).

[10] J. W. Burrow, *A Liberal Descent: Victorians and the English Past* (Cambridge, 1981).

[11] Ibid. 98–9.

[12] For an amplification of this point, see T. W. Heyck, *The Transformation of Intellectual Life in Victorian England* (London, 1982).

[13] Geoffrey Hawthorn, *Enlightenment and Despair: A History of Social Theory* (2nd edn., Cambridge, 1987).

[14] See Philip Abrams, *The Origins of British Sociology: 1834–1914* (Chicago, 1968).

[15] See J. W. Burrow, *Evolution and Society: A Study in Victorian Social Thought* (Cambridge, 1966).

[16] For details of the collapse of the ideology of political economy, see S. Collini, D. Winch, and J. Burrow, *That Noble Science of Politics: A Study in Nineteenth Century Intellectual History* (Cambridge, 1983).

[17] It is worth noting in passing, however, that the direction of much nineteenth-century French sociology was also conservative; but, by seeking to retain what was essential to the Revolution, its conservatism was once more different from that of British sociology. See Robert A. Nisbet, 'Conservatism and Sociology', *American Journal of Sociology* 58 (1952), 167–75.

The Meaning of Revolution in Britain 1770–1800

GEORGE WOODCOCK

THE French Revolution was a dramatic and decisive event in British history, most of all because the wars it precipitated dominated English politics and ruled the island economy for more than twenty years. The processes that in later generations were to be called the Industrial and Agricultural Revolutions were certainly accelerated by the increased need for war supplies and for food grown at home, and changes in the structure of society that had already begun in the late eighteenth century were hastened as the industrial cities grew in size and in population, a development that made inevitable, during the decades after the French wars came to an end, the beginning of that process of political reform which continued through the nineteenth century and into the twentieth and in part at least saved Britain from a revolution of the French kind.

In a more direct way the French Revolution influenced British political attitudes by creating a more articulate and more sharply focused kind of radicalism than that which had existed before and by changing in British minds the meaning of the word 'revolution', which was already such a familiar term—and concept—in eighteenth-century England; so much so that Edward Thompson was justified in warning us, in *The Making of the English Working Class*: 'Too often events in England in the 1790s are seen only as a reflected glow from the storming of the Bastille. But the elements precipitated by the French example—the Dissenting and libertarian traditions—reach far back into English history.'[1]

Within those traditions the idea of revolution was already important and, indeed, some of the excitement that English radicals experienced when they heard the news of the storming of the Bastille was due to an extraordinary synchronicity. Just over a hundred years before, the English had carried out their own Glorious Revolution, that of 1688 when James II was replaced by William III, and the French Revolution took place almost exactly a century after the English acquired in 1689 their own Bill of Rights, which they regarded as a protective constitution. The Revolution Societies established in 1788 to hold banquets and other celebrations of the Great Revolution served in the following year to celebrate what at first sight seemed like a very similar event in France.

But what the English meant by a revolution and the meaning that emerged across the Channel as events unfolded in their own unprecedented way were strikingly different, and one can fairly say that among the many things which the French Revolution changed drastically was the political meaning of the word 'revolution' itself. It was a word that had been used originally as early as the fourteenth century in astronomical contexts; it appears thus in Gower and Chaucer, and when it was transferred metaphorically to political events the cyclical connotations lingered. A political revolution in the seventeenth century meant usually not merely the overthrow of an usurpatory government but also the restoration of what contemporaries regarded as a desirable past state of affairs. Thus writers such as Clarendon and Burnet referred to the Restoration of Charles II after the interlude of the Commonwealth as a 'revolution', and the 'prodigious revolution' of 1688, as Evelyn called it in writing to his fellow diarist Pepys, was not merely seen as a return to the true English constitution after the attempted despotism of James II, but was accepted as necessary not only by Whigs and Radicals, but even by Tories such as Bolingbroke, who in 1752 remarked that the maladministration of James II had made a revolution necessary and possible.

Pride in the Revolution of 1688, which they regarded as distinguishing them from the people of the rest of Europe, was widespread among all classes in Britain. The upper classes regarded it as a guarantee of their position, their privileges, and their power; the great Whig lords, the county oligarchies of Tory squires, the city corporations—corrupt and uncorrupt—saw their roles as guaranteed by the Revolution, if not originating in it. Even the radical artisans who accepted the name of Jacobin and in the 1790s formed their organizations to fraternize with the French revolutionaries and further their own reformist aims, were proud of the fact that their freedoms were respected; even in 1793, when the reaction against events in France was beginning to limit liberties in England, the London Corresponding Society—the most prominent radical organization in the country at the time—compared favourably the condition of English common people in the eighteenth century with that of ordinary Frenchmen before the Revolution.

The cyclic view of revolution, as a swinging back towards a better and more innocent past, has never been entirely eliminated from radical thinking. The idea that men have been corrupted by civilization, that (as Thomas Paine put it in an early work) 'Government, like dress, is the badge of our lost innocence',[2] persisted among anarchist theoreticians well into the nineteenth century and even at times gave an archaicist flavour to the arguments of Marx and Engels. It was there in Rousseau and other European thinkers of the years before 1789, but it also had its English roots. Less prominent, because less politically dangerous, than its Jacobite counterpart, the tradition of the Commonwealth persisted among English dissenters, and in the earlier half of the eighteenth century it was manifest to such an extent that in 1743, just two years before the '45, the Earl of Egmont actually considered 'a republican spirit' the most serious threat at the time to the constitutional compromise achieved in 1688–9.

Certainly there were strong echoes of the programme of the Levellers of the Civil War period in the arguments of English radicals who appeared during the 1770s, before and during the insurrection in the North American colonies. Major John Cartwright, who lived to an extraordinary age for his period (dying at 84 years of age in 1824), spanned the era between the American Revolution and the Chartist movement, and, with a number of like-minded democrats whose roots were entirely British, helped pave the way for a sympathic reaction to the French Revolution.

Cartwright was a naval officer who fought in the Seven Years War, rose to the rank of lieutenant, and retired from the service in 1775 because of ill health; he owed the title by which he was generally known to his later service in the militia, from which he was dismissed in 1789 for welcoming the fall of the Bastille. On leaving the navy he immediately expressed his sympathy for the rebels in the American colonies, and combined his support of them with a more general attack on the undemocratic nature of the British parliamentary system which echoed the contentions of the Levellers, reviving their call for adult male suffrage and annual parliaments in *Take Your Choice*, the first of his many pamphlets, which he published in 1776; later, in 1780, he called for equal electoral districts and for the payment of members of parliament.

The continuity of the native English radical tradition would be shown by the eventual incorporation of the proposals of the 'good grey Major' in the People's Charter, the key manifesto of the Chartist movement, more than sixty years later in 1838. But Cartwright did not merely swing the political clock back to the Civil War. He argued that a genuine democracy of the kind he advocated had existed in Saxon times, and that he was therefore only proposing a return to the practice of the English peoples before the political structure was corrupted by the introduction of a Norman kingdom based on aristocratic privilege. Other pamphleteers of the 1770s had even more radical proposals for bringing about a return to the pristine political order they saw existing in the past. James Burgh and Obadiah Hulme actually suggested the foundation of a national association, which would be a kind of quasi-revolutionary convention, existing outside parliament and—having gained the support of the people—virtually dictating its terms for reform to the existing legislature.

One of the most important shifts of viewpoint that would emerge after 1789 under the influence of events in France was a change in the view of revolution (and even of reform), a feeling that it meant not the re-establishment of a lost and regretted past, but the creation of a new present flowing into a future that would be quite different from anything in the past. Such a concept had been transferred from millenarian religion to politics by a few chiliasts during the Civil War period (notably the Fifth Monarchy Men who inherited the theocratic utopianism of the Anabaptists), and in a different way by the Diggers, but it had been submerged during the eighteenth century by the view of the 'great' revolutions of the preceding century as occasions of restoration rather than of radical change.

The French Revolution, taking place in a country that had no radical traditions like Britain, and therefore no myth of revolution as a cyclic process, assumed an entirely different direction and opened the era that would be dominated by another myth, that of progress, whether revolutionary or evolutionary, which rejected the past as a model and set its goals in the future, during which humanity and human society would draw ever nearer to perfection. The emergence of this new view of social change was celebrated in one of the key books of the period, Paine's *Rights of Man*, in which he finally repudiated all searchings in the past for the precedence of a just society, and declared: 'Every age and generation must be as free to act for itself, *in all cases*, as the ages and generations which preceded it. The vanity and presumption of governing beyond the grave, is the most ridiculous and insolent of all tyrannies.'[3]

It was this encouragement to look forward rather than backward that was to distinguish the influence of the French Revolution from that of the American Revolution in Britain. The American insurrectionaries were revolutionaries in the old rather than the new style, and very few of them were true Levellers. What they mainly sought was to make real for themselves the gains of the Great Revolution of 1688, to have their own constitution based in the same principles, and if that called for total independence, as Thomas Paine advised them in his early pamphlet, *Common Sense* (1775), they were willing to seek it. But by no means all of the American revolutionaries were as willing as some of their English radical contemporaries to take up the arguments of John Lilburne and his fellows during the Commonwealth and call for universal adult male suffrage. The Declaration of Independence may have claimed that 'all men are created equal', but in practice the American Revolution modified the idea considerably; as Ian Christie has remarked, 'Property and the vote were still coupled after 1776, as they had been before', and when human beings were property, as the slaves remained, a radical transformation of society became impossible.[4] This explains why Edmund Burke, one of the more conservative among the Whig upholders of the settlement of 1688 and its constitutional compromise, could plead the cause of the American rebels, and yet, when the French Revolution brought a challenge to his idea of a constitutional system of checks and balances, he could break with his former associates, such as Charles James Fox, and denounce the events in France even before the Jacobins had moved into a position of control.

With all the extravagant generosity of his nature, Fox hailed the fall of the Bastille with uncritical enthusiasm; he saw it as 'much the greatest event . . . that ever happened in the world'; in a speech of April 1791 he declared that he admired the new constitution of France, describing it as 'the most stupendous and glorious edifice of liberty, which had been erected on the foundation of human integrity in any time or country'.[5] It was the voice of a classic English libertarian welcoming what he took to be the liberation of a fellow people long oppressed.

The political association and the long personal friendship between Fox and Burke was to break at this point, for Burke saw immediately in the French insistence on 'natural rights' a challenge to his belief in 'natural order', and he recognized in their proposal of a democracy that would dispense with aristocracy and monarchy the opposite of the constitutional balance achieved by the Revolution of 1688, and indeed a return to what for him were obviously the aberrations of the Commonwealth from which England had escaped through the restoration of the monarchy in 1660 and its modification in 1688. As early as 1790, speaking in the House of Commons on the Army Estimates, he prophesied that the French would establish a very bad government—a very bad species of tyranny.[6] He had this prescient insight at a time when not only Fox, but even William Pitt had great hopes for the outcome of events in France, the latter hoping that the 'present convulsions' might end in 'general harmony and regular order', with France enjoying eventually 'that just kind of liberty which I venerate'.[7]

It was Burke's reaction rather than Fox's or even Pitt's that in the end would prevail in Britain, dominating government policy, sharpening the lines of emergent class struggle, and isolating those who, as political circumstances changed and England became involved in warfare with Republican and Imperial France, persisted in manifesting their sympathies for the ideal of the French Revolution even if not always for the actual deeds of the revolutionaries. Yet, grafted onto the older stem of English radical traditions, the inspiration of the French Revolution continued to work in England, but so modified by local circumstances that the word *Jacobin*, applied to radicals indiscriminately by their opponents, meant something quite different from the kind of neo-totalitarian revolutionary centralism it connoted in France. Perhaps the best definition of English Jacobinism—one that would include Tom Paine, William Godwin, and William Hazlitt as well as the artisan leaders of the London and Sheffield Corresponding Societies—was that offered by John Thelwall in his *Rights of Nature*, published in 1796 when the anti-Jacobin persecution was reaching its height in Britain:

In this discussion I adopt the term Jacobinism without hesitation—

1. Because it is fixed upon us, as a stigma, by our enemies . . .

2. Because, though I abhor the sanguinary ferocity of the late Jacobins

in France, yet their principles ... are the most consonant with my ideas of reason, and the nature of man, of any that I have met with.... I use the term Jacobinism simply to indicate *a large and comprehensive system of reform, not professing to be built upon the authorities and principles of the Gothic custumary.*[8]

Here we are listening to the voice of mainstream English radical thought, most of whose spokesmen adapted their arguments to the circumstances of the time, taking inspiration successively from events in the Thirteen Colonies and in France, but never losing sight of the fact that they were seeking changes in society that would suit English conditions and manifest English libertarian traditions. And as we turn to the trends in English political and social life that were in some degree influenced by the French Revolution, we find that they arose among a series of interpenetrating groups that were already predisposed, by a radical view of the settlement of 1688, to be sympathetic to the movement that brought an end to Europe's most powerful autocratic monarchy.

Four groups can be roughly identified. First were the radical Whigs, the followers of Charles James Fox and his associates, drawn mainly from the younger aristocracy and the gentry, who considered themselves the true heirs of the Great Revolution, seeking to preserve the constitution which they saw threatened by the persistent efforts of the Hanoverian kings to influence political decisions; they had seen the American uprising as a vindication of their arguments against concentration of authority in a single person, place, or class, and they viewed the French Revolution in the same way; they were not afraid—at least in Fox's case—to talk of the sovereignty of the people and to contemplate the end of monarchy if the people willed it. Yet, like Thelwall and most of the other people who in Britain at this period became known as Jacobins, they were at heart reformers rather than revolutionaries (in the sense outlined above).

The second group consisted of the Dissenting intellectuals and their followers who, more than any other group in England, preserved the heritage of the Commonwealth period in their doctrinal inheritances from the seventeenth-century sectarians. Presbyterians, Congregationalists, Baptists, Quakers, and members of tiny offshoot sects like the Sandemanians, many of them had proceeded along the paths of heresy towards such quasi-rationalist doctrines as Unitarianism and even Deism, and their resistance to

religious authority inclined them to oppose secular authority. The
Dissenters of the eighteenth century maintained a high intellectual
tradition; excluded from the Anglican-dominated universities, they
ran their own academies, such as those as Hoxton and Hackney,
where a notable level of scholarship was sustained. Some of the
most prominent Dissenters were among the intellectual leaders of
Britain in the later eighteenth century, and even, like Joseph
Priestley, the discoverer of oxygen, had international reputations as
scientists and scholars.

The links were strong and often direct between the Dissenting
intellectuals and the third group who were stimulated—and later
often disillusioned—by the French Revolution, the radical writers
who provided the intellectual stimulus for the Romantic movement.
Hazlitt, the son of a Unitarian minister, attended the Hackney
Academy and studied there under Joseph Priestley. Godwin, in his
youth an adherent of the Sandemanians, who believed in sharing
property among the faithful, went to Hoxton, where he was taught
by one of Priestley's great rivals, Alexander Kippis. Tom Paine was
born a Quaker. William Blake, who wore the red cap of the
Jacobins in the streets of London and incorporated the Revolutionary
mystique into his millenarian visions, was brought up in a pious
nonconformist household, and Coleridge, though the son of a
Church of England parson, was attracted to religious as well as
political radicalism: he combined conversion to Unitarianism—and
a brief career as a preacher—with an enthusiasm for French
revolutionary principles, and later for the teachings of Godwin,
that led him and Robert Southey to conceive their quixotic plan of
creating a Utopian community, a 'Pantisocracy', on the shores of the
Susquehannah River in the Appalachian Mountains.

But the link between political dissent and dissenting religion was
not a necessary one. Shelley and Byron, belated Romantic
adherents of the ideals if not of the practices of the French
Revolution, had more in common, so far as origins were concerned,
with Fox, Sheridan, and the other radical Whigs of the 1780s than
with the puritanical middle-class moralists such as Joseph Priestley.
Wordsworth also stood outside the dissenting tradition, yet he
shared more directly through experience in the French Revolution
than any of his English fellow writers except Paine. His early life,
among the country people of Cumberland, had turned him into a
kind of natural populist, whose sense of how ordinary people spoke

and thought led him to conceive and attempt a poetry couched in the language of the populace.

In June 1790, less than a year after the fall of the Bastille, Wordsworth set off with his friend Robert Jones on a trip to France that was motivated as much by curiosity and a 20-year-old's sense of adventure as it was by radical idealism. But once he was there, he was caught up in the emotions of the time, so that he could look back and declare in *The Prelude*, that great verse autobiography which would not be published in his lifetime:

> Bliss was it in that dawn to be alive,
> But to be young was very heaven![9]

Yet he still saw the situation with the prosaic and practical eye of the poet who sought to speak like a common man and welcomed the pragmatic reality (congenial to a poet who would shortly deny any '*essential* difference between the language of prose and metrical composition')[10] of a situation in which 'the meek and lofty'

> Were called upon to exercise their skill,
> Not in Utopia,—subterranean fields,—
> Or some secreted island, Heaven knows where!
> But in the very world, which is the world
> Of all of us,—the place where, in the end,
> We find our happiness, or not at all![11]

Back in England, Wordsworth would become for the time being a devoted Godwinian, and though he soon moved in a conservative direction, and was bitterly reproached by steadfast Jacobin sympathizers such as Hazlitt for having betrayed the Revolution, it seems from his own account that his eventual desertion of the French cause sprang largely from his perception that it had itself betrayed the freedom of the ordinary man in Europe. In 1790 he had gone on from France to the forest cantons of Switzerland, where the Everlasting Compact of 1291 had created a viable peasant democracy almost five centuries before the fall of the Bastille. When the French armies, led by Napoleon, marched into Switzerland in 1798 and destroyed the liberties of that ancient confederacy, it seemed to Wordsworth that the Revolution had turned against real freedom. Long afterwards, thinking back to the 1790s and remembering the great conflict between the English and the French that began in 1793, he remarked: 'I disapproved of the

war against France at its commencement, thinking—which was
perhaps an error—that it might have been avoided; but after
Buonoparte had violated the independence of Switzerland, my
heart turned against him, and against the nation that could submit
to be the instrument of such an outrage.'[12]

Wordsworth was closer to the common man—the mountaineer
of Switzerland or the Lake District—in his feelings than in his way
of life or his political actions. But there were vital links between
other literary intellectuals of the time and the working radicals who
represented the fourth group to be deeply affected by the French
Revolution. These were the workers, and especially the artisans,
who at this time were beginning also to experience the effects of
that phenomenon which (perhaps significantly) the French economist Jérôme-Adolphe Blanqui (brother of the French nineteenth-
century neo-Jacobin Louis-Auguste Blarqui) would be the first to
call the Industrial Revolution.

It was during the 1790s, under the influence of events in France,
that the politically conscious working-class in England began to
develop, in bodies such as the Corresponding Societies, the kind of
organizational structures, controlled by themselves, that would
serve as models for later workers' movements, from Chartism
onwards, that appeared and reasserted an indigenous tradition
when the direct influence of the Jacobins had been diffused by time
and social change. But though a workers' movement inspired by a
consistent radical policy was a development of the 1790s, militant
expressions of unrest over social and economic issues had become
familiar features of English life much earlier in the eighteenth
century.

At that period, when the suffrage was so limited that the House
of Commons was elected by a tiny minority of the nation's
commoners, the ordinary people, having no formal voice in the
councils of the nation, resorted to direct action on a remarkably
wide scale, and at times they proved themselves a very effective
Third Estate. Almost any popular grievance was liable to bring the
rioters into the streets, and surprisingly often the authorities would
bow to the popular will expressed in this way.

Riots could take place over religion, such as those protesting
against concessions to the Jews in 1753 or the Gordon Riots of
1780 which, under the cry of 'No Popery!', helped to hinder and
delay the process of Catholic emancipation. Food riots were

particularly common at times of poor harvests, when the people suspected farmers and merchants of hoarding grain and waiting for prices to rise. Only a few of these riots aimed at mere looting; usually the rioters, led by artisans with some education, would seize stocks of grain and sell it at what were regarded as reasonable prices, handing the proceeds to the owners. Often the magistrates not merely condoned such direct action but actually supported it by issuing local regulations that sustained the will of the rioters. The great decentralization of eighteenth-century British society, which had no kind of regular police force and depended largely on the local gentry for the effective keeping of order, tended to favour such manifestations of the popular will.

The people rioted against the enclosure of land, against the militia laws, against the activities of the press gangs, against workhouses. When the government sought in 1736 to limit severely the scale and production of gin, widespread riots prevented the new laws from being applied. In the 1770s three thousand seamen took to the streets of Liverpool in protest against wage reductions, seized two cannon, and attacked the Exchange; the magistrates handled them leniently, releasing the ringleaders when they agreed to enlist in the Navy. And long before the advent of King Ludd, there were machine-wrecking riots protesting against new inventions that took work away from artisans and their families.

Indeed, there was hardly a decade in the eighteenth century, and hardly an industrial district, in which riots against innovatory techniques, usually accompanied by machine wrecking, did not take place. In the 1720s the Norfolk weavers rioted against the introduction of cotton printing, and in 1737 the women of Macclesfield destroyed looms and, when their leaders were arrested, went to jail and set them free. The Northumberland miners destroyed pithead gear in the 1740s and kept on doing it through the century. Hargreaves's first spinning jenny was destroyed by angry textile workers in 1767, and throughout the 1770s mobs rampaged through the Lancashire towns, destroying weaving machinery. The flying shuttle provoked similar direct action in the West Country during the 1780s, and in London the silk weavers of Spitalfields were so famous for their inclination to riot that in 1765 their actions prompted a scared Horace Walpole to speculate that the 'general spirit of mutiny and dissatisfaction in the lower people' posed a danger of rebellion and civil war.[13]

The general custom of referring to the protesting workers of the dawning industrial revolution as 'mobs' obscures the fact that a network of rudimentary organization had sprung up in the form of friendly societies and trade clubs, with quite elaborate structures and codes of behaviour. They were mainly local groups, but in some crafts the old custom of travelling journeymen had survived from the days of the medieval guilds; among the leather breeches makers, for example, local fraternities would provide a night's lodging and a shilling for the road for men who were tramping in seach of work, and in this way contact was maintained between workers in various parts of the country.

The aims of these groups were mainly economic, to organize mutual benefit systems and to protect the livings of their members, and they must be seen as the precursors of the trade unions rather than of working-class political parties, though their mode of organization would eventually be used as a model for the political clubs and societies of the French Revolutionary period.

Such clubs formed the nuclei for strike campaigns, and a revealing outburst by Chief Justice Lord Mansfield at the Lancashire Assizes in 1758 talked of 'several thousands' who had left their work and 'entered into combinations for raising their wages'. They had formed committees and 'established boxes and fixed stewards in every township for collecting money for such weavers as should by their Committee be ordered to leave their masters, and made other dangerous and illegal regulations'.[14] Despite repeated laws against combinations, the workers of eighteenth-century England kept on organizing to face the threats to their standard of living created by the industrial innovations of the period.

Most of the industrial direct action I have described took place in relatively small communities usually dominated by a single industry. London, which by the late eighteenth century was Europe's largest city, with a population nearing three quarters of a million, many times that of any other British community, presented an entirely different situation. There was no single dominant industry, and the vast heterogenous population, with its crowds of discontented apprentices and its swarms of destitute people living in the appalling slums known as rookeries, turned the city into a potential social volcano. There were thousands of people in London ready at any time and for any cause to go on the rampage, partly because it gave expression to their frustration and despair, partly because there was always something to be gained (even if their lives were risked in those hanging times) when the looting began, and partly because it gave them an illusory sense of power to threaten the lives of those in authority; William Pitt, just made Prime Minister, escaped with difficulty when his carriage was demolished by an angry crowd of Charles James Fox's supporters, and King George III was terrified when the mob attacked and stoned his coach in 1795.

If the lasting power of the mob was illusory, its immediate force was genuine, and mass political action in Britain sprang from the manipulation of the eighteenth-century London mob by political leaders, usually those out of power. At the very beginning of the Hanoverian period, riots by Tory and even Jacobite mobs were common in London, preluding the rising of 1715, and it was to deal with them that the Riot Act was passed in 1715.

Lord George Gordon used the mob for a bad end, to exploit religious intolerance, and Wilkes used it to enhance the drama of his personal battle against the establishment. Through that long battle, which lasted more than a decade, Wilkes won concrete victories for personal liberty. General warrants were declared illegal and a rigged parliament was finally forced by the obstinate voters of Middlesex to accept him as a member, partly through repeated re-elections and partly through tumultuous mass demonstrations. And though he himself lost interest in mass action once he was elected Lord Mayor of London in 1774 (and actually played an active part in suppressing the Gordon riots in 1780), the actions of Wilkes and his supporters changed the nature of political movements in England. Against the arguments of certain recent conservative historians, such as J. C. D. Clark, who in *English Society 1688–1832* described Wilkesism as 'a phenomenon which was as intellectually shallow as it was evanescent' and stated that Wilkes 'founded no tradition of mass action . . . and left no intellectual legacy',[15] one can quote, as a truer view of the role of Wilkes in the English radical tradition, the assessment of J. H. Plumb in *England in the Eighteenth Century*:

Wilkes by his actions and by his legal battles had confirmed important liberties, but his influence was more profound than this. He brought Parliament into great disrepute. He demonstrated by his actions its unrepresentative nature; its dependence on the Crown; its corruption and prejudice—facts known for decades, but never so amply demonstrated; nor had the danger to personal liberty, inherent in such a system, been so clearly proved. And the Wilkes agitation produced new political methods. The public meeting was born and stayed alive. The Supporters of the Bill of Rights Society was founded, the first political society which used modern methods of agitation—paid agents were sent round the country to make speeches, and the Press was deliberately and carefully exploited. Political dissatisfaction was given strength, and coherence, by deliberate organization.[16]

If Wilkes retired from the struggle, his associates often remained, so that there are direct links with later agitations through continuing organizations such as the Supporters of the Bill of Rights, founded in 1769, and through individuals such as John Horne Tooke, the philologist-revolutionary, who supported Wilkes in his agitations in the 1760s and was imprisoned for seditious libel because he defended the American rebels in 1778. For his support of the French Revolution Horne Tooke would be tried for high treason in 1794 and acquitted.

It is in fact from the Wilkesite agitation onwards that one can trace a confluence between radical trends in England and the trends in France that were moving towards the French Revolution. Horne Tooke had formed a Constitution Society during the early 1770s which in 1780 had turned into the Society for Constitutional Information, in which Tooke was joined by Major Cartwright, Capel Lofft, and Dr John Jebb, all of whom produced pamphlets dedicated to parliamentary reform and reviving the Leveller demands for equal representation, annual parliaments, and universal suffrage. John Jebb, in particular argued for campaigns of persistent agitation to achieve these aims, and proposed moving beyond normal parliamentary procedures, urging that the business of the reformers must be 'not to prevail with the deputies, but to animate the people'.[17] Somewhat less radical in their approach at this time were the dissenting leaders, well-known preachers or teachers at the nonconformist academies, largely Unitarians and Arians, who gathered at the 'Club of Honest Whigs' in London. They included not only men such as Richard Price and Joseph Priestley, who were to play notable roles during the era of the French Revolution, but also the Americans Benjamin Franklin and Josiah Quincy, who were in London during the 1770s, putting the case for the aggrieved colonies without much success. These men who combined religious and political dissent played their part in sustaining the continuity between late eighteenth-century English reformism and the ideas that were debated during the Commonwealth.

Even before the French Revolution the influence of what we generally talk of as the Enlightenment and of its writers was beginning to reach England and to have an effect on intellectuals that in various ways percolated to other parts of society. Earlier in the century it was the French, for instance Voltaire and Montesquieu, who came to England to learn from its examples of constitutional government, but by the 1770s English readers were beginning to find inspiration in the political and religious arguments and speculations of French or Swiss writers such as d'Holbach and Voltaire, Helvétius and Rousseau. As early as 1763 Peter Annet, an elderly schoolmaster, was imprisoned for blasphemy and put in the stocks because he had translated passages from Voltaire and published them in tract form. And William Godwin recorded how in 1781, while he was still a young dissenting minister, his faith was so shaken by the writings of Rousseau, Helvétius, and d'Holbach, that he took advantage of a dispute over alleged church discipline and left the pulpit for good. Later on, and especially after the French Revolution, the same writers reached a readership of educated artisans through being published in pamphlet form, and some years later Volney's *Ruins of Empire*, one of the classic works of the French Revolutionary era, enjoyed a similar vogue.

The French Revolution not only gave a new lease of life to existing reform organizations in England, but led to the establishment of radical organizations that for the first time began to organize working people on a political rather than an economic basis. The Society for Constitutional Information, which had become inactive in the mid-1780s, was revived by Horne Tooke, and at its meetings in the Crown and Anchor Tavern issued exhortations to the English to take heed of the French example. The Revolution Society, having in 1788 celebrated the centenary of the Glorious Revolution of 1688, met in 1789, with intellectuals such as William Godwin and John Thelwall present at its banquet, to send a congratulatory address to the French people and urge that, as the world's leading countries, France and Britain should work together and promote the cause of freedom worldwide. In 1791 Horne Tooke, ever active, summoned at the Thatched House Tavern in London a 'Select Meeting of the FRIENDS OF UNIVERSAL PEACE AND LIBERTY' which issued an 'Address and Declaration' calling on the British people to observe and profit by the French example. And in 1792 a group of the more radical Whig gentry, led by Charles Grey, founded the Society of Friends of the People; though Charles James Fox never joined it, it represented his particular type of aristocratic republicanism which was one of the several English responses to the French Revolution.

These were groupings of patrician or middle-class intellectuals or politicians. To the working population the appeal of the French Revolution was transmitted (insofar as the transmission was organizational) through avowedly plebeian organizations known as Corresponding Societies. On this level as much as any other, as E. P. Thompson has shown in his massive and classic book, *The Making of the English Working Class*, the French example was a precipitant of 'Dissenting and libertarian traditions' that 'reach far back into English history'. The agitation we associate with the Corresponding Societies 'was not an agitation about France, although French events both inspired and bedevilled it. It was an English agitation, of impressive dimensions, for an English democracy.'[18]

The initiative for founding the London Corresponding Society, the most important if not the first organization of its kind, came from the Scottish bootmaker Thomas Hardy. Hardy was typical of the serious-minded artisans who had formed the leadership of the trade clubs and friendly societies of preceding decades and had been active in the Wilkes campaigns for basic political liberties. He had been educated at a village school in Scotland where the pupils paid a penny a week, had been apprenticed to a shoemaker in Stirling, and had worked briefly as a bricklayer before he came to London as a journeyman in the boot trade during the later 1770s. He was a man of considerable piety, a pillar of the Scots Kirk in Covent Garden, and altogether an eminently sober and respectable citizen, shortly to set up as a master in his craft. In January 1792 he gathered a group of his friends, all of them artisans, for a meeting in the Bell Tavern in Exeter Street. He gave his own account of the meeting in a curiously detached manner, as if he were writing as an outside narrator:

They had finished their daily labour, and met there by appointment. After having their bread and cheese and porter for supper, as usual, and their pipes afterwards, with some conversation on the hardness of the times and the dearness of all the necessaries of life, which they, in common with their fellow citizens, felt to their sorrow, the business for which they had met was brought forward—*Parliamentary Reform*—an important subject to be deliberated upon and dealt with by such a class of men.[19]

Significantly, food prices, which had been the cause of riots throughout the eighteenth century, were pushed aside in favour not of the economic issues that had inspired earlier working men's organizations but of political action for a political end. Eight of the nine men agreed to form the London Corresponding Society, so called because it was intended to establish contact and co-ordinate activities by corresponding with like-minded societies that had already been founded in Sheffield, Derby, and Manchester, and with similar groups which it was expected would appear—as they did—in other provincial centres. The ninth man went home to think over his membership, and joined within a week.

The first rule of the society was that the number of its members be unlimited. A neophyte member had merely to answer affirmatively the question: 'Are you thoroughly persuaded that the welfare of these kingdoms require that every adult person, in possession of his reason, and not incapacitated by crimes, should have a vote for a Member of Parliament?'[20] Thomas Hardy became the Secretary of the Society, and its subscription was set at a penny a week to encourage a wide membership among working people.

The London Corresponding Society expanded rapidly. A fortnight after its foundation there were 25 members, but within six months this had grown to 2,000 and by the peak year of 1795 it reached, according to the most extravagant estimates, 30,000. The claims of the Society's leaders ranged between 2,000 (Francis Place) and 12–13,000 (Maurice Margarot) as an active membership; spies infiltrated by the government into the organization at this time, such as the famous 'Citizen Groves', gave lower figures, suggesting that Margarot's estimate took account of lapsed members still on the books, and we can probably accept as reasonably accurate E. P. Thompson's informed guess that there was an active membership of at least 2,000, a paying membership of 5,000, and a paper membership of 10,000.

The provincial societies, particularly in industrial cities such as Sheffield, may have had larger memberships in proportion to the local population. The Sheffield Society, founded late in 1791, already claimed 2,000 members by the spring of 1792, and this figure is given a degree of confirmation by the fact that the *Sheffield Register*, which supported the movement, reached the high circulation for that period of 2,000 copies weekly. The Sheffield Society in fact found its membership so unwieldy that it decentralized into small local divisions which were given the Old English name of 'tythings' and came together in a Grand Council.

The mass of the membership of these Corresponding Societies— shopkeepers, artisans, labourers—consisted of members of the working-class or the *petite bourgeoisie*, though there was a degree of cross-connection with the earlier patrician reform organizations, and among the active members of the London Corresponding Society were men such as Horne Tooke (the friend of Wilkes), the attorney John Frost, the playwright Thomas Holcroft, John Thelwall (the friend of Coleridge and Southey), and Maurice Margarot and Joseph Gerrald, members of the rich merchant class who would both eventually be paid for their enthusiasm with free voyages to Botany Bay.

Organizations such as the London Corresponding Society received the influence of the French Revolution in two ways: more or less directly, through their efforts to make and sustain contact with the revolutionaries in France and their eager and uncritical acceptance of the name of Jacobin and of revolutionary modes and manner; and directly through the mass of literature produced in Britain by the great intellectual debate that burst forth in the years immediately after the Revolution, and produced not only Edmund Burke's *Reflections on the Revolution in France*, but also no less than thirty-eight replies of various kinds, some of which, such as Tom Paine's *Rights of Man* and William Godwin's *An Enquiry concerning Political Justice*, were in the long run more influential than the book they answered, and others of considerable note in their time and in literary history, such as James Mackintosh's *Vindiciae Gallicae* and Mary Wollstonecraft's *A Vindication of the Rights of Man*.

Since its influence spread far beyond the English radical organizations of the 1790s, and perhaps represents the most important intrusion of the French Revolution into English intellectual life, I will deal with the literary controversy before the more directly political agitation of the Corresponding Societies and the reactions it evoked in British society.

The storm began in Burke's angry reaction to a discourse by Richard Price, one of the dissenting leaders who had given ardent support to the American rebels and in 1776 had published a book, *On Civil Liberty*, which became a quite remarkable best-seller for its period: 60,000 copies of the first edition sold immediately, and more than 100,000 copies of a later, cheaper edition. Price had also supported John Wilkes, and when the French Revolution came, the Bastille was taken, and Louis XVI was turned into a virtual prisoner in the Tuileries, he saw in this event, as did many of his dissenting associates, a reactivation not merely of the spirit of 1688 but also of that of the Commonwealth.

On 4 November 1789, Price delivered at the Meeting House in Old Jewry a kind of secular sermon at the celebration which the Society for Commemorating the Revolution in Great Britain held every year on William III's birthday. The Society claimed to have met in this way every year since 1688 without arousing much attention, but this year was different. Price took the opportunity to congratulate the French revolutionaries and to celebrate what he saw as the culmination of the aims of 1688. In doing so, whether aware of it or not, he was replacing the old cyclic concept of revolution by the new progressive one. Talking of the English Revolution, he stressed its incompleteness:

But the most important instance of the imperfect state in which the Revolution left our constitution, is the INEQUALITY OF OUR REPRESENT-ATION. I think, indeed, this defect in our constitution so gross and so palpable, as to make it excellent chiefly in form and theory. You should remember that a representation in the legislature of a kingdom is the *basis* of constitutional liberty in it, and of all legitimate government; and that without it a government is nothing but an usurpation.[21]

From this point Price went on to commend the French Revolution as if it offered a remedy to the deficiencies he had found in the settlement of 1688, and in his peroration he spoke, as H. N. Brailsford remarked, like Simeon hailing the coming of Christ and the salvation he brought.

I have lived to see THIRTY MILLIONS of people, indignant and resolute, spurning at slavery, and demanding liberty with an irresistible voice; their king led in triumph, and an arbitrary monarch surrendering himself to his subjects. . . . And now methinks, I see the ardour for liberty catching and spreading, a general amendment beginning in human affairs; the dominion of kings changed for the dominion of laws, and the dominion of priests giving way to the dominion of reason and conscience.[22]

To give emphasis to his admiration for the French revolutionaries and their actions, Price printed as an appendix to his Discourse the French National Assembly's *Declaration of the Rights of Men and of Citizens*.

At this time the French Revolution was still observed with widespread benevolence. True, as Price exulted, a king 'had been led in triumph' when the Parisian mob had marched out to Versailles in the October Days of 1789 and had forced the royal family to return to Paris where they could live under the supervision of the revolutionaries;[23] there had been some violence and bloodshed associated with that incident and with the assault on the Bastille a few months before. But the September massacres of 1792, the execution of the king in January 1793, and the subsequent Terror when the tumbrils rolled through the streets of Paris to the beat of drums as the Jacobins liquidated first the aristocrats, then the Girondins, and finally each other, still lay in the future, and were foreseen by few people in Britain, where the native tradition of the Glorious Revolution tended to mask the fact that in France a quite different series of events was unfolding.

Burke thus had a free field when he published his reply to Price, the *Reflections on the Revolution in France*, in 1790. He had grown steadily more conservative in his interpretation of the British tradition since the days when he had argued that the American rebels were acting in the spirit of the Revolution of 1688. He looked back now with nostalgia to a mythical past of aristocratic nobility in which he, the Dublin lawyer's son, would hardly have found a place, and lamented:

But the age of Chivalry is gone.—That of sophisters, oeconomists, and calculators, has succeeded; and the glory of Europe is extinguished for ever. Never, never more, shall we behold that generous loyalty to rank and sex, that proud submission, that dignified obedience, that subordination of the heart, which kept alive, even in servitude itself, the spirit of an exalted freedom. The unbought grace of life, the cheap defence of nations, the nurse of manly sentiment and heroic enterprise is gone![24]

Such a nostalgic evocation of the medieval world of the Normans and the Plantagenets, with its stress on submission, obedience, subordination, even servitude, as the conditions of an 'exalted freedom', were far removed from the concepts of those who even before the French Revolution had found the sources of their politics in memories of the Commonwealth days or in an equally nostalgic evocation of a Saxon past of sturdy farmers. But, combined with a natural inclination to regard the future with apprehension, such an attitude enabled Burke to foretell with striking accuracy the degeneration of the French Revolution into violence and tyranny, and to perceive the threat it would pose to the rest of Europe if it seriously undertook—as it eventually did—to spread its revolutionary doctrines by force.

Burke was particularly enraged by a phrase in Price's discourse claiming that among men's natural rights were 'the right to chuse our own governors; to cashier them for misconduct; and to frame a government for ourselves'.[25] The basis of his reply was that political structures rest on natural order rather than on natural rights, and that the Glorious Revolution had in fact been a conservative act which sustained the traditions of the English people by creating a balanced structure of king, lords, and commons and thus giving a political expression to natural order. It had done this without bloodshed; clearly Burke expected there would be more bloodshed in France, perhaps even touching the king, and behind his denunciation of events in France lurked the fear that the English might be led to repeat what for conservatives was the great crime of seventeenth-century radicalism, regicide. Even the enemies of the French Revolution were hesitant openly to stir that skeleton in the English past until Louis XVI was actually killed; then, a few days afterwards, on 30 January 1793, Bishop Samuel Horsley sounded the charge for the counter-revolutionary offensive by linking the two regicides in his Sermon to the House of Lords on the Anniversary of the Martyrdom of King Charles the First. In his peroration Horsley thundered: 'This foul murther, and these barbarities, have filled the measure of the guilt and infamy of France. O my Country! read the horror of thy own deed in this recent heightened imitation! lament and weep, that this black French treason should have found its example, in the crime of thy unnatural sons!'[26]

Burke was writing in 1790, three years before such a comparison was possible, but he perceived that the French Revolution was very different from the compromise between varying factions that had led in England to the Glorious Revolution, and by and large he was

correct in arguing that France would produce the antithesis to the
settlement of 1688 rather than the fulfilment of it as Price assumed.
 Many of those who so numerously sprang to counter Burke's
arguments and to justify the radical viewpoint as well as the French
Revolution itself tacitly accepted in their own special ways the
argument that the French Revolution was not in fact a fulfilment of
English constitutional traditions. Certainly both Thomas Paine and
William Godwin, Burke's principal and most influential antagonists,
recognized that with the French Revolution an entire reassessment
of the principles and priorities of political life was called for. Paine
attempted it in his *Rights of Man*, which was designed to appeal to
ordinary literate people and show them how the new view of social
and political relations posed by the French Revolution might be
translated into British terms and be used in practice to improve
their standards of living and broaden their freedoms. Godwin took
the stance of the detached philosopher, aiming his *An Enquiry
concerning Political Justice* principally at his fellow intellectuals,
and embarking on a thoroughgoing examination and criticism of
political institutions, an examination whose anarchistic conclusions
were all the more striking because Godwin deliberately detached
them from the particular circumstances in which he wrote. Like his
great French contemporary Condorcet, who went into hiding
during the Terror to write his great work *The Progress of the
Human Mind*, Godwin withdrew from the active political circles of
his time to write the masterpiece which he regarded as timely in its
appearance but lasting in its implications.
    Paine was already a veteran rebel by the time he set out to answer
Burke's *Reflections on the Revolution in France*. Born in 1737, he
had started out in life as an apprentice corset-maker, and had then
become an excise officer, but eventually was dismissed for
publishing a pamphlet suggesting that better pay might be the best
way to diminish corruption within the service. By now he had
already begun to move in reformist circles, where he met Benjamin
Franklin, who suggested he move to the North American colonies
and gave him introductions there. Doubtless it was Paine's Quaker
affiliations that led him to start in Philadelphia, where he was soon
able to make a living as a journalist.
    Less than six months after he arrived, the differences between
the colonists and the British reached the point of bloodshed with the
battle of Lexington, and Paine immediately took the side of the

rebels, writing his pamphlet, *Common Sense*, and in the process revealing a vivid colloquial style and a power of sustaining his arguments with arresting images, so that *Common Sense*, which urged the Americans to strive for complete independence, was an immediate success, achieving a sale of half a million copies by the time the Declaration of Independence was accepted by the colonies in July 1776. Paine took an active part in the War of Independence, but he made as many enemies as friends, and in 1787 he returned to England where shortly afterwards he became preoccupied with the French Revolution. He joined the Constitutional Society and his fellow members encouraged him in writing his book, which achieved publication thanks to the efforts of an *ad hoc* committee consisting of William Godwin, Thomas Holcroft, and Thomas Brand Hollis. On the day in March 1791 when *Rights of Man* appeared, Holcroft sent his famous whimsical note to Godwin:

I have got it—If it do not cure my cough it is a damned perverse mule of a cough—The pamphlet—From the row—But mum—We don't sell it—Oh, no—Ears and Eggs—Verbatim, except the addition of a short preface, which, as you have not seen, I send you my copy—Not a single castration (Laud be unto God and J. S. Jordan!) can I discover—Hey for the New Jerusalem! The millenium! And peace and eternal beatitude be unto the soul of Thomas Paine.[27]

Rights of Man was an eloquent indictment of the effects of arbitrary government in Europe; somewhat simplistically, Paine saw this as the main cause of poverty, illiteracy, unemployment, and war, and he suggested, with an assurance that developments in France would soon show to be naïve, that a republican order might prove itself exempt from such consequences. Essentially, in this work which he himself declared to be 'written in a style of thinking and expression different from what had been customary in England', he adopted the progressive urge of French revolutionism, deliberately avoiding the kind of constitutional arguments that depend on precedent, whether Norman as evoked by Burke or Saxon as evoked by Major Cartwright. Burke, he asserted, wanted to 'consign over the rights of posterity for ever, on the authority of a mouldy parchment'. Paine saw himself as 'contending for the rights of the *living*, and against their being willed away, and controlled, and contracted for, by the manuscript-assumed authority of the dead'.

Rights of Man was an immediate popular success. While Burke's *Reflections on the Revolution in France* took two years to sell 30,000 copies, *Rights* had already sold 50,000 copies by the end of 1791, and Paine was inspired to write a second part, in which he moved from political revolutionism to radical social reform, and sketched out what was virtually a welfare society, making advanced proposals for helping the poor at the expense of the wealthy by establishing popular and universal education, poor relief, old age pensions, family allowances, and public works for the unemployed, all to be financed by progressive income taxes.

The conservative and the rich were scandalized by such proposals, as were William Pitt and his associates in Government, but *Rights of Man* became popular among working people, according to some observers rivalling *Pilgrim's Progress* among the few books in their homes. The second part, so much concerned with the needs of the common people and how to meet them, almost coincided in its publication with the rise of the Corresponding Societies, and cheap reprints and abridgements of it became one of the staples of their propaganda. In Ireland, where hatred of a foreign oppressor was an added reason for discontent and rebellion, it became even more popular than in Britain, and Paine's claim that nearly half a million copies had been sold by the end of the eighteenth century was probably justified.

Paine's book was low-priced—first at three shillings and then, as a reprint, at sixpence, whereas Godwin's two-volume *An Enquiry concerning Political Justice*, which appeared in 1793 (the year after the second part of *Rights of Man*), was priced at thirty-six shillings, which is said to have been the reason why it did not suffer the same proscription as Paine's book. It was even more radical in its conclusions than *Rights of Man*, since it condemned not only monarchies, but all governments, and its thoroughgoing anarchism ran counter to Paine's ideas of state-operated welfare schemes; Godwin wanted men to co-operate voluntarily in small flexible units without centralized authority. And perhaps because in this way it carried the subversive doctrines of the time to a logical conclusion, it also played its part in the propaganda battles of the time; the Corresponding Societies made extracts from *Political Justice* which they distributed as political tracts, and groups of working men would subscribe a few pence each to buy copies and read in their circles. Yet Godwin's appeal was mainly complementary to Paine's, for it was in the intellectual circles of his time that the response to him was strongest; as Hazlitt recorded when he told of the impact of *An Enquiry Concerning Political Justice*: 'No work in our time gave such a blow to the philosophical mind of the country as the celebrated *Enquiry concerning Political Justice*. Tom Paine was considered for the time as a Tom Fool to him, Paley an old woman, Edmund Burke a flashy sophist.'[28]

Coleridge, Wordsworth, and Southey were immediately bedazzled by Godwin's vision, and when they fell into disillusionment, there was still Shelley, and again, at the end of Godwin's long life, Bulwer Lytton and Robert Owen would draw inspiration from the first of the great anarchists. But that takes us beyond the age of the French Revolution, into the age of the Reform Parliament, under which, ironically, Godwin was to end his life in a government sinecure as Yeoman Usher of the Exchequer, and English politics would seem to be running in their own course once again, undisturbed by foreign influences.

Before that, English radicalism had to go through the difficult days of the 1790s, when its links with the French Revolution would almost destroy it. The so-called Jacobins of the early 1790s in Britain were neither conspirators nor insurrectionaries. The leaders and members of the London Corresponding Society and its provincial counterparts never talked openly of violent revolution, and made no effort to further it while their organizations were still in legal existence. Their efforts, like those of the Chartists later on, were directed mainly towards parliamentary reform and adult suffrage, which in fact meant male suffrage; even the feminists of the time, such as Mary Wollstonecraft, did not go so far as to ask that women should vote. And though Tom Paine's proposals for ameliorating the lot of the poor at the expense of the rich were among the reasons for the great popularity of *Rights of Man*, the radical movement never as whole adopted them.

At the same time, the English reform movement adopted the forms and rhetoric of the French Revolution. Even the moderate Society for Constitutional Information elected some of the Girondin leaders as honorary members in the early days. Both the London Corresponding Society and the Scottish reformers in November 1792 sent delegates to the National Convention in France, where one of the deputies made a speech of welcome in which he prophesied a new republic would arise on the banks of the Thames.

John Frost, one of the London delegates, actually attended the trial of Louis XVI. Tom Paine was already there, having fled to France (warned, it is said, by a hunch of William Blake) just ahead of a trial which in November convicted him of treason; he was elected to the Convention to represent the Pas de Calais, but eventually fell out of favour for speaking against the King's execution, and himself narrowly escaped the guillotine.

Paine's trial in Britain and his sentence to death *in absentia* took place even before the execution of Louis XVI and the entry of Britain into war against France in February 1793. Once revolutionary France had become an enemy in fact as well as feeling it was natural that the British government should see those who still supported the regime in Paris and accepted the title as Jacobin as potential traitors, even if they were not technically involved in treason. In fact, though the radicals in Ireland—notably the United Irishmen—were closely involved with France and were promised French arms and armed forces to assist them in their rebellions, there is no evidence that the London Corresponding Society or its members ever plotted any action that would call on French help and turn them into virtual fifth columnists acting for the enemy.

Nevertheless, from this time onward the radicals and the government were set on a collision course it was difficult to avoid. The execution of Louis XVI and the coming of the Terror scared the British upper and middle classes who had at first welcomed the Revolution with liberal good will, and very soon Fox and his few supporters stood isolated among the patrician Whigs in still supporting radical ideals and opposing the war. The conservatives took courage from this, and aroused their own Church and King mobs such as that which in July 1791 rioted for three days in Birmingham, attacking dissenting meeting houses and the homes of those who were regarded as sympathetic to the French Revolution, and destroying the precious library and laboratory of Joseph Priestley, one of the great scientists of the time. So much feeling was aroused that at first the government tended to rely on groups of reactionary private citizens such as John Reeves's Anti-Jacobin Society to organize threatening demonstrations against the radicals, and on existing statutes against sedition and blasphemy.

The radicals met the growing reaction with a great deal of courage as they set about defending their rights to free speech and free publication. But in doing so they tended towards what in the context can only be regarded as provocative displays of defiance, whose consequences many of them must have anticipated. The members of the societies addressed each other as 'Citizen' in imitation of the French revolutionaries, took Jacobin oaths, and in several provincial centres planted the Tree of Liberty. French revolutionary songs such as the *Carmagnole*, *Ça Ira* and the *Marseillaise* were played or sung at their meetings, and toasts were offered not only to the Rights of Man but also to 'the Armies contending for Liberty', which clearly meant the enemies of Britain. At one meeting an ode was read, composed by no less a figure than the great orientalist Sir William Jones; it was based on a translation of the old Athenian song in praise of the tyrannicides Harmodius and Aristogiton, and it could only be regarded as expressing approval of the recent regicide in France.

It was when the radicals decided to follow the suggestions made by James Burgh in the 1770s and call a National Convention (using a title favoured in Paris) to frame proposals that would be presented to Parliament and the people, that the government, seeing the possibility of a parallel authority emerging, as it had done in France, determined to act decisively. The first National Convention was held in Edinburgh in December 1792 and consisted entirely of Scottish delegates, who met again in April 1793 and decided to call a larger meeting in the autumn to which delegates from England would be invited. Before that third gathering could assemble in November, the authorities had already started their persecution by arresting one of the Scottish leaders, Thomas Muir, who was convicted after an unfair trial and transported to Australia. Scottish law was in some ways more severe than English, and allowed less scope for the jury to make independent decisions than in England, and so it was in Scotland that the authorities struck again. The Convention assembled on 19 November, with delegates from London and Sheffield joining the Scottish ones, and carried on until 5 December, when the Scottish authorities terminated it and arrested a number of the leading participants, including Margarot and Gerrald from the London Corresponding Society; they also were sentenced to transportation by the vindictive Scottish judges.

Far from discouraging the radicals, these incidents provoked the English societies into greater activity and widespread indignation revivified the movement, which in May 1794 led Pitt and his associates to decide on an even stronger attack on the radicals.

Twelve leading members of the London Corresponding Society, including Thomas Hardy, John Thelwall, Horne Tooke, and Thomas Holcroft, were arrested and lodged in the Tower on the much graver charge of high treason, and the threat to the accused of suffering the macabre penalties then imposed for that crime (hanging, drawing and quartering, beheading, and other cruel refinements) was increased by a charge that Chief Justice Eyre made to the grand jury, extending the interpretation of treason to include virtually any attempt to change the form of government. William Godwin wrote a famous reply to Eyre which was published in the *Morning Chronicle* and profoundly influenced London opinion at the time, and Thomas Erskine pleaded so brilliantly in court that the jury acquitted the first three defendants and the trials were abandoned by the prosecution. This triumph led the radicals to their highest point of activity and popularity, and at the end of 1795 they began to hold great mass rallies such as that of 26 October, when a hundred thousand people gathered to hear speakers call for political reform and peace.

It was in response to such manifestations of popular support for the radical cause that the government, which had already suspended Habeas Corpus in 1794, set about framing legislation aimed at destroying the reform movement. The Seditious Meetings and Treasonable Practices Acts of 1795 forbade political meetings of more than fifty people, and when this failed to prevent the members of the Corresponding Societies continuing to meet in smaller groups, the Combination Acts of 1799 and 1800 effectively prevented anything but illegal underground organization. Then insurrection was indeed plotted, often with the complicity of government spies, and links with the French did emerge, largely through the importance of the United Irishmen in this last obscure phase of the British Jacobins.

When radicalism began to emerge into the open again early in the nineteenth century, the period of French influence was virtually at an end; Napoleon had destroyed what Robespierre had left of the idealism of 1789. Those indefatigable figures of the days before the storming of the Bastille, Major Cartwright, John Horne Tooke, and Christopher Wyvill, returned to do battle, and fresh figures such as William Cobbett, Francis Burdett, and Henry Hunt gave a new English aspect to the reform movement. No one looked back now to the Glorious Revolution of 1688 for inspiration or sought to reestablish the primitive democracy of Good King Alfred's day. The influence of the French Revolution, passing though it may have been, had turned the direction of radicalism in England towards the future, towards the progressivism that was characteristic of the nineteenth century; its aims were now to meet Tom Paine's revolutionary requirement that each age must find its own political forms without being bound by the dead hand of past traditions, institutions, or constitutions.

NOTES

[1] E. P. Thompson, *The Making of the English Working Class* (Harmondsworth, 1968), p. 111.
[2] Cited in H. N. Brailsford, *Shelley, Godwin and Their Circle* (Oxford, 1913), p. 53.
[3] Thomas Paine, *The Rights of Man*, ed. H. Collins (Harmondsworth, 1969), pp. 63–4.
[4] Ian Christie, *Stress and Stability in Late Eighteenth Century England* (Oxford, 1984), p. 13.
[5] Charles James Fox, cited in L. G. Mitchell, *Charles James Fox and the Disintegration of the Whig Party 1782–1794* (London, 1971), pp. 154 and 160.
[6] See Edmund Burke, *Substance of the Speech on the Army Estimates* (London, 1790).
[7] Cited in Lord Rosebery, *Pitt* (London, 1892), p. 120.
[8] John Thelwall, *The Rights of Nature* (London, 1796), ii, 32.
[9] *The Poetical Works of Wordsworth*, ed. Thomas Hutchinson, rev. E. de Selincourt (London, 1965), *The Prelude*, xi. 108–9.
[10] 'Preface' to *The Lyrical Ballads*, ibid. 736.
[11] *The Prelude*, xi. 139–44.
[12] Cited by Robert Greacen, 'Wordsworth as Politician', in Muriel Spark and Derek Stanford, eds., *Tribute to Wordsworth* (London, 1950), p. 213.
[13] Cited by Tony Hayter, *The Army and the Crowd in Mid-Georgian England* (London, 1978), p. 130.
[14] Dorothy George, *England in Transition* (London, 1931), pp. 142–3.
[15] J. C. D. Clark, *English Society 1688–1832* (Cambridge, 1985), p. 311.
[16] J. H. Plumb, *England in the Eighteenth Century* (Harmondsworth, 1950), p. 123.
[17] *The Theological, Medical, Political and Miscellaneous Works of John Jebb* (London, 1787), i. 161.
[18] E. P. Thompson, op. cit. 111.
[19] Thomas Hardy, *Memoir of Thomas Hardy, written by himself* (London, 1832), p. 13.
[20] Ibid. 108.
[21] Richard Price, *A Discourse on the Love of Our Country* (London, 1790), p. 39.
[22] Ibid. 49.
[23] See ibid. 48–9.
[24] Marilyn Butler, ed., *Burke, Paine, Godwin and the Revolution Controversy* (Cambridge, 1984), p. 44.
[25] Price, op. cit. 34.

²⁶ Samuel Horsley, *A Sermon Preached before the Lords Spiritual and Temporal . . . on Wednesday, January 30, 1793; Being the Anniversary of the Martyrdom of King Charles the First* (London, 1793), p. 23.

²⁷ George Woodcock, *William Godwin* (London, 1946), p. 37.

²⁸ William Hazlitt, 'William Godwin' in *The Spirit of the Age; or Contemporary Portraits* (Oxford, 1954), p. 20.

The Impact of the French Revolution on British Politics and Society

CLIVE EMSLEY

THERE are two traditional assessments of the impact of the French Revolution on British history which are common in English popular historiography: first, that the Revolution fostered a conservative backlash which put reform back for more than a generation, and second, that those seeking reform in Britain who fell victim to this conservative backlash were non-violent, constitutional reformers, with only a lunatic fringe advocating insurrection and revolution on the French model. Irish popular historiography is rather different; in this the French Revolution is seen as giving hope and, belatedly and insufficiently, military assistance to a nation struggling for its freedom and independence. Over the last three decades, beginning perhaps most notably with E. P. Thompson's *The Making of the English Working Class*, much in these traditional views has been challenged.[1] The aim of this essay is to re-assess the old view of the Revolution's impact on British politics and society as a whole—that is, recognizing the differences between England and Wales, Scotland, and Ireland. The first and largest section here chronicles the effects of the different stages of the Revolution on Britain; the second looks in more detail at questions of interpretation, the extent of repression and the extent of revolutionary activity.

Britain in 1789 was aggressive and booming: she had recovered from the loss of her thirteen colonies in their War of Independence (1775–82). The fiscal policies of the younger Pitt had stabilized the nation's finances. Trade was prospering even with recent enemies like the infant United States and France. A century of generally successful wars had left Britain with a considerable Empire even without her American colonies. Agricultural improvements had given England (as opposed to parts of her Celtic appendages) a solid, capitalist agriculture. Industrial developments and expansion promised new benefits. The political and constitutional structure of the country was a source of pride to many, though there were critics, most notably among Protestant Dissenters, who found themselves technically barred from political life by the Test and Corporation Acts. Englishmen prided themselves on possessing liberties unique in Europe. These notions of liberty had been central in the campaigns of John Wilkes during the 1760s and 1770s; and Wilkes's activities, besides extending—rather than simply, as he claimed, preserving—the bounds of these notions, sharpened perceptions of liberty across the social spectrum. The political and constitutional structure had been challenged by the American troubles; and, significantly, the colonists had based their initial demands on their rights as Englishmen. The dark days of the American war had prompted demands for reform at home: in England the County Association Movement united in a call to end gross abuses in public expenditure and make some moderate improvements to the parliamentary system (a radical wing of the movement went rather further). In Ireland armed volunteers, who had come forward to defend their country against possible invasion, forced some reforms out of Westminister, notably legislative independence for the separate Irish Parliament which met in Dublin. In Scotland, fully integrated into the English parliamentary system, moves for the reform of Scottish representation at Westminster did not gain much momentum until the County Association Movement and the Irish Volunteer Movement were, after partial success, in decline. By the end of the 1780s the reform movements brought to life by the American war had petered out except for feeble demands for improvements in Scottish representation and more forceful demands for reform on behalf of the dissenters.

The beginnings of the revolutionary upheavals in France coincided with the centenary of the Glorious Revolution of 1688–9, which had formed the climax of the constitutional struggles within seventeenth-century Britain. Most members of the political nation, as well as those rarely enfranchised participants in the lively political debates which were part of eighteenth-century British artisan culture, looked to the Glorious Revolution as one of the key elements in establishing the liberty which, they believed, marked the British off from their continental neighbours. However, the centenary celebrations were temporarily overshadowed in November 1788 by George III's mental illness. For four months the king lay ill and parliament showed itself in its worst light arguing over the question of regency. Pitt sought to maintain his position and his ministry by providing for a limited regency; Charles James Fox, Pitt's arch parliamentary enemy, hastened back from an Italian holiday to demand full powers for the Prince of Wales which, he confidently expected, would lead to a new ministry with a significant post for himself. Even years after the event, at least one astute commentator of the British political scene regarded George III's recovery as a more significant event than the beginning of the French Revolution.[2] Indeed, the summoning of the Estates General, the Tennis Court Oath, the storming of the Bastille, prompted little agitation or excitement in Britain. Most of those who did take an interest in events in France viewed them as weakening the old enemy and, possibly, leading the French to enjoy constitutional benefits similar to those enjoyed in Britain for a century.

Some reformers, notably those among the dissenters, took encouragement from events in France. In May 1789 a bill for the repeal of the Test and Corporation Acts was narrowly defeated; disappointed dissenters took comfort in the kind of principles expressed in the French Declaration of the Rights of Man and Citizen and in the end of French absolutism which they saw as opening a new era for all mankind. Anna Leticia Barbauld, the wife of a dissenting clergyman, directed the opponents of repeal to what was happening in France: 'Nobles, the creatures of Kings, exist there no longer; but Man, the creature of God, exists there. Millions of men exist there who, only now, truly begin to exist, and hail with shouts of grateful acclamation the better birth-day of their country. Go on, generous nation, set the world an example of virtues as you have of talents. Be our model, as we have been yours.'[3] The London Revolution Society, revived during the centenary celebrations in 1788, was chiefly composed of dissenters. At its annual meeting on 4 November 1789 Dr Richard Price, a unitarian minister and noted economic expert, preached a sermon praising the achievements of the Glorious Revolution, notably the establishment of three principles:

First; The right to liberty of conscience in religious matters.

Secondly; The right to resist power when abused. And,

Thirdly; The right to choose our own governors; to cashier them for misconduct; and to frame a government for ourselves.

Yet for all that the Glorious Revolution was 'a great work', it was 'by no means a perfect work': the laws against dissenters remained, and there was gross inequality in parliamentary representation. Price welcomed recent events in France and looking beyond them saw 'the ardour for liberty catching and spreading; a general amendment beginning in human affairs; the dominion of kings changed for the dominion of laws, and the dominion of priests giving way to the dominion of reason and conscience.'[4] At the dinner following the meeting the Revolution Society unanimously adopted Price's motion to address the National Assembly in France. It was Price's sermon and this address which indirectly sparked off the English debate on the French Revolution.

In his private correspondence Edmund Burke, one of the most eloquent and powerful voices among the parliamentary opposition, had shown considerable reserve towards events in France as early as the summer of 1789; by November he was concerned that France was becoming a threat to general order and liberty.[5] Price's sermon brought matters to a head. In his *Reflections on the Revolution in France*, published at the beginning of November 1790, Burke denied Price's interpretation of 1688; it had not established the rights of the people of England to choose their governors, to cashier them for any misconduct, or to frame a government for themselves. He went on to condemn the ideas of natural, abstract rights as meaningless and to insist that such rights as existed for man in society were inherited and embodied in constitutional precedent. Furthermore it was both foolish and dangerous to proceed as the French National Assembly had done 'to commence their schemes of reform with abolition and total destruction'.[6] In Burke's opinion the English Constitution had evolved and mellowed over centuries; it contained no notions of abstract or natural rights, it needed no drastic reformation and certainly no innovation. The *Reflections* brought forth a crop of replies. The most able and literary was James Mackintosh's *Vindiciae Gallicae* which expressed the kind of sentiments espoused by the Foxite Whigs, notably doubting whether governments were ever prepared to improve themselves without the promptings of the people in general and enlightened politicians in particular. But the most long-lasting and popular of the replies was Tom Paine's *Rights of Man*. In Part One of this pamphlet, published in March 1791, Paine argued that Burke had misunderstood the French Revolution totally and he ridiculed Burke's reliance on constitutional precedent. But the pamphlet was much more than a repudiation of Burke, and contained vigorous attacks on hereditary government, on state religions, and particularly on the English constitution, crown, and parliament. Paine hoped that his book might have a galvanizing effect similar to that of his pamphlet *Common Sense* which had been so influential in focusing colonial discontent in America in 1776. Part Two of *Rights of Man*, publication of which was delayed until February 1792, was even more radical: it outlined the principles and practices of both the old and the new systems of government—the new were to be found in the United States and France; it put forward proposals for a prompt reduction of taxes and government expenditure, together with schemes for social welfare which would improve education for the young and help to maintain the very poor and the aged. What most alarmed members of established political society was the way in which *Rights of Man* was adopted as a key text by the new kinds of political clubs which began to be established in the winter of 1791–2—clubs at least partially organized by, and drawing their principle membership from, artisans and working men; clubs which demanded a thoroughgoing reform of the political system.[7]

The excitement generated by the French Revolution itself, then by the pamphlet controversy, and finally by the dramatic and public rift between Burke and Fox in the Commons in May 1791, had prompted gentlemen reformers to revive the old political campaigns from the American war years. This was most notable in the north of Ireland where the Volunteer Movement had continued its political activities and where a core of advanced radicals existed among the Ulster Presbyterians. In the summer of 1791 men from this group established the United Irish Society, demanding the political emancipation of Roman Catholics and a radical reform of the Dublin parliament to throw off the last vestiges of dominance from Westminster; they did not, however, call for an independent Ireland. Other progressive Whig groups in England and Scotland began to correspond with French political clubs and individuals visited what appeared to them to be the new land of liberty. Prominent among these progressive reformers were the members of the Society for Constitutional Information (SCI) which had first been organized within the radical wing of the County Association Movement to provide, as its name implied, cheap constitutional information for 'the Commonality at Large'.[8] The membership of this society was small; the subscription of one guinea a year, or thirty guineas for life, kept it exclusive. Tom Paine was a member and while not every one of his fellow members wholeheartedly agreed with his sentiments, in general the membership appears to have regarded *Rights of Man* as a useful instrument for reopening the debate on parliamentary reform. The excitement revived the SCI's correspondence with its country members who, like Thomas Cooper and Thomas Walker in Manchester and John Audley in Cambridge, organized similar societies in their own localities— stimulated as much, if not perhaps more, by the political and social tensions of those localities as by events in far-away France. Yet these societies were quite different socially from those which began to appear at the close of 1791; they were societies of men of some wealth and social standing—Cooper was a barrister and a chemist, Walker was a prominent businessman and had been Boroughreeve of Manchester. The new societies established in the winter of 1791–2 contained a sprinkling of such men and were nurtured by the SCI and its provincial counterparts, but their membership was drawn primarily from artisans and simple working men, while their low membership fees—a penny a week in the London Corresponding Society (LCS)—were designed to keep membership open to all.

The Sheffield Constitutional Society, formed probably in November 1791, seems to have been the first of these popular societies. Notable among its four or five founding members was John Gales, a bookshop owner who published and edited the weekly *Sheffield Register*; this gave the society a mouthpiece for its opinions from the very beginning. Sheffield was a fast-growing town, full of small masters and highly skilled and relatively well-paid craftsmen with a reputation for resilience and self-reliance. Lord Loughborough concluded that one principle reason for the appearance of the Sheffield Society was that the staple manufacture of cutlery was carried on by journeymen and apprentices who could 'earn a full maintenance without employing their whole time'; they therefore had time on their hands to dabble in politics.[9] At the end of May 1792 the society claimed a membership of 2,400;[10] by then it was affiliated to the SCI, having requested that twelve Sheffield men be admitted to honorary membership of the London Society. The Sheffield Society's correspondence with the SCI set a precedent for intercommunication and co-operation between the new societies. Others followed Sheffield's lead in affiliating with the SCI, the best known being the London Corresponding Society which eventually replaced the SCI as the focal point in the metropolis for the correspondence of the provincial popular societies.

In London, at roughly the same time as the formation of the Sheffield Society, Thomas Hardy, a 40-year-old shoemaker from Scotland, re-read some old SCI pamphlets. Hardy, a devout dissenter, was excited by the French Revolution which he considered to be one of the greatest events in the history of the world. This excitement, coupled with the ideas he drew from the SCI pamphlets, led him to formulate the idea for the LCS. After a lengthy debate with some friends as to whether tradesmen, shopkeepers, and mechanics had the right to demand and agitate for parliamentary reform, an inaugural meeting of the society was held in a pub in the Strand on 25 January 1792. Eight men were present and Hardy was chosen as both secretary and treasurer. The society's initial growth was not as spectacular as that experienced in Sheffield, and in its first few months of life the LCS proceeded cautiously, taking advice and encouragement from members of the SCI, notably the Revd. John Horne Tooke. At the beginning of April, with a membership of about seventy, the LCS presented an address to the public and published its resolutions calling for 'a fair, equal and impartial Representation of the People in Parliament' and for the abolition of corruption and privilege.[11]

By the time of this address there were several other popular societies at least in an embryonic state. Norwich, a hotbed of unitarian dissent, had several separate societies by the spring of 1792. Delegates of the United Constitutional Societies of Norwich transmitted their resolutions to the SCI in March. In the following month the Norwich Revolution Society requested that twelve of its members be admitted to honorary membership of the SCI. The Manchester Patriotic Society was formed in May and the Manchester Reformation Society in June; they were both assisted by Cooper and Walker's Constitutional Society. Other, smaller clubs wrote to Sheffield for advice on how to organize themselves into regular bodies.

The growth of such societies and their eager acceptance of Paine's theories turned some reformers of the more traditional stamp away from reform. Some men resigned from the SCI or declined to attend functions at which Paine would be present. The Revd. Christopher Wyvill, the prime mover of the old Association

Movement and still an advocate of reform, deplored Paine's 'unconstitutional ground' and believed that he had 'formed a party for a Republic among the lower classes of people by holding out to them the prospect of plundering the rich'.[12] But their disapproval of Paine did not prevent moderate reformers from being eyed with suspicion themselves. Indeed all reformers began to be tarred with the Paineite brush, whatever their platform. Samuel Hoare, treasurer of the Committee for the Abolition of the Slave Trade, found that members of the Church of England had adopted the idea 'that the dissenters wish for a revolution; and that the Abolition of the Slave Trade is somewhat connected with it'.[13] Lord Auckland expressed such ideas to Lord Grenville, the Foreign Secretary, in March 1792: 'Nor would it be difficult to show that many of the doctrines bringing forwards in this country under cover of the slave question and of religious toleration, are in unison with those *des vainqueurs de la Bastille.*'[14]

In April 1792 a group of young Whig aristocrats formed the Society of the Friends of the People. Wyvill and his associates were delighted that a reform society which rejected Paine had at last been established. But the prevailing attitude towards the Friends was one of distrust, even among their own parliamentary allies. On 30 April Charles Grey, one of the Friends, declared his intention of bringing a motion for parliamentary reform before the House of Commons in accordance with a promise he had made to the society. Pitt opposed him, arguing that while he was a friend to reform, any action at that moment would be dangerous since there were now two kinds of reformers in the country: those who sought a moderate reform, and those who wanted to subvert the constitution, depose the king, and establish a republic. To what extent Pitt believed his arguments, and to what extent he was seeking to widen the split in the opposition, is open to debate, but he carried the House and many appear to have accepted his words at face value. The political situation was polarizing and the time had come for men to take their stand. Lord Loughborough, a leader of the conservative faction of the Whig opposition, but enjoying close links with Pitt's ministers, wrote to Henry Dundas, the Home Secretary, that 'The Times are now too serious for any Play of Party. The Bp. of Autun [Talleyrand] said in a public company here that there were not 200 Persons in all of France who meant the Revolution. I hope there are not so many who mean a change of this Government, but they will count on this side all who appear indifferent. The Lookers on make the mob.'[15]

Three weeks after the Commons debate on reform, Pitt's government took its first overt measures against the popular societies, Paine, and 'French principles'. On 21 May a royal proclamation was published against seditious meetings and writings. The proclamation split the parliamentary opposition, although every effort was made to preserve the show of unity. The Foxites thought it unnecessary, the conservative Whigs led by the Duke of Portland supported it; Pitt exploited the division to the full by throwing out suggestions for a coalition with the Portland group. The popular societies opposed the proclamation. The LCS spoke of living 'under a worse political tyranny than that of Venice'.[16] The Norwich Revolution Society and the Sheffield Constitutional Society showed their opposition, and their strength, by successfully opposing town motions of thanks to the king for the proclamation.[17] But there were many more elsewhere who supported the measure and who hoped, in the words of James Bland Burges, the Under Secretary of State in the Foreign Office, that it would provide 'a complete antidote to the Jacobinical poison'.[18] The *Annual Register* for 1792 reported that by 1 September the king had received 341 loyal addresses thanking him for the proclamation and acclaiming the existing constitution.[19] On 10 September two lists were compiled in the Home Office: the first named all those places which had sent congratulatory addresses to the king, the second was ominously headed 'counties, Cities, and Towns from whence addresses have not been received'.[20]

The great *journée* of 10 August 1792 finally toppled the French monarchy; three weeks later the *sans-culottes* of the Paris sections, fearing an uprising in support of the Duke of Brunswick's approaching armies, massacred the captives in the city's prisons. Fox felt, on reflection, that he could forgive the killings of 10 August because of the reluctance of Louis XVI and his ministers to act in unison with the National Assembly; but for the September massacres he could find not 'a shadow of excuse . . . not even the possibility of extenuating it in the smallest degree'.[21] Samuel Romilly was so revolted by the September massacres that he confessed to having lost all the hope that he first had in the Revolution. The pro-government newspapers fed the British public on a harrowing diet of French butchery. The *London Chronicle* spoke of 'deliberate slaughter more cruel than ever stained the ferocity of savage warfare'. *The Times* believed that the 'French barbarians' were far worse than the Goths and Vandals who had sacked Rome. Even the opposition *Morning Chronicle* spoke of 'furies' in the Paris streets in September and commented that 'the heart is torn with the afflicting idea that such a scene could have been acted by beings who call themselves human'. It subsequently modified its position and printed an account which sought to understand the prison massacres.[22] The LCS drew a parallel between the French overthrow of the Bourbons and the English overthrow of the Stuarts, and attributed the September massacres to 'cruelty and revenge . . . among a few inhabitants of the capital', brought on by the threatening manifesto addressed to the Parisians in Brunswick's name.[23] The Manchester reformers went further and immediately leapt to the defence of the *septembriseurs*. On 10 September the editors of the *Manchester Herald* printed a special handbill which contained reports from correspondents in France emphasizing the atrocities of the Austrian and Prussian armies and playing down the massacres in Paris. The editors had no doubt about the guilt of those killed in Paris: 'we have no hesitation in declaring, that in our opinion, it will eventually prove the truest mercy; and we sincerely hope, it may prove an extensive and salutary warning.'[24] The *Manchester Herald* of 15 September again justified the massacres, arguing that the prisoners had brought their fate upon themselves.[25] But such justifications or explanations were only received sympathetically by those already staunch in the French cause. For those Englishmen who had been eyeing events in both France and England with increasing suspicion, the overthrow of the French monarchy, the September massacres, and the English reformers' justifications of these events only confirmed their suspicions. For the *Leeds Intelligencer*, the mouthpiece of the Anglican merchant community in Leeds, the Manchester justification was astonishing: 'A vindication of murder the mind naturally revolts at—what, then, can be expected from such principles—such actions—and such an overthrow of Justice, Humanity, and Order?'[26]

The unexpected French victories at Valmy and Jemappes were welcomed with enthusiasm and rejoicing by radical reformers and those who had any sympathy left for France. Fox could not recall a public event, 'not excepting Saratoga and York Town', which gave him as much delight as the news of Valmy.[27] In Sheffield a massive demonstration celebrated Brunswick's defeat. In London 'the Committee' and their supporters executed an effigy of Brunswick on Kennington Common.[28] The radical societies sent encouragement to the new French National Convention and the 'soldiers of liberty'. Delegates crossed the Channel to present congratulatory addresses to the Convention. Many of the phrases contained in these addresses were injudicious and fed their opponents' suspicions. The LCS proclaimed: 'Frenchmen you are already free, but Britons are preparing to be so.' The SCI announced that they were 'burning with ardour in the [Convention's] cause'. The president of the Convention replied in the same vein, addressing the SCI's delegation as 'generous republicans'. He went on: 'the moment cannot be distant when the people of France will offer their congratulations to a national convention in England.'[29] Nor was the encouragement given to the French merely verbal. The SCI's delegates could tell the Convention that a thousand pairs of shoes for the 'soldiers of liberty', paid for by 'patriotic donation' in England, had arrived in Calais; more were promised. The *London Chronicle* described a Gravesend boat arriving at Calais laden with 'twenty large packets filled with shoes, clothing, and blanketing, and ammunition'.[30] The Dover customs house reported that nine cases of daggers were shipped to France.[31] (Probably these were the daggers ordered by a Dr Maxwell of Birmingham; and it was probably with one of the same that Burke made his histrionic gesture of hurling a dagger into the floor of the Commons.)[32]

The closing weeks of 1792 saw the beginning of serious conflict between the two extremes of political opinion in Britain. The British Jacobins advocated support for France against the confederation of European princes with whom she was at war; in Britain itself they demanded a fundamental reform of Parliament, leading to an end to 'old corruption' and a chamber composed of men elected by universal manhood suffrage. Possibly some sought more far-reaching changes, but no one openly called for a republic. The loyalists, on the other hand, feared the advance of the French armies in the Low Countries, which threatened both Britain's trade and her Dutch ally. They were appalled by events in France, as indeed were many who had earlier been sympathetic to parliamentary reform. Many of the propertied classes were unable to differentiate between reformers and revolutionaries. Benjamin

Vaughan, MP for Calne and himself a moderate reformer, wrote of 'a terror' in the country 'lest Republicans should use violence to change the government and the division of property; a terror, common to many who are themselves Republicans'.[33] This terror was aggravated by fears of a deficient harvest and by serious industrial disorders particularly along the east coast in November. Members of the propertied classes began advocating philanthropic measures born out of self-interest. One Anglican vicar asked: 'Was not the wretchedness of the french Peasantry, of the french Mechanics and labouring Manufacturers, the grand Instrument of the Tiers Etat, and of ambitious ruffian Demagogues to accomplish the Ruin, and to deluge in Blood the finest Country in Europe? May not similar Causes at home produce similar Effects?'[34] A gentleman of Brentford suggested that 'Winter Gifts' would be 'an effectual, and an economical means of keeping a number of poor creatures quiet, whose necessities, unless timely relieved will expose them to the arts and delusions of designing men'.[35] Some gentlemen simply raised wages. There were rumours of French spies and saboteurs concealing themselves among the thousands of émigrés seeking refuge in Britain. There is fragmentary evidence that even members of the Cabinet were swept along on this current of fear, and expected some sort of insurrection in London at the beginning of December. The government's response was a second round of repressive measures: a royal proclamation deploring the ineffectiveness of its predecessor; and the embodiment of ten county militia regiments. For Pitt this response had the added benefit of widening the rift in the opposition.[36]

The propertied classes reacted to the fears of civil disorder by establishing Associations for the Preservation of Liberty and Property against Republicans and Levellers. The first of these was organized in London by John Reeves, Receiver of the London Police and formerly a chief justice in Newfoundland. Reeves's society held its inaugural meeting on 20 November 1792. Its aims were to support the laws, suppress seditious publications, and defend persons and property against the threat of Jacobinism and 'French principles'. The idea was taken up by loyalists throughout the country. Not every loyalist association was composed of rabid Burkeites and anti-reformers—Fox sat on the committee of the association of St George's Parish, Hanover Square, while the association meeting in the Merchant Taylors' Hall openly expressed sympathy for reform—but in general the tone was one of opposition to reform and particularly to all manifestations of popular radicalism. A counter-attack was mounted against sedition with pamphlets, broadsides, and prints. Some of the loyalist associations organized demonstrations which often ended with Paine being burned in effigy, and occasionally with violent attacks on reformers. Loyalists collected information which could be used in prosecutions for sedition; some organized such prosecutions and, on occasion, they also organized the jury.[37] The government was well satisfied with these manifestations of loyalty. 'Nothing can exceed the good disposition of this country at the present moment,' wrote Lord Grenville in mid-December. 'The change within the last three weeks is little less than miraculous.'[38]

The National Convention declared war on Britain on 1 February 1793. Predictably British attitudes to the war divided along those lines already drawn by the debates on the French Revolution and reform. Loyalists, now further outraged by the execution of Louis XVI, welcomed the conflict. In general, those in favour of reform, from the moderates such as Wyvill and the Friends of the People to the most extreme members of the popular societies, opposed it. The popular societies, whose membership seems to have declined from the beginning of the new year, initially condemned the war because of their sympathy for the French; but as the economic effects of the conflict developed, more personal reasons came into play, for the war dislocated trade and threw men out of work.

The main effort in the reform campaign during 1793 centred on the motion which Charles Grey had promised to introduce into the Commons on behalf of the Friends of the People. The popular societies were suspicious of the Friends, but the motion promised a public airing of the arguments for reform and the societies consequently decided to petition parliament alongside the Friends. The result of the debate was a forgone conclusion; Grey's motion was rejected by 282 votes to 41. The Commons refused to accept the petition from the Sheffield radicals on the grounds that its content was derogatory to the dignity of the house. The petition from Norwich was refused on the ground that the 3,700 signatures were attached to a printed copy. But the total number of petitions did not suggest that there was an overwhelming movement in favour of reform within the country; there were thirty-six in all, and twenty-four of these came from Scotland, underlining the strength that ideas of reform had gained in that country in the wake of the French Revolution.

In June 1793, the month following the defeat of Grey's motion, the popular societies in Norwich listed the alternatives open to reformers as: 'An Address to the King—futile; a Petition to Parliament (as a conquered People)—tolerable; a National Convention (if circumstances admitted)—best of all.'[39] The idea of a convention, or extra-parliamentary assembly, exerting pressure on parliament to reform itself, was not new in the 1790s. James Burgh, a dissenter and prominent political theorist, had put the case forcefully in his *Political Disquisitions* (1774–5). These ideas had attracted considerable interest among the radical wing of the Association movement. The Irish Volunteers had met in a national convention in 1783 to bring pressure on the Dublin parliament to reform itself. A national convention was mooted in 1790 as part of the campaign for the repeal of the Test and Corporation Acts. In December 1792, and again in the following April, Scottish reformers had met in a convention in Edinburgh. Yet these precedents hardly gave the idea respectability. Furthermore, events in France, where the legislative body of the new republic had taken the name National Convention, gave the idea of a British National Convention sinister connotations.

At the end of 1793 societies in England were invited to send delegates to a second Edinburgh convention. The LCS sent two men, Maurice Margarot and Joseph Gerrald; the SCI also chose two delegates, Charles Sinclair and Henry 'Redhead' Yorke, though illness prevented the latter from going. The Sheffield Society sent Matthew Campbell Brown. The societies in Norwich agreed to share Margarot's expenses; that in Leeds agreed to share Brown's. The Scottish authorities and judiciary had already shown their hostility to reform by imposing savage sentences of transportation on two moderate reformers, Thomas Muir and the Revd. Thomas Fyshe Palmer. The British Convention, by its very existence, was a provocation to the Edinburgh authorities; the more so because of its conscious imitation of French republican forms. After seventeen days it was dissolved by force. Gerrald, Margarot, and William Skirving, the Convention's secretary, who between them had dominated the proceedings, were charged with sedition and subsequently each was sentenced to fourteen years transportation.

The closing of the British Convention and the subsequent trials, together with the passage of legislation in Ireland forbidding the meeting of any assembly called a convention, generated a desperate excitement among English radicals. Thomas Hardy urged the societies in Norwich that 'Now is the time for us to do something worthy of *Men*. The brave defenders of Liberty south of the English Channel are performing wonders driving their enemies before them like chaff before the whirlwind.'[40]

The SCI proclaimed that the law ceased to be an object of obedience when it became an instrument of oppression, adding that those who imitated 'the infamous' Judge Jeffries by passing iniquitous sentences deserved to share his fate—'torn to pieces by a brave and injured People'. The society saw 'with Regret, but . . . without Fear, that the Period is fast approaching when the Liberties of Britons must depend not upon Reason, to which they have long appealed, nor on their Powers of expressing it, but on their firm and undaunted Resolution to oppose Tyranny by the same Means by which it is exercised.'[41]

Demanding peace with France, demanding that the sentences on the Scottish 'martyrs' be quashed, and agitated lest legislation similar to the Irish Convention Act be introduced at Westminster, the popular societies talked of holding a new convention. Mass open-air meetings were held in Sheffield and London. On 14 April 1794 an open-air meeting held by the LCS at Chalk Farm proclaimed that Britons had now lost their liberty and suggested that the government should consider whether it was guilty of high treason since its actions savoured of the days of the Star Chamber, Charles I, and James II; these resolutions did not fail to point out that Charles had been executed and James banished.[42] Given the events in France such comment was as inflammatory as the use of the word 'convention'.

The government did not remain idle. It was anxious about the possibility of a desperate French landing on the coasts; its agents closely watched William Jackson, a secret emissary from France, as he sought information on the possible reception of an invasion force in England and Ireland. The popular radicals' behaviour led the Home Office to take a closer look at the societies with a view to prosecution. In January 1794 more spies were infiltrated into the LCS and their reports increased concern by drawing attention to a group undergoing military training as the Lambeth Loyal Association. Possibly this was similar to other volunteer companies

organized from 1793 onwards to aid the civil power and oppose
invasion—late in the 1790s several persons got into trouble with
magistrates for practising arms drill illegally, even though their
intentions were clearly loyal—but the spies did not consider that
the Lambeth Loyal Association could be regarded in any way as
'loyal'. The association could not have been a serious instrument of
insurrection (it never reached its quota of sixty men, and did not
succeed in getting similar corps organized) but, obviously, this does
not mean that certain of its members may not have had hopes in
this direction. In parallel with the investigation by spies and secret
agents, from the beginning of the year, the crown law officers were
approached for advice on possible legal proceedings against
members of the popular societies. Early in May, leaders of the LCS,
the SCI, and some provincial societies were arrested on warrants
specifying suspicion of 'treasonable practices'. The Habeas Corpus
Act was temporarily suspended. The understanding between Pitt
and the Duke of Portland was formalized in a ministerial coalition.

In the summer of 1794 the Jacobin terror in France was checked
with the fall of Robespierre. But the events of Thermidor had little
impact in Britain where the tension was maintained by the exposure
of two plots. In Edinburgh the authorities unearthed the conspiracy
of Robert Watt and David Downie and some extremist remnants of
the British Convention. Watt and Downie were condemned to
death; Downie was reprieved, but Watt, a former government spy,
was executed. At the end of September the Pop-Gun Plot—an
unlikely plan to assassinate George III by firing a poised dart
through an airgun disguised as a walking-stick—was exposed in
London. The membership of the popular societies melted away.

About two dozen men were held under the suspension of the
Habeas Corpus Act. Of these, twelve were charged with treason but
only three—Hardy, Horne Tooke, and the radical lecturer John
Thelwall—were tried. All three were acquitted, to the great joy of
the crowds which assembled daily outside the Old Bailey during the
trials; after the third acquittal the government gave up and released
its other prisoners. Hardy believed that there were 800 warrants
ready to be issued had he been convicted; whether this was true or
not, and there appears to be no other evidence to support it,[43] the
fears were real. Major John Cartwright had been warned by the
Attorney General that he was implicated; he expressed his relief to
his wife that the acquittals had checked 'a system of prescription

and terror like that of Robespierre'.[44] The majority of those who continued to espouse the cause of reform could take similar comfort and boast that the accusation that they planned an armed insurrection had been rejected by that fine institution, the English jury. Anti-reformers could take comfort from the fact that there were no martyrs to focus a radical opposition and possibly provoke it to foolhardiness; they could also argue that the acquittals themselves demonstrated the leniency and superiority of the British constitution, especially in contrast to what was happening in France. Hostility and suspicion continued to cloud the way in which reformers and anti-reformers regarded each other, but it was the more traditional eighteenth-century problem of food shortages which occasioned the crisis of the following two years.

The wheat yield of 1794 was one-fifth below the ten-year average; the resulting shortage of bread affected the whole country. The government began buying wheat abroad to ease the shortage; but these efforts, those of local authorities, and those of private individuals were insufficient to prevent a considerable number of disturbances. The riots followed a traditional pattern; some barns were burned, some mills and bakehouses were attacked; waggons, barges, and ships transporting corn were stopped and their cargoes seized. Most common were the disturbances in markets where crowds fixed what they considered to be fair prices for foodstuffs and sold the goods at those prices. Several of these disturbances assumed an ominous character when soldiers, most commonly from the embodied county militia regiments, participated on the side of the rioters. But although the troubles followed a traditional pattern some gentlemen saw the corn shortages and the riots as deliberately engineered. One Wiltshire attorney had 'reason to believe that the present scarcity of provisions is not occasioned by real want of anything but that the Corn etc. is bought up by our rascally English Jacobins and hid on purpose to starve the people into a Rebellion against Government'.[45]

Others thought that the Jacobins were using the high prices as an opportunity to stir up trouble; as one magistrate in Norfolk lamented, high prices gave 'to every ill disposed person but too plausible a ground to harangue the common people'.[46] Some pamphlets and handbills published by the radical press during the year only served to aggravate such fears: *A Picture of the Times* declared that the war was the cause of high prices and insisted that

it was an insult to those who had overcome the oppression of the
Stuarts to fight the French who, 'following their glorious example',
had overcome the oppression of the Bourbons;[47] *The Rights of
Swine* also blamed the war, but criticized the behaviour of 'the
wealthy and voluptuous' and dismissed charity and other forms of
assistance as 'nothing more than the appendages of Corruption,
Extortion and Oppression'.[48] Yet whatever the fears of loyalist
gentlemen, it was only in isolated cases that overt French principles
were reported among the food rioters. The *London Chronicle*
printed a letter from Exeter claiming that during an attack on a
mill, rioters in Devon had raised red and white flags: 'the white flag
was for an avowal of French principles; the red flag that they would
spill their blood in support of such principles.'[49] During disorders
in Haverfordwest a woman was reported to have cried that 'in less
than a Twelve month she should see the downfall of the Clergy and
of every Rich Person'; some of the women with her declared their
intention of living 'as well as the Gentry'.[50]

Towards the end of 1795, circumstances suggested a close link
between the popular radicals and popular disturbance in the
metropolis. The success of an open-air meeting in June, together
with a dramatic increase in membership, encouraged the LCS to
arrange another open-air meeting on 26 October in fields surrounding a tavern, Copenhagen House, in Islington. The meeting
was chaired by a young Irishman, John Binns, and heard speeches
from Thelwall, Richard Hodgson, a hatter who had evaded an
arrest warrant for treasonable practices in the preceding year, and
John Gale Jones, a Welsh 'surgeon' who was making a name for
himself as a radical orator. A series of resolutions was passed, an
address was issued to the nation on the critical and calamitous state
of the country, and a remonstrance was sent to George III. The
meeting passed off peacefully; and while there remains dispute
about its actual size, it clearly was a very large gathering.[51] Three
days later, as George III rode in state to the House of Lords, angry
and disorderly crowds thronged the streets demanding bread and
an end to the war. Several of their Lordships were jeered and
hooted; the Duke of Portland was, according to the *Annual
Register*, 'very much hooted'.[52] The king himself was jeered and a
pebble broke a window of his coach—initially the king, and several
others, appeared to have believed it was a shot. When George
returned from Parliament to St James's Palace, crowds pursued

him; he transferred from his state coach to his private coach for the journey to Buckingham Palace. The private coach was pursued into St James's Park where it was jostled and, allegedly, one man tried to drag the king from his seat. A troop of horseguards galloped up in the nick of time to rescue the king and disperse the crowd. The precise events surrounding the attack remain a mystery. Francis Place, the radical tailor, named the man who opened the carriage door as John Ridley, a bootmaker and member of the LCS, but insisted that the whole incident was an accident.[53] John Binns, writing twenty years after Place and over fifty years after the event, also identified the 'attacker' as a member of the LCS, but implied that opening the carriage door was no accident.[54] Whatever the truth, a flood of addresses congratulated the king on his escape, and while the LCS was probably guiltless of any attempt of engineering the trouble, the proximity of the Copenhagen House meeting to the disturbances was too much of a coincidence for most loyalists. A proclamation was issued against seditious assemblies, and the government hastily introduced two bills into parliament. The first made it a treasonable offence to incite hatred of the king, his government, or the constitution either by speech or in writing. The second restricted public meetings to less than fifty persons, unless a magistrate was notified well in advance; it gave magistrates wide powers over such meetings and enabled them to strike at radical lecturers like Thelwall, whose lecture rooms could now be closed as 'disorderly houses.'

The two bills provoked a passionate debate in the country and brought the Foxite Whigs together in alliance with the popular societies. But such an alliance stood little chance against the scale of loyalist outrage and the dominance of the Pitt–Portland coalition in parliament. The bills became law in December. It has been common to portray the passage of the two acts as a significant moment in Pitt's repression of radicalism and the undermining of English liberties. The new treason legislation, however, was never invoked; the Seditious Meetings act was rarely used. Probably their existence on the statute book did frighten some reformers, yet many continued to soldier on: the difficulties which beset the LCS in 1796 resulted less from legislation and government action than from internal disputes, notably about religion. Food rioting eventually subsided with a bountiful harvest in 1796, but internal tranquillity was not restored; indeed the first half of 1797 was the most gloomy

period for Pitt's administration. Towards the end of 1796, as the
remnants of the First Coalition crumbled and as invasion by the
French seemed more likely, the government introduced bills for
raising supplementary auxiliary troops which would reinforce the
English militia in case of invasion and free regular troops for
offensive action. The passing of the bills was the cue for widespread
disturbances in England and Scotland. On two separate occasions
French troop transports penetrated the Royal Navy's defence
cordon: only a stormy sea prevented Lazare Hoche from landing in
the south-west of Ireland at the end of 1796; in February 1797
William Tate and his *légion noire* landed in Pembrokeshire. Tate's
landing was a fiasco but it brought to a climax the deteriorating
position of the Bank of England which, subsequently, called a halt
to payment *in specie*. The popularity of Pitt's government reached
its lowest ebb; the *Annual Register* recorded that during March,
'most of the counties, cities, and towns of the kingdom, petitioned
his Majesty for the removal of ministers, and the consequent
restoration of peace'.[55] April, May, and June saw the largest and
most serious combination to affect Georgian England when the
home fleets mutinied, first at Spithead and then at the Nore. Again
it was feared that the British Jacobins were engineering the trouble.
Probably there was a politically conscious radical minority among
the mutineers, especially at the Nore; there were certainly agitators
on shore who also circulated handbills in the hope of prompting
mutiny in the army. The attitudes of the majority of the seamen are
more difficult to assess. Obviously they backed the aims of the
mutinies for improvement in pay and conditions; yet mutiny in
the Georgian Navy appears in many respects to have mirrored the
legitimizing notions of the eighteenth-century food rioter—mutiny,
like rioting, was the last resort in bringing a social superior's
attention to grievances or problems which required speedy resolution. A majority, at least of those at Spithead, had no intention
of being dictated to by the French and appear to have been fully
prepared to set sail and fight should an invasion be attempted or
should a French fleet put to sea. In 1798 there were abortive
attempts to provoke more mutinies in the fleet; this time politics
were central.[56] The ringleaders of the trouble in 1789 were,
generally speaking, United Irishmen; over the preceding three years,
the United Irishmen had evolved into an insurrectionary organization seeking aid from France.

The arrest and trial of William Jackson had demonstrated to some of the more extreme Irish radicals the possibility of French aid, and their minds raced to hopes of what might be achieved. The brief tenure of the liberal-minded, pro-Catholic Earl Fitzwilliam as Lord Lieutenant of Ireland in 1795 had excited hopes of reform, which were cruelly and rapidly dashed when he was recalled. Economic distress sparked off disorder, brutally suppressed in the north by an alliance of upper-class Protestants and their plebeian co-religionists organized in the Peep o' Day Boys. In the aftermath of the 'Armagh outrages' it appeared to many Catholics that there was a government-backed campaign against them; many joined the militant Catholic Defender associations which responded to Protestant violence in kind, and while individuals joined the United Irish, many Defender groups also attached themselves to the society. The United Irishmen were transformed from a body of radical, but essentially Whig, constitutional reformers into a group of insurrectionary republicans negotiating French assistance, and eventually backed by thousands of Catholic peasants. In March 1798 the Irish authorities sought to forestall insurrection by arresting the leaders of the United Irishmen who were meeting in a house in Dublin. The arrests were partially successful but they sparked off a rebellion which, for all that it was largely leaderless, initially humiliated the British troops in Ireland and shook the existing political system of the country. Cruelty and brutality marked the behaviour of both sides before the rebellion was crushed and General Humbert and his thousand French veterans surrendered to overwhelming odds.[57]

Thousands of Irish had emigrated to England during the eighteenth century looking for work; the United Irish society found members among the Irish communities in England and, among the extremist elements of the popular societies, United Englishmen and United Scotsmen appeared to be espousing conspiratorial means to republican ends. The government received warnings about these societies during 1797: there were allegations of arming and drilling; United Scotsmen may have encouraged the disorders provoked by the Scottish Militia Act.[58] As rebellion flared in Ireland the government in Westminster struck at the United societies in England and Scotland with the suspension of the Habeas Corpus Act and a new round of arrests. George Mealmaker, one of the leaders of the United Scotsmen, was tried and sentenced to fourteen years' transportation; a weaver arrested with him was sentenced to five years and another, who absconded, was outlawed. Upwards of eighty men were held in England for various periods under the suspension of the Habeas Corpus Act; not all of them were offenders, for the lists of those held also includes the government's spies; but no one was ever brought to trial and a few men remained in prison until 1801. The government was reluctant to embark on a new round of prosecutions probably for a variety of reasons: their previous rate of success in the courts had been poor—all of those charged with treason in 1794 had been acquitted, and of the five United Irishmen arrested on the south coast seeking ship for France at the beginning of 1798, only one, the Revd. James Coigley, had been convicted; furthermore the government appears to have preferred to keep its spies functioning secretly in the societies rather than exposing them publicly in the courts and having, in consequence, to infiltrate new agents into any rump that remained.

For a year following the arrests of April 1798 the government spies, William Gent and John Tunbridge, continued to send in reports of meetings of the LCS. The society they described struggled to act much as before: corresponding with the surviving provincial societies, publicizing the ideas of Paine and similar reformers, and now having to find financial assistance for its imprisoned members. Members of the society were also closely linked with the remnants of the United Irishmen and United Englishmen; and there were extravagant stories of arming and drilling. In the spring of 1799 more arrests were made in London of United Irishmen and United Englishmen. A secret parliamentary committee reported on the revolutionary aspirations of these groups and, in July, an act of parliament outlawed by name both the LCS and the different United Societies.

The arrests and the legislation of 1798 and 1799 could not, however, prevent the wave of unrest which swept through Britain during the following two years. As in 1795 and 1796 the disorders of 1799 to 1801 were sparked off, initially, by bad harvests and high prices. Again there were those who saw the economic crisis as something engineered by the British Jacobins 'that they may with more facility bring on a revolution by their destructive principles of Jacobinism',[59] and there were those who believed that rioters were prompted by 'active and ill disposed Persons, who instigate the boys and women to be riotous, in hopes of promoting general confusion'.[60] Particularly noticeable about the disorder of these years is the way that French revolutionary language and example had percolated into the threats of the plebeian classes:

> Peace
> and Large Bread
> or
> a King without a head

began one notice pasted up in Bath.[61] A paper circulating in the neighbourhood of Malden warned:

> On swill and Grains you wish the poor to be fed
> And underneath the Gullintine we could wish to see your heads.[62]

In Banbury 'Cheap Bread or no King' was written on the church door.[63] A paper pasted up in Ramsbury, Wiltshire, urged: 'let us true Britons loock to our selves let us Banish some to Hannover where they came from. Downe with your Contitucion Aret a rebublick'.[64] Social protest mingled with the threats and warnings. The officers of the West Bromwich Volunteers were damned: 'We dont care a dam for your big Devils as wear that damnation bloody bloody rag about your damned paunch bellys.' The ordinary privates, however, were consoled as 'poor fellows' for whom the officers had no care or interest.[65] A Manchester magistrate was urged to reduce food prices: 'if not you may depend a sivel Wars this hardship to put an aend against your fine halls and your pleashuars ground We Will Destroy eather by fire or sword'.[65] Handbills posted in Kidderminster encouraged the people to 'crush' monopolizing farmers and all tyrants; it added:

> The Bishops, Vicars, Curates
> Parliament and things
> not only evils are
> but worthless things.[67]

In the winter of 1800/1 and in the following spring, large open-air nocturnal meetings were held in the industrial districts of Lancashire and the West Riding; there were reports of revolutionary organization and oath-taking, and rumours of planned risings. The resignation of Pitt and his replacement by Addington, the preliminaries of the Peace of Amiens, and, in the autumn, a reasonable harvest combined to reduce the agitation.

It is not the possible to argue that the French Revolution produced a conservative backlash in Britain which held reform in check without also acknowledging that the Revolution, as well as generating the fears which led to the conservative backlash, also contributed greatly to the revival of reformers' hopes. This double impact is reflected in the two greatest political pamphlets to appear in Europe during the revolutionary decade, both of which, ironically, were first written in English and first printed in England—Burke's *Reflections*, which remains perhaps the most powerful statement of political conservatism, and Paine's *Rights of Man*, the classic text upon which many a nineteenth-century radical activist was weaned.

By its double impact the French Revolution helped to polarize politics in Britain, though to do this it had to build on the potential for friction already present within British society: the Anglican–Dissenter rivalry; debates over the meaning of English liberty, which had already provoked conflict during the Wilkes episodes and the American war; emergent class conflict; and, in Ireland (where Catholic–Protestant rivalry was potentially far more dangerous than Anglican–Dissenter rivalry in Britain) a leavening of national sentiment. At both ends of the political spectrum men drew parallels with events in France to spice their propaganda and blacken their opponents. Reformers branded Pitt as 'the English Robespierre' and likened Pitt's 'reign of terror' to that of the extreme Jacobins who, in the eyes of many British reformers, had perverted the course of the French Revolution. Such parallels were ludicrous, but they were potent. For loyal supporters of church, king, and constitution, wishing to score in the propaganda battle, it seemed sufficient to point to the excesses in France and to note how these had followed in the wake of a supposed moderate reform. The proud use of French terms by British reformers who wished to demonstrate their solidarity with the French in what appeared to be a struggle for mankind and liberty in general, only served to confirm the loyalists' worst fears, especially after war had been declared. 'Citizen' John Harrison, who had connections with the popular clubs in both Sheffield and Birmingham, declared himself 'a Lover of my Country! A promoter of love and good-will amongst men! A Friend to Freedom!' and equated these attitudes with being a *sans-culotte*, a title which he also took for himself.[68] For loyalists the *sans-culottes* were the monsters described in the press as responsible for the butchery in the Paris streets; they appeared as half-human, and cannibalistic in the powerful images of cartoonists such as Gillray.

Many moderate reformers were concerned, indeed appalled, by the violence of the Jacobin republic. The threat of invasion by the French led many to declare that their first loyalty was to Britain. The LCS general committee meeting broken up by the Bow Street police officers in April 1798 was discussing what action to take should the French land, and one leading member was reported as opining that the society should offer its services to government to fight an invader since the French seemed 'more desirous of establishing an extensive military despotism, than of propagating republican principles'.[69] At the same time, however, it must be noted that others appear to have been ready to join the French and looked forward to their coming. In Ireland the French were welcome; but Humbert's men arrived too late to assist the main rising which had already been cannonaded to oblivion on Vinegar Hill, and his force was probably too small to have tipped the balance in favour of the United Irishmen. Tate's landing in Wales was of no military significance, and if the *légion noire* was expecting mass support from the Welsh it was to be sadly disappointed. Had the French landed near a large town on the British mainland, and specifically a large town with a significant Irish population and British popular radicals, then the situation might have been different. But it also needs to be borne in mind that revolutions generally begin in capital cities; the overthrow of the Hanoverian regime would have required either the taking of London by the French, or a massive popular insurrection and a crisis of confidence among ministers and within the armed forces. Such an insurrection never materialized. Neither did such a crisis of confidence within Pitt's government, even in the bleak days of 1795 with its food riots and the presence of soldiers among the rioters, or in 1797 when the fleet was in mutiny and attempts were made to subvert the army, or in 1800–1 when food rioters were, on occasions, assisted by military volunteer corps and when activists organized large nocturnal meetings in the industrial districts. The men who ruled England during the decade of the French Revolution may on occasion have been shaken by events, but they were generally ready to take firm action and, when necessary, they found the coercive power and parliamentary support that they required.

Yet the determination, toughness, and internal success of Pitt's government did not dampen the hopes of conspirators, and recent research has suggested an ambivalence to conspiracy among many of those lionized in Whig historiography as constitutional reformers.[70] Fox and his faction seceded from parliament in July 1797 in protest at the behaviour of Pitt's government and their own inability to promote reform. Fox and other leading figures of his parliamentary circle were in close communication with leaders of the United Irishmen in 1797 and early in 1798. The Foxites were probably not fully aware of the insurrectionary nature of the Irish society at this time, but the United Irish appear to have been fortified by a belief in the Foxites' tacit support. Furthermore the secession from parliament, the intemperate speeches of some, and the intemperate behaviour of a few in attempting forcibly to prevent the re-arrest of Arthur O'Connor on an Irish warrant after his acquittal in an English court, all led to contemporary suspicion. The destruction of the papers of the Fifth Duke of Bedford and of the Earl of Stanhope ('Citizen Stanhope') have helped to prompt suspicion among recent historians. Fox's assertion that Pitt had no evidence of conspiracy and that all those arrested under the suspension of the Habeas Corpus Act towards the end of the 1790s were innocent of any crime, is clearly erroneous. In 1803 Colonel Despard was tried for a treasonable conspiracy in London, found guilty, and executed. Despard's plot had definite links with Ireland, and while Fox and his immediate circle were not implicated on this occasion, other radicals, generally portrayed as essentially constitutional, were clearly sympathetic to the seditious men even if their actual involvement remains conjectural.[71]

The conservative backlash frightened many reformers; it angered many others who saw parallels with the French experience and spoke of a 'terror'. Yet the components of the repression, and the different local environments of repression, are as important in any full understanding of the impact of the Revolution on Britain as the components and local environments of radicalism. Pitt's government did not have at its disposal a national police force, nor the local agents of central government who were to be found in many contemporary European states. Local administration was in the hands of local gentlemen: where a local élite opposed the government, as in Nottingham for much of the 1790s, radicalism could enjoy virtual immunity. Where a tradition of conflict existed between an Anglican élite and reformers, generally unenfranchised Dissenters, the political controversies of the 1790s added new, and sometimes particularly vicious, elements to old enmities. In general the old landowning élite which dominated the county benches was suspicious of the British Jacobins and their proposals. Furthermore this élite had considerable power over its tenantry or workforce. In England and Wales, Jacobins could find themselves prosecuted for seditious libel (the publishing of Paine or his ilk especially in 1792–3) or for seditious words (a crime much more noticeable towards the end of the 1790s). The prosecution was generally brought by local gentlemen, often in the early years by members of a Reeves society; the jury might be packed, and the bench of magistrates partial. Jacobins might also find themselves the victims of mob violence. Sometimes the mob was stirred up and encouraged by loyalist gentlemen and was allowed to proceed unchecked by partial magistrates, as appears to have been the case when the house of the prominent dissenter and scientist Joseph Priestley was sacked in Birmingham in July 1791. But it would be wrong to see every attack on English Jacobins as inspired by the élite: in Liverpool William Roscoe and his circle were suspect in the eyes of the populace for their stance against the slave trade—the Liverpool populace recognized that their town's prosperity depended upon slaves. Some of the Paineite burnings, moreover, have all the hallmarks of traditional, folkloric rough musicking and were rather different from the more organized bonfires and celebrations laid on by gentlemen. Some of the volunteer corps organized from the early stages of the war were as much, possibly more, concerned with a counter-revolutionary role than with an anti-invasion one. During the economic crisis of 1799–1801 some of the poorer volunteers, especially those in urban infantry corps, became distinctly unreliable against food rioters. Yet patriotism and determination to oppose a French landing were clearly present as reasons for many plebeian volunteers joining these corps in the first place.

The behaviour of the local élites towards the British Jacobins was conducted under the umbrella of government exhortation and legislation. Beyond exhortation the government had no means of ensuring that magistrates took what the government might consider to be appropriate action. The government's law officers conducted only a very few of the political prosecutions in England and Wales during the 1790s. Generally, when invited to prosecute in the provinces by local magistrates, they declined. The much criticized repressive legislation of 1795 was scarcely used. Unquestionably a few of the arrests and prosecutions authorized by the central government had a profound effect. The arrests of 1794 do appear to have been a key element in prompting men to leave the popular clubs in droves, yet membership increased again significantly in the following year. The prosecution of Gilbert Wakefield in 1798 for seditious libel under an *ex-officio* information led to several pamphlets by moderate reformers being rejected by nervous printers; yet these pamphlets were published the following year. While the repressive behaviour of Pitt's government left a legacy of anger and hatred, the impact of certain key incidents in that repression would appear to have been of a relatively short duration. The numbers frightened off reform activity by the repression, as opposed to the numbers who joined during periods of particular excitement and/or economic hardship, and who fell away as rapidly, can only be guessed at. But to attribute the defeat of the reformers during the 1790s to Pittite repression is to overrate both the scale of the latter and the intensity of support for the former.

The repression in Scotland was conducted under a different legal system. Scottish law, unlike the law in England and Wales, allowed men to be transported for sedition. The transportation of the Scottish martyrs and later of George Mealmaker may have had a more profound and discouraging effect on Scottish reformers. From time to time there was concern south of the border that Pitt was contemplating legislation to enable similar sentences to be passed in the English courts, but no such legislation was ever introduced, and in England and Wales sentences for seditious libel were rarely of more than two years' imprisonment. The manner in which Lord Braxfield taunted the accused from the bench may equally have unnerved faint hearts; but the scale of repression in Scotland, outside of these celebrated incidents, awaits a historian and it probably differed little from the overall pattern in England and Wales. Official oppression in all three countries was, by and large, conducted under the existing law. What the 1790s did was to demonstrate the legal powers available to the British government to maintain itself, and the limits on the boasted rights of Englishmen when the government and the ruling élite perceived itself under threat.

In Ireland the repression might justifiably be given the name 'terror'. The activities of the authorities at Dublin Castle caused concern among, and prompted rebukes from, the government at Westminster. Out in the countryside the repression conducted by the military was ferocious. Sir Ralph Abercrombie, the commander-in-chief in Ireland, resigned partly in disgust at the brutal behaviour of the yeomanry and the militia in the weeks before the 1798 rebellion; when Lord Cornwallis assumed command in the aftermath of the rebellion, he expressed his horror at 'the ferocity of the troops'.[72] The rebellion resolved the government at Westminster to incorporate Ireland fully into Great Britain; the Act of Union was passed in 1801. But the cruel history of the rebellion and its repression, and the rising of Robert Emmet in 1803, left future Irish patriots with a gallery of martyrs; furthermore, while the United Irishmen had not begun as anti-English or anti-Protestant, or as social reformers, in the mythology of the movement as proclaimed by subsequent Irish republicans, they tended to assume all of these forms.

Mythology was also to play a potent role in political radicals' portrayals of the 1790s in England and Scotland. In 1832 the editor of the *Scotsman* saw in the agitation for the Great Reform Act the climax of 'the Forty Years War', a war which had been declared on 21 May 1792 with the royal proclamation against seditious meetings and publications, 'an act forever memorable as the commencement of the struggle between the House of Commons and the People'.[73] Like the use of the term 'Pitt's reign of terror', the word 'war' here illustrates the passion of the continuing reform debate rather than helping towards a meaningful explanation of events. The agitation for reform survived the 1790s; considerable continuity in the membership of reform and radical groups has been detected in London and the provinces from the revolutionary decade, through the Napoleonic wars, and beyond. There was also continuity among those who participated in the twilight world of conspiracy in England, Scotland, and Ireland. The French Revolution put the debate about the structure of British politics and the parliamentary system at the top of the political agenda. The fury and venom of this debate built on the arguments raised in the Wilkite disorders of the 1760s and the disputes over sovereignty and representation inherent in the American troubles. The intensity of the debate probably also contributed to its longevity. Wilkes had received massive plebeian support and had played upon this in his appeals to the rights of the free-born Englishman; artisan groups had shown a strong interest in events in America. A key legacy of the French Revolution's impact on Britain was the way in which it encouraged self-taught plebeians to agitate for change on their own behalf. After the winter of 1791–2 British radicalism was always to be infused with plebeian activists, no longer prepared simply to follow, but ready publicly to argue their own political case and to push their own political demands.

NOTES

[1] E. P. Thompson, *The Making of the English Working Class* (London, 1963).

[2] Sir Nathaniel Wraxall, *Historical Memoirs* (2nd edn., London, 1815), i, p. iii.

[3] Anna Leticia Barbauld, *An Address to the Opposers of the Repeal of the Corporation and Test Acts* (1790), quoted in Alfred Cobban, ed., *The Debate on the French Revolution 1789–1800* (London, 1950), p. 50.

[4] Richard Price, *A Discourse on the Love of our Country* (1789), quoted in Cobban, pp. 61 and 64.

[5] T. W. Copeland, ed., *The Correspondence of Edmund Burke* (9 vols., Cambridge, 1958–70), vi. 39–50.

[6] Edmund Burke, *Reflections on the Revolution in France* (London, 1910), p. 164.

[7] The best and most recent study of both popular and genteel radicals during the revolutionary decade is Albert Goodwin, *The Friends of Liberty: The English Democratic Movement in the Age of the French Revolution* (London, 1979). Unless otherwise indicated, material on the societies is drawn from Goodwin.

[8] This phrase is taken from the SCI's 'First Address to the Public'. See E. C. Black, *The Association: British Extraparliamentary Political Organisation, 1769–1793* (Cambridge, Mass., 1963), p. 178.

[9] S[cottish] R[ecord] O[ffice], Melville Castle Muniments G.D.1.17.2 Loughborough to Dundas, 24 Apr. 1792.

[10] [Public Record Office] T.S.11.952.3496(2) Ashton to Adams, 26 May 1792.

[11] Thomas Hardy, *Memoir of Thomas Hardy* (London, 1832); Mary Thale, ed., *Selections from the Papers of the London Corresponding Society 1792–1799* (Cambridge, 1983), p. 10.

[12] *The Wyvill Papers* (York, 1794–1804), v. 50.

[13] R. I. and S. Wilberforce, *The Correspondence of William Wilberforce* (London, 1840), i. 290.

[14] H[istorical] M[anuscripts] C[ommission] *Dropmore Papers*, ii. 236.

[15] SRO Melville Castle Muniments G.D.1.17.2 Loughborough to Dundas, 24 Apr. 1792.

[16] Thale, op. cit. 15.

[17] T.S.11.952.3496(2) Goff to Adams, 19 June 1792, and Ashton to Adams, 3 July 1792.

[18] Bishop of Bath and Wells, ed., *Journal and Correspondence of William, Lord Auckland* (London, 1861–2), ii. 411.

[19] *Annual Register* (1792), p. 36.

[20] [Public Record Office] H.O.42.21.

[21] Lord John Russell, ed., *Memorials and Correspondence of Charles James Fox* (London, 1853–7), ii. 368.

[22] Sir Samuel Romilly, *Memoirs of the life of Sir Samuel Romilly written by himself* (ed. by his sons, London, 1840), ii. 4–5 and 8–9; *London Chronicle* (13 Sept. 1792); *The Times* (10 Sept. 1792); *Morning Chronicle* (8 and 11 Sept. 1792).

[23] *Address of the London Corresponding Society to the other Societies of Great Britain*, 29 Nov. 1792, copy in T.S.11.952.3496(2).

[24] H.O.42.21.52b.

[25] *Manchester Herald* (15 Sept. 1792).

[26] *Leeds Intelligencer* (17 Sept. 1792).

[27] Russell, ii. 372.

[28] H.O.42.22.208 'The Committee' to Fournier, 6 Nov. 1792.

[29] T.S.11.952.3496(2) contains copies of all of these addresses.

[30] *London Chronicle* (11 Dec. 1792).

[31] H.O.42.22.203 Newport to Nepean, 5 Nov. 1792.

[32] *Parliamentary History*, xxx. 189.

[33] H.O.42.22 Vaughan to Nepean, 30 Nov. 1792.

[34] B[ritish] L[ibrary] Add[itional] MSS 16920 ff. 17–20, Howlett to Moore, 1 Dec. 1792.

[35] BL Add MSS 16923 ff. 47–50, Trimmer to Reeves, 22 Dec. 1792.

[36] Clive Emsley, 'The London "Insurrection" of December 1792: Fact, Fiction, or Fantasy?', *Journal of British Studies* 17, 2 (1978), 66–86.

[37] Black, op. cit., ch. 7 *passim*; Donald E. Ginter, 'The Loyalist Association Movement of 1792–93', *Historical Journal* 9, 2 (1966), 179–90. Robert R. Dozier, *For King, Constitution and Country: The English Loyalists and the French Revolution* (Lexington, 1983), is disappointing.

[38] *HMC Dropmore*, ii. 359.

[39] *Second Report of the Committee of Secrecy of the House of Commons* (London, 1794), Appendix E.

[40] T.S.11.953.3497 Hardy to Cordell, 11 Jan. 1794.

[41] *Second Report of the Committee of Secrecy*, Appendix C.

[42] *First Report of the Committee of Secrecy of the House of Commons* (London, 1794), pp. 30 ff.

[43] Hardy, op. cit. 42–3 and 121. The *Courier*, 14 Nov. 1794, reported that there were eighty warrants ready to be issued on Hardy's conviction.

[44] Frances Dorothy Cartwright, *The Life and Correspondence of Major Cartwright, edited by his niece* (London, 1826), i. 210 and 213.

[45] H.O.42.35.197 Garnett to Portland, 18 July 1795.

[46] H.O.42.36.235 Fellows to Portland (?), 19 Oct. 1795.

[47] *A Picture of the Times, in a Letter, addressed to the People of England by a Lover of Peace* (2nd edn., London, 1795).

[48] *The Rights of Swine. An Address to the Poor* (London, 1795). This was one of a series of pamphlets published by 'Citizen' Richard Lee from his bookshop 'The British Tree of Liberty' which changed its address three times during 1795. Many of Lee's publications suggest a predilection for the Jacobin Terror and can only have served to aggravate loyalist fears: *Block the Third*; *King Killing*; *The Happy Reign of George the Last*; *The Reign of the English Robespierre*; *Citizen Guillotine (with a Caricature Copperplate)*. Lee eventually emigrated to the United States.

[49] *London Chronicle* (3 Aug. 1795).

[50] H.O.42.35.213 Philipps to Portland, 24 Aug. 1795.

[51] Compare the estimates in Thompson, pp. 157–8, and Goodwin, pp. 384–5.

[52] *Annual Register* (1795), p. 37.

[53] BL Add MSS 27808 ff. 47–9.

[54] *Recollections of the Life of John Binns, by himself*, (Philadelphia, 1854), pp. 55–6.

[55] *Annual Register* (1797) p. 18; see also p. 83.

[56] Conrad Gill, *The Naval Mutinies of 1797* (Manchester, 1913), remains the best account of the 1797 mutinies. For the mutiny attempts in 1798, see Roger Wells, *Insurrection: The British Experience 1795–1803* (Gloucester, 1983), pp. 145–51.

[57] For events in Ireland during the revolutionary decade, see Marianne Elliott, *Partners in Revolution: The United Irishmen and France* (New Haven, 1982).

[58] Kenneth J. Logue, *Popular Disturbances in Scotland 1780–1815* (Edinburgh, 1979), pp. 110–13. There has been no detailed study of Scottish radicalism in the revolutionary decade since H. W. Meikle, *Scotland and the French Revolution* (Glasgow, 1912).

[59] H.O.42.50 Packes to Portland, 16 May 1800.

[60] H.O.42.50 Legge to John King (?), 1 May 1800.

[61] H.O.42.50 George to Master of the Rolls, 13 and 16 Mar. 1800.

[62] [Public Record Office] WO.47.17 Lee to Windham, 6 Feb. 1800.

[63] H.O.42.49 Walford to Morice, 27 Apr. 1800.

[64] H.O.42.50 Meyrick to Portland, 12 June 1800.

[65] H.O.42.49 Jesson to Gower, 11 Apr. 1800.

[66] H.O.42.50 Bayley to Portland, 23 June 1800.

[67] H.O.42.55.116–19 Bailiff of Kidderminster to Portland, 17 Dec. 1800.

[68] John Harrison, *A Letter to the Rt. Hon. Henry Dundas M.P., or an Appeal to the People of Great Britain* (London, 1794), p. 27.

[69] Thale, op. cit. 430.

[70] Elliott, op. cit. 209–12; J. Anne Hone, *For the Cause of Truth: Radicalism in London 1796–1821* (Oxford, 1982), pp. 42–7 and 113–17; Wells, op. cit. 65–9, 175–6, and 201–5.

[71] The following paragraphs are based largely on Clive Emsley, 'An Aspect of Pitt's "Terror": prosecutions for sedition during the 1790s', *Social History*, 6 (1981), 155–84; and id., 'Repression, "terror" and the rule of law in England during the decade of the French Revolution', *English Historical Review*, 100 (1985), 801–25.

[72] Elliott, op. cit. 191–2 and 207.

[73] BL Add MSS 27809 ff. 268–72.

Radical Spectators of the Revolution: the Case of the *Analytical Review*[1]

BRIAN RIGBY

IN this essay I shall try to describe some of the ways in which an important group of British writers wrote about France and the French Revolution from 1788 to the end of the 1790s. In order to do this I have chosen to look closely at the *Analytical Review*, perhaps the most important intellectual radical monthly of the period.[2] An important part of my intention is to show how the French Revolution crystallized various contradictions in British radical thinking of the time. The *Analytical Review* was published by Joseph Johnson[3] and edited initially by Thomas Christie.[4] Johnson played a central role in Unitarian and dissenting circles and his publishing activities were of considerable significance in the late eighteenth century. His circle of literary, intellectual, religious, and political associates was extensive, and he drew on the rich resources of provincial literary and intellectual life, as well as on those of London. The small army of reviewers required to furnish material for the 133 numbers of the *Analytical* represented an important body of radical intellectuals active throughout the 1790s. However, although we know the identity of certain reviewers, for instance Mary Wollstonecraft[5] and Henry Fuseli,[6] we remain in ignorance with regard to the vast majority. The *Analytical* emerges as a collective venture, as the expression of the opinions of an influential section of the intellectual classes, as the voice of the educated, professional, and dissenting middle class which supported progressive reform and sympathized with the cause of the French Revolution in the late 1780s and throughout the 1790s. There are, of course, differences of opinion among reviewers; none the less, it is possible to isolate and describe the review's stance on a range of issues thrown into prominence by the events of the Revolution.

It would, however, give a false impression of the intellectual activity of the *Analytical* were we to forget that, even at the height of the most passionate debates about the Revolution, the journal continued to devote an enormous amount of space to scholarly topics which had no direct bearing on contemporary politics in Britain or in France. The educated classes of the late eighteenth century aspired to a kind of universal knowledge, and it was assumed that readers of the *Analytical* would take a lively and informed interest in a range of scholarly areas. The first issue (May 1788) contained the following headings: Theology, Sacred Criticism, Ecclesiastical History, Philosophy, History, Biography, Law, Natural Knowledge, Botany, Chemistry, Medicine, Anatomy, Surgery, Mathematical Sciences, Music, Poetry, and finally Miscellanies (as if the rest had not been miscellaneous enough). The contents may strike the modern mind as uncompromisingly erudite; moreover, one cannot but be impressed by the range of material, by the expertise demonstrated, and, above all, by the degree of intellectual curiosity that informed the journal. In a characteristically eighteenth-century manner critical debate co-existed with scholarly matters. We find political concerns arising in contexts which might at first sight seem somewhat remote, for example in connection with theology and law. More pressing political preoccupations were not absent from the journal, but they were more obviously felt in some issues than in others.[7] This was the case, for instance, in the late 1790 and early 1791 issues which contained extensive discussions of the *Reflections on the Revolution in France* and the replies to Burke.[8] This was also the case throughout 1794 and early 1795, when the *Analytical* devoted a considerable amount of space to reviewing and publishing extracts from the proceedings of the British Treason Trials.

In a manner representative of late eighteenth-century culture, the review aspired to a comprehensive, even universal knowledge and prided itself on its scholarly impartiality. Indeed, one of the most interesting aspects of the *Analytical* is the way in which it set itself up as the epitome of impartiality, objectivity, and universality at the very time when such values were being challenged and when political opinion, under the impact of the Revolution, was being severely polarized. In his prefatory address 'To the Public' in the first number of the *Review*, the young Scottish Unitarian editor, Thomas Christie, enlarged upon a passage from Francis Bacon which served as the epigraph to each issue.[9] The quotation recommended that reviewers analyse their subjects, not in the manner of critics who waste their time praising or finding fault, but rather in the manner of scholars, who set down the facts historically

and are sparing with their opinions. In this spirit, Christie lamented
the condition of modern journalism: contemporary critics were
only interested in flaunting their own opinions and judgements.
They failed to give a fair hearing to the author under review and
neglected their responsibility to encourage the reader to judge for
himself on the basis of the facts set before him.[10] Christie insisted
that the dominant quality of a reviewer should be 'modesty': his
task was not to give personal opinions to make polemical points,
but to perform the purely 'analytical' task of setting out and
explaining the contents of the books reviewed.[11] 'Could we pursue
our own plan,' Christie remarked, 'it would be to have one purely
analytical. The true idea of a Literary Journal is to give the history
of the republic of letters.'[12] However, Christie admitted that such a
journal would only be 'esteemed by the learned and thinking few
[and] would not be sufficiently adapted to the taste of the public at
large'.[13] In order to reach a wider public and to make the review an
economic proposition a compromise was effected. The journal was
still to have 'more of an analytic cast in it than any other',[14] but the
editors judged that there needed to be some expression of
opinion—although for modern readers the amount of opinion
seems rather small in comparison with the number of austere
articles of scholarly analysis. Christie ended his prefatory address
by asserting that 'it will be our highest ambition to give to the world
a respectable Journal, one that shall tend to diffuse knowledge, and
to advance the interests of science, of virtue and morality'.[15] But
whilst the *Analytical* remained predominantly a scholarly review,
whose standard reviewing procedure was limited to giving substantial extracts and minimal critical comment, this was far from
the whole story. At those points where the *Analytical* departed
from the scholarly procedures which it set itself, we can discern the
strain which contemporary events in France and Britain were
putting on the values of impartiality and objective analysis: the
stances of 'modesty' and 'respectability' gave way to polemic and
partisan passion.

The *Analytical*'s claim to be an impartial, scholarly journal was,
of course, ridiculed by its political opponents, who simply lumped
it into the same Jacobinical bag as reviews such as the *Monthly* and
the *Critical*.[16] These reviews were seen by anti-Jacobins as totally
ungodly and unpatriotic and were regularly singled out and
stigmatized in the fight against the spread of 'French principles'.[17]

British conservatives pursued all in Britain who showed sympathy for anything French, branding them as 'TRAITORS, persons leagued with the enemy for the overthrow of the British constitution'.[18] The main purpose of the *Anti-Jacobin Review*—as its prospectus made clear—was to counter the influence of such treacherous and infidel publications as the *Analytical*.[19] And when, in December 1798, the original series of the journal came to an end, the *Anti-Jacobin* clearly believed it had played a significant role, not only in scrutinizing the Jacobinical reviews, but also in actually destroying the *Analytical*:

Of the *utility* of our past labours, (and, we must observe that *our* ambition is not *to shine*, but *to be useful*), a full conviction may be acquired by a careful comparison of the *late* numbers of the *Monthly* and *Critical Reviews*, with any of those that were published previous to the month of August last, when our first number appeared. The other object of our immediate attacks, the *Analytical Review*, has received its death-blow, and we have more reason to congratulate ourselves upon the share which we have had in producing its dissolution, than it would be expedient here to unfold.[20]

The *Anti-Jacobin* was of course correct in its assessment that the *Analytical* was in profound sympathy with the early stages of the Revolution in France as well as with the radical causes championed by middle-class Rational Dissenters in Britain.[21] The *Analytical*'s true position was clearly expressed in its judgement of Burke's *Reflections on the Revolution in France*:

It is obvious, that one of Mr. Burke's leading principles is, that it is wiser and better to ground our claim to liberty, and a free and equal government on prescription, local custom, or what he calls *inheritance*, than on the abstract principles of truth and reason, as 'the rights of men'. This we confess appears to us a monstrous and extraordinary doctrine—a doctrine which places an effectual bar to all progressive improvement, immerges the human mind in all the darkness of the darkest ages.[22]

As middle-class dissenters, keen for reform, and intensely aware of their own exclusion from full civic and political dignity, the *Analytical* reviewers were bound to react violently to Burke's assault on 'innovation'. Indeed, it is when they speak for the dignity of the middle ranks of society and against the pretensions of the aristocracy, that they speak with most passion:

We cannot, as cool and dispassionate persons, subscribe to Mr. Burke's extravagant idolatry of ancestry and rank. He seems to intimate, that a person of ignoble birth, intruding himself into a legislative station, commits an usurpation on the *prerogatives* of *nature*, and that in lowering certain individuals, (the nobles we presume), the French have lowered the *dignity* and *importance* of the *state*. To the present legislators of France, Mr. Burke proudly opposes the Guises, the Condés, the Colignis, and the Richelieus.— We would only wish to know, what service these *great* men rendered to mankind? Or whether the 'taylors and carpenters of Paris,' are not better citizens, if they prove instrumental in rescuing their fellow-creatures from oppression and injustice? We know of no rule for judging of men but by their conduct. Mr. Burke may tell us of 'every thing illustrious in rank, in descent, in hereditary and acquired opulence;' and of men of liberal professions not being 'habituated to sentiments of dignity.'—But we can see no reason why lawyers, and curates, may not prove as able legislators as dissipated men of family, who have lavished their patrimony in the most profligate pursuits; and we are confirmed in this sentiment (by a fact which indeed is immediately contrary to another of our author's assertions) that is, that we fear *men of family* are in general very far from being the best educated persons in any nation.[23]

Since the educated middle-class dissenters did not have rank or power, they constantly looked to their moral qualities and intellectual capacities as signs of their dignity, worth, and even superiority over aristocratic 'men of family'. It was, indeed, one of the major radical strategies of the period to place the highest significance on intellectual capacities in order to advance the claims of the educated middle classes over the inherited privileges of the aristocracy. The strategy of the *Analytical* reviewers was precisely this, for in their cool and dispassionate examination of the facts they claimed to speak for Reason, as opposed to alleged aristocratic superstition and irrationality. The radical response to Burke focused on his brilliant oratory, for it was this that had to be conjured away: Burke's rhetorical skills were interpreted so as to suggest that he was 'the dupe of his imagination or his passions'.[24] The Rational Dissenter's view was that the Burkean sublime was simply the mask of injustice and irrationality. The *Analytical*'s editor, Thomas Christie, was suspicious of the power of Burke's eloquence: the ideal stance of the Rational Dissenter required a calm, reasonable examination of the facts, and involved a refusal to be duped by the false and the meretricious.[25] The dissenters associated Burke's defence of ancient privilege with what they saw as the irrationality and gaudiness of Roman Catholicism. In their eyes Burke's ornate style was the style of ancient monarchy. Thomas Paine, on the other hand, was considered to possess a style to match his egalitarian and democratic sentiments, a style which seemingly depended on unadorned rational argument.[26] In fact, so profound was the *Analytical*'s agreement with Paine on political matters—on, for example, the 'despotism of the English system[27]— that it could hardly bring itself to criticize his attitudes to religion and morality.[28] This is significant, for it was on these issues that the rather puritanical and pious dissenting reviewers of the *Analytical* differed markedly from many of their political allies, whose critique of despotic monarchy was rooted in French eighteenth-century materialistic philosophy and whose writings were imbued with the spirit of *libertinage*. In fact it is ironic that the anti-Jacobins consistently chose to represent the *Analytical* as thoroughly pro-French and therefore in total sympathy with scepticism and licentiousness. The evidence of the *Analytical* does not bear out this picture of a review intending to subvert traditional 'English' moral and religious values. Its treatment of Voltaire, for example, fell well within the standard English conservative response to France:[29]

Every one knows with what pleasure Voltaire diffused the poison of Scepticism and infidelity through his voluminous works. There is scarcely a single production of his in prose, that does not contain some impious ribaldry, or indecent scoffing at the truths of Divine Revelation. So fond was this versatile genius of aiming the shafts of ridicule at objects, which every good man regards with pious reverence or respectful silence, that he would often wander from his subject for the sake of indulging a pitiful witticism, or starting an idle cavil.[30]

The very term 'the poison of Scepticism and infidelity' could come straight out of an anti-Jacobin tract. What is more, the violence of the objection to Voltaire's 'impious ribaldry' and 'indecent scoffing at the truths of Divine Revelation' shows to what extent the *Analytical* itself still held to the 'truths' of Divine Revelation. As to the charge that it was eager to introduce all things French, one only has to see how it reviewed a translation of Voltaire's *La Pucelle or the Maid of Orleans* in April 1789 to realize that, like the staunch British conservatives, it wanted to keep England, and particularly the common man, free from being infected by such material.[31] And in November 1790 the reviewer of Condorcet's *Life of Voltaire* made explicit the degree of difference between English Unitarians and French free-thinkers. Here Condorcet's religious and political sentiments were described as being even 'more licentious and more extravagant' than those of Voltaire:

Not content to correct the errors and expose the superstitions of a fraudulent and corrupt system; not disposed to separate Christianity from the mass of folly and corruption, which the vice and ignorance of ages have heaped on it, our author would destroy every form of religion, and break the tie which connects the human soul with the Deity: but he might as well attempt to extirpate from our bosoms the passions of hope and fear.[32]

Reservations were also expressed when the *Analytical* looked at Condorcet's *Esquisse d'un tableau historique des progrès de l'esprit humain*. Initially the reviewer was happy to envisage Condorcet as a philosophical martyr to the revolutionary cause, even comparing his death to that of Socrates.[33] But the sense of awe aroused by the fate of the modern philosophical martyr soon gave way to dismay: the *Analytical* found unacceptable what it judged to be the flippant and irresponsible manner in which French progressive philosophers dismissed Christianity out of hand.[34] For despite the progressive, unorthodox views of some dissenters, and despite the way in which anti-Jacobins branded them as infidels, most Unitarians were still very much part of a pious and strict non-conformist culture which considered that fundamental religious and moral principles should be inculcated in the population at large, and not least in the poor and the young—a point much in evidence in the favourable reviews given by the *Analytical* to works devoted to the Sunday-School movement.[35]

The British Rational Dissenter, caught between his two contradictory political and religious impulses, was also faced with the dilemma of how to argue for his political, religious, and moral principles, while advocating the notion of impartiality. The case of Condorcet illustrates the predicament of the *Analytical*. Here was a philosopher who by his immoderate, impassioned, and partisan attacks on Christianity, was no better than those he claimed to be attacking: 'In the violent invectives which we find against Christianity, the author [Condorcet] forgets, that there may be a species of fanatic philosophy, and a degree of bigotry, or wild enthusiasm in politics, as dangerous as ignorance, and as corrupt as tyranny.' The *Analytical* not only takes issue with Condorcet's characterization of all religion as 'bigotry, superstition and fraud', it also rejects his pretensions to an 'exclusive power to pronounce the oracles of truth'. The *Analytical* thought of itself as part of a community of 'men . . . of disinterested sincerity', and considered that all such men were bound to feel indignation at Condorcet's habit of hurling 'opprobrious epithets' at the Christian religion. However, it was so attached to its ideal of a measured philosophical stance that it felt that 'men . . . of disinterested sincerity' should not retaliate in kind: 'were they to retort them [these opprobrious epithets], what would ensue, but mutual hostilities, and an infringement of that toleration and forbearance, which every good man wishes to promote?'[36] This passage is reminiscent of a section of Thomas Christie's *Letters on the Revolution of France*, in which he objected to Burke's lavish use of 'abusive epithets': 'If a man let loose his over-heated imagination, and accuses others of being plunderers, confiscators, atheists, and even murderers, they may be stimulated to retaliate, by calling him court-flatterer, turn-coat, toad-eater, knave, pensioner and slave. Thus a war of abusive epithets and malignity is begun, which troubles the peace of society, and often produces dreadful consequences.'[37] While condemning the 'war of abusive epithets' Christie managed, however, to let fly a few of his own at Burke's expense. Nevertheless, the main point remains that as editor of the *Analytical* Christie wished all debate about the Revolution to be carried out in a scholarly and rational manner. To resort to abuse was not only to fall below the standards of rational debate, it was also to encourage populist passions. Political debate should remain the preserve of 'the reflecting and enlightened part of the community'.[38]

The *Analytical* thought that since everyone who wrote on the Revolution viewed it 'through a coloured medium',[39] it was necessary to make an open declaration of one's partisanship, so that the reader could make up his own mind as to the worth of the testimony and interpretation being offered. Best of all, of course, was to raise the debate onto the level of rational and philosophical analysis, to try and arrive at exact historical truth, not by looking through the 'magnifying medium of prejudice' or applying 'the secret bias of a pre-established theory',[40] but by standing back from the immediate political context and transcending one's own personal enthusiasm and involvement: 'In truth, the merits of the great political and ecclesiastical questions now before the public can never be examined fairly, till they are detached from all those adventitious circumstances, which have been associated with them by passion and interest.'[41]

Although the *Analytical* reviewers strove to adopt this measured, unbiased, and philosophical stance while discussing contemporary political issues, they also realized that such objectivity could only be fully achieved by posterity: 'It must be the business of the future historian to disentangle the threads of the complicated events which are now passing.'[42] A review in 1795 of William Playfair's *The History of Jacobinism* categorized three kinds of 'historians' of the Revolution. The first kind encompassed 'those who, though they may detest some characters, and abhor some measures, which have disgraced it, heartily approve of the general principles upon which the revolution has been founded'; the second consisted of those who 'choose to suspend their judgment concerning the utility of a republican plan of government, and to wait till the present great struggle is terminated before they pronounce directly on its merits'; the third was made up of those who regarded 'every advance in political freedom as a step towards anarchy, and more jealous for the honour of princes than for the rights of the people, condemn the revolution *in toto*, both in principle and in execution'.[43] On the basis of what I have already said, the *Analytical* clearly placed itself in the second group, occupying the comfortable middle ground, remaining sympathetic to the friends of freedom in England and France but refusing to be drawn into precocious and ill-considered enthusiasms. It objected violently to being tarred with the same brush as more intemperate enthusiasts of the Revolution, even when some of these (such as Mary Wollstonecraft) were to be found among its own ranks. The *Analytical* well understood that, as a political strategy, anti-Jacobins such as Playfair were seeking to designate as 'Jacobins' a range of people with different opinions: 'Nothing is easier than to proscribe any class of citizens by means of an appellation, first rendered odious to the multitude: we ourselves have had some instances of this in our own history, one of which is still fresh in our memory.'[44] The *Analytical* may have had in mind the British Treason trials of 1794–5 when it highlighted this strategy. Or more probably, it was thinking of the Birmingham Riots of July 1791, when the Unitarian preacher, philosopher, and scientist Joseph Priestley found himself the victim of a Church and King mob which burned his house down and effectively hounded

him out of the town because of his alleged Jacobinism. The
persecution of Priestley was an event of critical importance for the
Analytical, for it occasioned an analysis of the effects of industrialization, as well as a critique of those conservative political forces
which were manipulating the working population for their own
purposes:

It is a melancholy reflection, that manufactures, as at present conducted,
seem to debase the human mind. The children of manufacturers in the
town of Birmingham, being employed in the unceasing circle of manual
labour from their earliest youth, become mere pieces of mechanism by the
time that they attain the usual age of discretion. Deprived of education by
the poverty of their parents, they are equally incapable of judging and of
acting for themselves; thus they are at every instant liable to be misled by
the arts of the malicious, and the counsels of the profligate and the
designing, and it may so happen, while the wealth of the kingdom is
increasing, and its commerce extending by their efforts, that the beings by
whose agency those blessings are secured, are themselves relapsing into a
state of deplorable ignorance and barbarity. It is undoubtedly a *desideratum*
in morals as well as in politicks, that men should be taught to think as well
as act.

These short reflections are not suggested by the *wounded spirit* of a
dissenter, who has either experienced, or is exposed, to oppression; they
are the suggestions of a man who thinks that society has no controul over
religious opinions; that the diffusion of knowledge tends to the promotion
of virtue; and that morals can form the only stable basis of civil liberty.[45]

This was both a plea for religious tolerance—in this case on
behalf of Unitarians—and a plea for education as the only possible
basis for civic well-being in an age of industrial progress which was
witnessing the painful emergence of democratic politics. But
awareness of the cynical manoeuvres of men of power did not
lessen the *Analytical*'s fear and distrust of the unthinking mob. In
his *Letters on the Revolution*, Thomas Christie made clear that,
even before the Revolution, Rational Dissenters had few populist
illusions. At a time when dissenters were being denied full
citizenship, their main aim was to achieve civic and political power
for the educated middle classes. The 'uninformed multitudes' had
nothing worthwhile to offer in the making of a democratic society:

If Governors would know the secret of rendering their Government firm,
and their situations tranquil, let them respect *public opinion*, and watch its
progress. I do not mean the opinion merely of numbers, the predominant

opinion of uninformed multitudes, who may be said to have no opinion, because they have no *principles*, and consequently no *fixed* opinions; but I mean the opinion of the reflecting and enlightened part of the community.[46]

Early British sympathizers with the Revolution thought that it signalled the emergence of 'a civilization founded on reason and morality'.[47] In reality, the 'enthusiasm' of the dissenters was significantly tempered by their cautious, scholarly, and rational mentality.[48] They thought that the Revolution, even in its first stages, should be subjected to reasoned analysis. Thus Thomas Christie and the *Analytical* could not see what possible contribution might be made by the 'uninformed multitudes', or how they could understand the significance of the event or appreciate its magnitude. But on the other hand, Christie was genuinely dumbfounded that a man of Burke's intellectual capacities could fail to respond to the Revolution with a due sense of its importance:

That the French Revolution should have been misunderstood by the weak, the thoughtless, and superficial, who constitute but too great a portion of mankind; that this immense event should have been ill appreciated, by men who neither possessed acquired learning to judge of the past, nor vigor of intellect to anticipate the future—that it should have excited the hatred of bigots, or the contempt of triflers, and the *fruges consumere nati* of human society, was what I should have expected. Nor was I surprized to find *some* men of superior sense and uncontested discernment, who, immersed in the occupations of business, and viewing the French Revolution only through the faithless medium of newspapers, had formed an unfavourable opinion of it;—but that a politician and a philosopher should so judge, that a man grown old in the observation of political business, and the affairs of nations, should so far mistake the matter—that a *master in Israel* should not know these things, was an event so extraordinary and unexpected, that when I first discovered it, I was stupified with astonishment.[49]

These comments follow a familiar pattern. The Revolution's British radical sympathizers always considered their conservative, anti-Jacobin opponents to be 'narrow-minded', lacking sufficient generosity of spirit or expansiveness of vision to appreciate its full significance and its contribution to human progress. The conservatives, on the other hand, followed Burke in believing that a man's primary attachment and 'affection' was for the 'little platoon', his own family, neighbourhood, and country, and not for some abstract, general notion such as humanity.

In its review of Condorcet's *Life of Voltaire* the *Analytical* expressed its fundamental belief in the need for tolerance of others and for acceptance of difference of opinion: 'It is, indeed, the peculiar delusion of every narrow-minded sect to suppose, that all mankind will, or ought to embrace their tenets.'[50] In saying this, the reviewer saw in Condorcet an example of a radical philosopher who, in his pursuit of liberty, had himself become a prejudiced fanatic. The reviewer would inevitably also have had in mind the intolerance displayed within Britain to dissenters and to radical sympathizers with the revolutionary cause. However, it must be said that the *Analytical* reviewers themselves fell far short of the ideal of tolerance towards all parties. Their technique was to brand as 'narrow-minded' all who did not share their own political views.[51]

Contrary to what has often been thought, Voltaire and Rousseau were not always bracketed together in the minds of eighteenth-century Englishmen.[52] I have already pointed out that it was not only the conservatives who objected to Voltaire; the dissenters also found his scoffing irreligion unacceptable. It was rather the response to Rousseau which separated the two camps.[53] The publication of the *Letter from Mr Burke to a Member of the National Assembly* (1791), singling out Rousseau as the evil genius of the Revolution, spurred many to leap to his defence. But even here the situation was not clear-cut, for although the *Analytical* found the *Letter* a lamentably weak production, it made an exception of the highly damning section on Rousseau. In so doing the *Analytical* refused to follow the many radicals, such as Capel Lofft, who idolized Rousseau and were passionate in his defence; its reviewers regarded the philosopher in a more ambiguous light. Furthermore, a review in October 1790 devoted to a volume entitled *A Tour through Part of France, containing a Description of Paris, Cherbourg, and Ermenonville: with a Rhapsody composed at the Tomb of Rousseau ...* (1789), expressed reservations concerning the Rousseaumania current among radicals. The reviewer mocked the author's exalted enthusiasm for Rousseau which 'borders on the ridiculous'.[54]

A more important *Analytical* reviewer of Rousseau was Mary Wollstonecraft. No unqualified supporter (Rousseau's ideas about women were, after all, her main target in *A Vindication of the Rights of Women* (1792)[55] she none the less emerges from the pages of the *Analytical* as an enthusiast. For example, in her July 1789 review of the English translation of Madame de Staël's *Letters on the Works and Character of J.-J. Rousseau*, she criticized those who, in attacking Rousseau, revealed their inability to appreciate or tolerate individuality and originality. It is interesting to see how, in the very month of the fall of the Bastille, one of the most radical of English radical reviewers spoke not for equality and sameness, but for genius, originality, and difference. Reviewing the second part of Rousseau's *Confessions* in April 1790, Wollstonecraft went even further in her praise, making Rousseau the criterion by which to distinguish between the enlarged and generous view of human nature held by radicals, and the narrow, self-interested views of conservatives:

Without considering whether Rousseau was right or wrong, in thus exposing his weaknesses, and shewing himself just as he was, with all his imperfections on his head, to his frail fellow-creatures, it is only necessary to observe, that a description of what has actually passed in a human mind must ever be useful; yet, men who have not the power of concentering seeming contradictions, will rudely laugh at inconsistencies as if they were absurdities; but their laugh is the crackling of thorns, the empty noise of insensible ignorance. . . . His extreme timidity and awkward bashfulness, which made him speak with difficulty in company, utter foolish things in his confusion, and behave rudely when he was abruptly roused out of his reveries, drew on him the reproach of misanthropy, which he certainly did not deserve; yet the excess of his affection for his fellow-creatures, his exquisite sensibility, and that panting after distinction, so characteristic of genius, all contributed to render his conduct strange and inexplicable to little minds; for experience seems to prove, that a man of genius is seldom respected by his inferiors, if they live within his vortex, nor are his moral virtues allowed to be pure, because he is a rule to himself.[56]

The most intriguing aspect of this passage is Wollstonecraft's implication that superior minds are those which have 'the power of concentering seeming contradictions'. Rousseau had always been charged with being 'paradoxical'. Such had been the principal accusation levelled by commonsensical English readers; his ideas were constantly characterized as inconsistent, contradictory, and far-fetched; and there was the notorious gap between his ideas and his own personal practice. For Burkean conservatives, with their preference for the 'little platoon', Rousseau's treatment of his children was not only proof of his wickedness, but also a demonstration that his ideas on virtue and community were purely abstract and theoretical. Mary Wollstonecraft, on the other hand, though not condoning Rousseau's behaviour, argued that humanity might have profited in the long run from his decision to fulfil his destiny as a philosopher and writer, rather than his duty as a father. What is more, this manner of arguing corresponded exactly to that employed by radicals when dealing with the French Revolution itself, particularly when they felt called upon to justify or explain its 'errors', 'evils', or follies.[57] This rhetorical tactic is in evidence in Christie's *Letters on the Revolution of France*:

If a people suddenly let loose from bondage, had committed some follies in the first moments of exultation, on the recovery of their liberty, if their conduct had been enthusiastic, or even riotous, a wise Statesman would not have been surprised, and a candid Statesman would have forgiven them. To judge of such a people from ourselves, who never experienced anything like their situation—to measure the feelings and conduct of men at once brought into a new world, by our own old ideas—to launch forth into elaborate criticism or tragical declamation on their errors, marks a want of political sagacity, an ignorance of human nature, and a narrowness of mind ill concealed under the mask of superior wisdom.[58]

The British radical, therefore, liked to see himself as one who had the required historical knowledge and breadth of imaginative vision to understand and explain the French Revolution, even when it took a course which was unexpected, irrational, and violent. In a period when the norm was to impose one's own cultural standards upon the feelings and conduct of others, to encounter any justification of 'otherness' was rare. Even when faced with acts of great cruelty and savagery, Thomas Christie sought to find explanations for them, rather than resorting to condemnations of senseless violence:

[The] tyrannic acts they had seen or heard of, practised on their fellow-citizens, had inured their minds to scenes of horrour and barbarity. The *Bastille* had accustomed them to condemn and punish without trial or accusation; the frequent repetition of *public capital punishments* . . . had familiarized them with putting men to death; the *gibbets* of the State point to the *lanterne*, and the *racks*, *stakes* and *wheels* of established authority, had fatally habituated them to shut their ears against the cries of the dying, and to abuse the bodies of the dead.[59]

If the Revolution was indeed constructing a civilization founded on reason and morality, it was too important an event to be undermined by seeming contradictions between means and ends. The *Analytical* reviewers recognized that the Revolution had unleashed a terrific supply of 'energy', some of it stored up in the long years before the event, and some of it generated during the Revolution itself by the process of destroying the old political framework. During the Revolution's early years the *Analytical* reviewers were happy to regard 'disorders' as 'temporary irregularities' and as 'inseparable from the energies attending the destruction of an old, and the formation of a new government'.[60] For one thing, they tended to think of revolutionary energy as virtuous, having an irresistible power to defeat evil and oppression, capable of creating the new society of reason and justice.[61] After the September Massacres and the Terror, it became much more difficult for British radicals to retain this notion of virtuous energy, although there was a significant attempt to salvage important aspects of it. Writing in July 1795 about the Jacobins, one reviewer remarked: 'We can at one and the same time admire their energy, and condemn their ferociousness.'[62] In the same number another reviewer went further in attempting to characterize the notion of virtuous energy:

The energy displayed by the jacobins deserved the thanks of their contemporaries, and became entitled to the eulogiums of posterity, for it is the first duty of every citizen to save his country. Their conduct upon that occasion ought to be liberally constructed, and it was impossible to repel a mighty combination of foreign enemies, and check the efforts of numerous intestine foes, without the commission of many irregularities, which their opponents, with a considerable degree of justice, might fairly term oppression. But no sooner were the protectors and assertors of royalty within and without the republic humbled, and the safety of France ensured, that every degree of unnecessary severity became at once highly critical and impolitic.[63]

Although the reviewer thought the actions of the Jacobins should be 'liberally constructed', he was clearly uncertain how to describe these actions—whether by the evasive euphemism of 'irregularities', or by the less equivocal term 'oppression'. He evidently considered that on balance political and military considerations justified the early actions of the Jacobins, but that once a certain point was passed, 'unnecessary severity' could no longer be condoned. The dissenting and radical reviewers, therefore, found themselves constantly engaged in assessing degrees of good and evil, weighing means and ends. These subtle acts of discrimination, although in a sense imposed on them by the course of events, none the less reinforced the reviewers in their estimation of themselves as careful, sophisticated, rational thinkers. Christie described the initial act of rebellion against political authority in terms of a scrupulous examination of the nature and extent of duties and obligations. Hence political 'wisdom' was defined as the capacity to make distinctions such as these:

Wisdom . . . is as far removed from that blind obstinacy that opposes every change, as from the childish weakness that would be perpetually changing. The enlightened statesman is neither an admirer of novelty because it is new, nor a worshipper of antiquity because it is old. He is characterized by that *discriminating* mind, which discerns what ought to be preserved, and what it has become fit to alter.[64]

Even at the height of the Terror, when it is commonly thought that British liberal and radical sympathizers were finally repelled by events in France, we still find the *Analytical* taking the long historical view:

While recent horrours make a strong impression upon the imagination, it ought not to be forgotten, that if the phrensy of liberty have driven the french nation into shocking excesses, the phrensy of conquest has often produced excesses still more shocking; and that if civism and philosophy have slain their thousands, tyranny and superstition have slain their ten thousands. The Bartholomew massacre furnished scenes of savage butchery and studied cruelty, not to be parallelled in the recent history of the french revolution.[65]

Nevertheless, the *Analytical* reviewers were in the end drawn into 'the anguish of sympathy'.[66] This is evidenced when in late 1795 and early 1796 the periodical devoted several long reviews to Helen Maria Williams, an author with whose political and religious views the reviewers had a profound affinity. William's work, *Letters Containing a Sketch of the Politics of France, from the 31st of May 1793, till the 28th of July 1794, and of the Scenes which have passed in the Prisons of Paris*, was principally concerned with telling the story of the imprisonment and execution of the Girondins and with describing their heroic and stoical behaviour as they went to the scaffold.[67] Williams (a friend of the Girondist,

Madame Roland) emphasized the most sensational examples of 'the horrid work of revolutionary murder' (the 'noyades' and the 'fusillades').[68] Her account was designed to condemn the Jacobins and to attract the reader's sympathy for the Girondins, considered as the true martyrs of the Revolution.[69] So convinced was she that the Girondins represented the very essence of the Revolution that she violently rounded on those English friends of freedom who dared to besmirch their memory. In showing sympathy for Williams's view of the Revolution and the course it had taken, the *Analytical* demonstrated that it too thought that there was only one 'real' Revolution—the rationalist, humanist, constitutionalist Revolution of the Girondins. The reviewers considered the Girondins as they regarded themselves, not as a 'party' or a 'faction', but as representatives of humanity itself, impartial spokesmen for truth, reason, and justice. This belief in their own rationality, however, blinded them to the extent to which they were partisan, and also to the degree to which they (like other participants in, and spectators of, the Revolution) were not guided by facts, but seduced by visions and trapped by myths.

There is nothing new in the claim that British middle-class radicals had Utopian visions at the time of the French Revolution. However, such visions involved profound contradictions. What has been insufficiently stressed is that such hopes were in a constant tension with a rationalist ideology which valorized intellectual caution and a scholarly respect for facts. What also seems clear is that despite their occasional acknowledgement of the possibility of other political values, the Rational Dissenters remained convinced of the rightness of their own political and religious positions. As a consequence, their dedication to reason, which at the time of the Revolution could be seen as a radical gesture against the unexamined prejudices of the conservatives as well as a defence against the 'irrationality' of the mob, was now beginning to look much more like the narrow-minded, materialistic, and positivistic religion of the nineteenth-century middle class and its devotion to the world of 'fact'. Indeed in one of the last numbers of the *Analytical* published by Johnson the ideas of Godwin and Condorcet were likened to the religious enthusiasms of Brothers and mocked as 'pleasing dreams':

The imaginations of men, which are ever soaring above the reality of things, and prepared to take wing upon every remarkable occasion, have conceived, that a new era is about to commence, and that the future history of our species will resemble the past in nothing. Mr. Condorcet, Mr. Godwin, and Mr. Brothers have, indeed, been differently affected by the astonishing events which have lately occurred; but it would be difficult to say of the three which has reasoned and prophesied with most extravagance.[70]

NOTES

[1] This essay is a companion piece to a paper I presented at the 1988 Colston Symposium at the University of Bristol. The paper was entitled 'The French Revolution and English Literary Radicals: the case of the *Analytical Review*'. It is to be published in the proceedings of the conference, *The Impact of the French Revolution upon European Consciousness*, ed. W. Doyle and H. T. Mason (Gloucester, 1989). Henceforth the periodical will be designated in references as *AR*.

[2] The first number appeared in May 1788 and the last in June 1799. The 1799 issues were published by T. Hurst; Joseph Johnson had published all the previous issues.

[3] On Johnson see in particular G. P. Tyson, *Joseph Johnson: A Liberal Publisher* (Iowa City, 1979). On the *Analytical Review* see D. Roper, *Reviewing before the 'Edinburgh' 1788–1802* (London, 1978).

[4] Thomas Christie translated the French Constitution and was the author of *Letters on the Revolution of France* (London, 1791).

[5] See R. Wardle, 'Mary Wollstonecraft, *Analytical Reviewer*', *PMLA*, 62 (1947), 1000–9; D. Roper, 'Mary Wollstonecraft's Reviews', *Notes and Queries*, 203 (1958), 37–8.

[6] See E. C. Mason, *The Mind of Henry Fuseli* (London, 1951), pp. 354–9.

[7] See Tyson, op. cit. 160–1.

[8] A very full review is in the November 1790 issue (pp. 295–307).

[9] 'At haec omnia ita tractari praecipimus, ut non, Criticorum more, in laude et censura tempus teratur; sed plane *historice* RES IPSAE narrentur, judicium *parcius* interponatur' (Bacon, *De Historia Literaria Conscribenda*).

[10] *AR* 1 (May 1788), 'Prefatory Address', p. i.

[11] Ibid. ii.

[12] Ibid. iii.

[13] Ibid. iv.

[14] Ibid.

[15] Ibid. v.

[16] See the *Anti-Jacobin Review* 1 (July 1798), 109.

[17] See for instance the title of the pamphlet reviewed by the *Anti-Jacobin* in December 1798 (pp. 691–2): *An Oblique View of the Grand Conspiracy against Social Order; or, a Candid Inquiry, tending to shew what Part the Analytical, the Monthly, the Critical Reviews and the New Annual Register have taken in that Conspiracy.*

[18] *Anti-Jacobin Review*, 1 (July 1798), 107.

[19] The editor of the *Anti-Jacobin Review* was John Gifford. For a discussion of his anti-French activities on behalf of the British government see E. Lorraine de Montluzin, *The Anti-Jacobins 1798–1800: the Early Contributions to the 'Anti-Jacobin Review'* (London, 1988). Gifford was in fact a pseudonym for John Richards Green.

[20] *Anti-Jacobin Review*, 1 (July 1798), 'Prefatory address', pp. iv–v.

[21] The *Anti-Jacobin* was already exulting over the final demise of the *Analytical* in the 'Preface' to its April 1799 number (pp. vi–vii).

[22] *AR* 8 (Nov. 1790), 303.

[23] Ibid. In its review of Capel Lofft's *Remarks on the Letter of the Right Hon. Mr Burke, concerning the Revolution in France*, the *Analytical* quoted approvingly a similar passage from Lofft where he rhapsodized over the new age in which the new rational man inherits the earth. See *AR* 8 (Dec. 1790), 425.

[24] *AR* 8 (Nov. 1790), 307.

[25] See *Letters on the Revolution of France* (London, 1791), p. 7.

[26] The *Analytical*'s review of Paine's *Rights of Man* makes this opposition clear: 'elegant and declamatory, Mr. Burke seduces us along by the charms of his eloquence; plain, but forcible, Mr. Paine carries us away with him by the invincible energy of truth and sense. Fanciful and excursive, Mr B. delights the imagination by the beauty of his metaphors, and the splendour of his ornaments; while his opponent holds our judgment captive by the native vigour of his arguments, the originality of his sentiments, and the pointedness of his remarks. Mr. B. is the polished and playful courtier, who dances in his chains; Mr. Paine is the stern republican, who exults in his liberty, and treats with equal freedom the monarch and the peasant' (*AR* 9 (Mar. 1791), 312–13).

[27] *AR* 12 (Mar. 1792), 302.

[28] Cf. *AR* 22 (Nov. 1795), 499.

[29] For a fully documented account of eighteenth-century English responses to Voltaire, see B. N. Schilling, *Conservative England and the Case against Voltaire* (New York, 1950).

[30] *AR* 3 (Feb. 1789), 215.

[31] *AR* 3 (April 1789), Appendix, 537–8.

[32] *AR* 8 (Nov. 1790), 284.

[33] *AR* 22 (Sept. 1795), 225.

[34] '[T]he question respecting the truth of christianity is, by the learned on the continent, unfortunately supposed to be long ago decided. They read nothing more on the subject' (*AR* 22 (Oct. 1795), 337).

[35] In 1788, for example, the *Analytical* examined two works by Mrs Trimmer published by Johnson, *The Sunday-School Catechist* and *The Sunday Scholar's Manual*. The reviewer's comments were favourable: 'These corresponding works are designed as a specimen of a mode of religious instruction, peculiarly adapted to the capacities and stations of the poor. Mrs. Trimmer very benevolently dedicates a great part of her time to the improvement of that class of her fellow-creatures which has hitherto been too much neglected. We perfectly coincide with her in thinking, that by the means of Sunday Schools, the poor and the rich being brought together, the most salutary effects may be produced' (*AR* 1 (Aug. 1788), 475).

[36] *AR* 8 (Nov. 1790), 285.

[37] *Letters on the Revolution of France*, pp. 49–50.

[38] Ibid. 44. It is to be remembered that the *Analytical* would have liked to address itself exclusively to 'the learned and thinking few' (*AR* 1 (May 1788), 'Prefatory Address', p. iv).

[39] *AR* 22 (July 1795), 12.

[40] *AR* 25 (Jan. 1797), 70.

[41] *AR* 18 (April 1794), Appendix, 515.

[42] *AR* 16 (June 1793), 131. This assertion comes in the course of a review of John Moore's *A Journal during a Residence in France* (London, 1793). The passage is worth quoting at length since it shows the *Analytical*'s constant concern with objectivity and impartiality and its quest for historical exactness and fairness: 'In such great public commotions as have recently happened in France, nothing is more difficult, than to arrive at the knowledge of the exact truth concerning those great events, which it is the business of the journalist to record as they happen, and of the

historian to transmit, in a regular narrative, to posterity. While transactions of such magnitude are passing, multitudes are interested in misrepresenting them; and almost every one views them through a different medium, or under a different aspect, according to the opinions he entertains and the party he espouses. Dr. M., in drawing up the present journal, met with many difficulties of this kind; and acknowledges, that, "on some of the most interesting occurrences, the various accounts which poured in from all quarters, crossed, jostled, and confounded each other in such a manner, that he has sometimes been tempted to suspect, that as his information increased, his knowledge diminished." It is therefore no reflection either upon his judgment or his candour, to consider the minute detail of events contained in this volume rather as materials, from which, upon a due comparison with other accounts, a judgment may be formed, than as, in itself, affording an ultimate decision on questionable points. Dr. M. may perhaps have been as impartial a spectator of what passed during his residence in Paris, as any other man; but he will not claim such a perfect exemption from the common infirmities of the human mind, as to entitle his representation to implicit confidence. It must be the business of the future historian to disentangle the threads of the complicated events which are now passing. In the mean time minute journals of every kind are valuable registers of facts; and such a journal as Dr. M.'s, in which the results of diligent inquiry are adorned with the graces of elegant writing, will not fail to be highly acceptable to the .public.'

[43] *AR* 22 (Nov. 1795), 457.

[44] *AR* 22 (July 1795), 100.

[45] *AR* 11 (Oct. 1791), 175.

[46] *Letters on the Revolution of France*, pp. 43–4.

[47] Mary Wollstonecraft, *An Historical and Moral View of the Origin and Progress of the French Revolution and the Effect it has Produced in Europe* (London, 1795; 1st edn., 1794), p. 226.

[48] This is one of the main themes of my paper to appear in the volume edited by W. Doyle and H. T. Mason.

[49] *Letters on the Revolution of France*, pp. 57–8.

[50] *AR* 8 (Nov. 1790), 285.

[51] In the following quotation from Christie's *Letters on the Revolution of France* we can see how he makes the response to the Revolution a *test* of man's humanity, and how he is willing to regard those who attack the Revolution as guilty of a crime against humanity: 'For my part, Sir, I believe the French Revolution to be the greatest and most glorious event that ever took place in the history of the world. It is the only revolution that has *completely* respected the rights of mankind. It is the only revolution that is likely to change the object of ambition amongst men, and to convert it into an emulation of superior wisdom and virtue, instead of a lust of power and conquest. I believe that in process of time it will enlighten the darkest corners of the globe, and diffuse every where the salutary rays of freedom and happiness. To arraign such a revolution is, in my opinion, to plead against mankind; it is to involve one's-self in the *crimen laesae majestatis generis humani*' (pp. 58–9). This is one of the rare occasions on which Christie allows himself an 'enthusiastic' welcoming of the Revolution.

[52] As in the famous line of Blake: 'Mock on, mock on, Voltaire, Rousseau!' (*Complete Poems*, ed. W. H. Stevenson (London, 1971), p. 481).

[53] On Rousseau in England in this period see in particular J. Voisine, *J.-J. Rousseau en Angleterre à l'époque romantique* (Paris, 1956), and H. Roddier, *J.-J. Rousseau en Angleterre au XVIIIe siècle* (Paris, 1950).

[54] *AR* 8 (Oct. 1790), 159.

[55] In its review of *A Vindication of the Rights of Women* the *Analytical* agreed

with Mary Wollstonecraft's criticism of Rousseau's attitudes to women and female education. See *AR* 13 (July, 1792), Appendix, 481–2.

[56] *AR* 6 (April 1790), 386 and 389.

[57] This 'power of concentering seeming contradictions' is an issue which appears also in an anti-Jacobin work entitled *A Residence in France, during the Years 1792, 1793, 1794, and 1795; Described in a Series of Letters from an English Lady, Prepared for the Press by John Gifford*. The 'English Lady' highlights the way in which much of the violence and cruelty of the Revolution was executed with suavity and sensibility, and ventures to suggest that this capacity to act in one way and behave in another is essentially French: 'Our country, like every other, has doubtless produced too many examples of human depravity; but I scarcely recollect any, where a ferocious disposition was not accompanied by corresponding manners—or where men, who would plunder or massacre, affected to retain at the same time habits of softness, and a conciliating physiognomy. . . . I must still persist in not thinking it a defect that we are too impetuous, or perhaps too ingenuous, to unite contradictions' (*A Residence in France* (London, 1797), ii. 215 and 216).

[58] *Letters on the Revolution of France*, pp. 133–4.

[59] Ibid. 126.

[60] *AR* 8 (Nov. 1790), 308.

[61] Cf. Mary Wollstonecraft on the fall of the Bastille: 'The accounts of the slaughter . . . were certainly very much exaggerated; for the fortress appears to have been taken by the force of mind of the multitude, pressing forward regardless of danger.' A similar attitude underlay her explanation of how the Revolution destroyed the Ancien Régime: 'The irresistible energy of the moral and political sentiments of half a century, at last kindled into a blaze the illuminating rays of truth, which, throwing new light on the mental powers of man, and giving a fresh spring to his reasoning faculties, completely undermined the strong holds of priestcraft and hypocrisy' (*An Historical and Moral View of the Origin and Progress of the French Revolution*, pp. 192 and 12).

[62] *AR* 22 (July 1795), 35.

[63] Ibid. 100.

[64] *Letters on the Revolution of France*, p. 41.

[65] *AR* 18 (April 1794), Appendix, 515.

[66] *AR* 24 (July 1796), 11.

[67] *AR* 22 (Aug. 1795), 137–45. The work is also discussed in the January and July 1796 numbers.

[68] *AR* 24 (July 1796), 12.

[69] It is ironic that Helen Maria Williams refused to extend her sympathy to the aristocratic and royal 'victims' of the earlier stages of the Revolution. See *AR* 8 (Dec. 1790), 434.

[70] *AR* 28 (Aug. 1798), 119.

The Impact of the French Revolution upon British Statecraft, 1789–1921

LORD BELOFF

WHEN the war ended in November 1918, the allied governments faced the question of what to do with their victory, but also, no less difficult, what to do about the Bolshevik regime in Russia. In the British cabinet, opinions were divided. Churchill, confident in his belief that the Bolsheviks represented only a minority of the people, was in favour of military intervention to enable the Russians to set up a democratic form of government. Lloyd George was opposed to intervention, partly for domestic reasons but also because he doubted whether the British government was fully informed about the actual situation. There was, however, another argument, that by historical analogy. During the French Revolution there had been horrors 'as bad as, or worse' than any perpetrated by the Bolsheviks. But British intervention had enabled Danton 'to rally French patriotism and make the terror a military instrument'. France had thus become organized 'as a great military machine imbued with a passionate hatred' of Great Britain. The way to perpetuate Bolshevism was to try to suppress it with foreign troops.[1]

At the first meeting in Paris of the Council of Ten which was to be the directing body of the Peace Conference, Lloyd George returned to his theme in opposing the proposal that the various Russian exiled groups in Paris should be given a status at the Conference. It was wrong to hear them and not to seek representation from the Bolsheviks, the *de facto* rulers of the country. During the French Revolution, the British government had said that the émigrés represented France, 'a mistake which led to a quarter of a century of war'.[2]

No one would have thought Lloyd George a statesman particularly prone to historical musings, so his suggested parallel with the French Revolution and the dilemmas it had presented to British statecraft must have seemed part of accepted wisdom. Indeed he could have added that the two revolutions had also in common their ability to command support and sympathy among elements of the population in countries whose governments were deeply hostile to them.[3] It was common knowledge that this had been so in the Britain of the revolutionary era.[4] Lloyd George was fully aware of the sympathies of many in the British Labour movement now being played upon by Bolshevik propaganda.[5]

It was therefore arguably the reappearance in a new form of a dilemma that had faced British statesmen ever since the days of Pitt and Fox. How did a country devoted to constitutional continuity and to only such reform as could be reconciled with its existing institutions and its own political traditions deal with a regime that claimed to embody a universalist appeal, and had not renounced the use of force to make that appeal effective? It is hardly necessary to stress the difference between the two revolutions or the social forces which gave them their weight. More important is to note at the outset a difference between the two countries in which they took place, in respect of their relations with the United Kingdom. Russia in 1918–19 was partly of Europe and partly not of it. Its contacts with Britain, although long-standing—particularly in commerce—had never been intimate. The conflict of recent times, whether overt as in the Crimean War or covert as in the 'great game in Asia', had been on the periphery of British concerns. Not so with France.

From the time of the creation of modern France its growth and national self-image had been conditioned by rivalry with the Plantagenet monarchy of England. The fortunes of the two countries had been inextricably interwoven as had their cultural development. The history of neither can be understood without the history of the other. Only six years before the Revolution, France had been a principal instrument of the destruction of the British Empire in North America. Nothing that happened in France could leave Britain indifferent, and so it was to prove throughout the nineteenth century.

After Waterloo, Britain was never again in direct conflict with France, though there were some near misses; Lloyd George had been eight years in the House of Commons at the time of Fashoda. By that time fears of France as the source of revolutionary upheavals were a thing of the past. The Third Republic, relying as it did on its alliance with Tsarist Russia, was hardly in a position to play such a role. When at a gala banquet for the officers of the French fleet paying a ceremonial visit to the Russian naval base at Cronstadt in July 1891, Tsar Alexander III, even if reluctantly and impatiently, stood bareheaded for the opening bars of the Mareillaise, it could have been said that the French Revolution had come to an end.[6] But from 1789 until at least 1871 and the Paris Commune and perhaps for some years afterwards, France to British statesmen spelled trouble whether they were conservatives who resented all change, or reformers who felt that their cause might be damaged by connections with French revolutionary ideas. The many changes of regime that France underwent between 1789 and the establishment of the Third Republic, some of them the fruit of direct action in the streets, was a constant reminder of the differences between the two countries. No doubt the British record was not as smooth as some would have liked the world to believe: 1815–17, 1830–2, and 1846–8 were unquiet yers. But two major extensions of the franchise, the gradual diminution of royal influence, and the reform of municipal government hardly balance France's record of upheaval. How to explain it? How to guard against it? These were the questions to which British public figures gave a variety of answers. In giving them they were no doubt affected by the popular image of the Revolution of 1789 itself. The drama and terror of those years were given body by Carlyle's *The French Revolution*, published in 1837, and in fictional form by Dickens's *A Tale of Two Cities*, published in 1859.

In assessing British statecraft it must be remembered that not everyone has been in agreement either on the impact of the Revolution on Britain or on Lloyd George's view that Britain had gone to war to stem the tide of Jacobinism. Long-standing political and economic rivalries dictated the policies of Britain and France as they did those of the other European powers. Indeed the Revolution in its earlier phases seemed welcome news to the British government, making it likely that France would be too preoccupied with internal problems to give any cause for anxiety abroad. It was the attack upon the Austrian Netherlands and the threat to Holland as much as the universalist rhetoric with which these aggressions were justified that finally caused Britain to abandon its neutrality. The function of ideologies in the long cycle of wars that followed was largely to confuse the view of each side about the other's strength and intentions.[7]

It is nevertheless true that there was, as earlier in the century, some interpenetration of ideas and attitudes between British and

French political leaders and thinkers. Some British constitutional theorists hoped to persuade the French in 1789 that Britain provided the best model for the defence of liberties and there was some reciprocal interest in the ideas of the French Enlightenment. Popular enthusiasm for the Revolution was slower to awaken in Britain and reached its peak only in 1792 when it was largely discredited by the advent of the Terror. Indeed, Pitt's ability to take the country into the war depended upon the strong tide of anti-revolutionary patriotic feeling that then made itself manifest. The question of the importance of the sympathies with France that survived the British entry into war and the degree of British support for the view that the armies of the Republic and even of Napoleon carried liberty on their banners is a more difficult one. But that it should have existed, as a historian of the period has pointed out, comes as no surprise to those who have witnessed similar stalwartness in defence of the Russian Revolution by British sovietophiles even at the height of the Stalinist repression.[8]

It is a commonplace that the Revolution gave rise in Britain to a major debate about political and social reform and the methods for achieving them, a debate in which Edmund Burke and Thomas Paine represent the two main positions.[9] But not everyone would agree that it was Burke who, by initiating the debate as early as 1790 in his *Reflections on the Revolution in France* (that is to say before the Revolution had revealed its full scope and accompanying horrors), gave an impetus to radicalism on the other side.[10]

With the coming of war the situation changed. The conservative elements in British society developed a counterbalancing ideology of their own.[11] The radicals, having tried and failed to use pressure to force the government to maintain its neutrality, were in some cases tempted into direct collusion with what was now the national enemy. Just as French émigré aristocrats tried to commit Britain to restoring the Ancien Régime, so British political exiles in Paris tried to persuade the French government that an invasion would lead to a rising in their favour, once French troops had landed. It was only between 1797 and 1799 that such a movement came to a head even on a small scale. And by then it was inextricably bound up with events in Ireland. Despite the economic burdens of the war and their impact upon the working classes it was on Irish immigrants in England, particularly in the north-west, that the French pitched such hopes as they had. Ireland itself did indeed appear to present the most hopeful prospect for the French, who made contacts with the United Irish and attempted to raise the country against British rule by expeditions poorly managed and in their upshot disastrous for the Irish who were left to bear the burden of repression.[12] The French hoped to take revenge on the British for their support of the Royalist rebels in the Vendée. Their failure was not only due to military miscalculations. The Irish leaders themselves were suspicious that the French might simply be using them to help establish their own rule, as had happened elsewhere in Europe. Nor, despite the contrary views expressed by the British government, were the philosophy or objectives of the movement akin to those of the French revolutionaries: 'The United Irish leaders were misfits among the revolutionaries of the 1790s. The American system of democracy rather than the French remained their ideal model. To most revolution and bloodshed were distasteful.'[13] What they hoped for from a French invasion was that British rule would be withdrawn and the invasion force itself agree to be controlled by an interim government formed by the Irish leadership. The possibility of exploiting Irish national sentiment was kept alive by Napoleon, though without commitment. With regard to relations with Britain, the situation in Ireland continued to attract French attention until the international situation underwent the transformation of the 1870s.

The renewal of large-scale social discontent in Britain at the conclusion of the Napoleonic wars once again provoked governmental attention to its possible links with radical movements on the continent still inspired by the French example. A Secret Committee of the House of Commons in 1817 claimed to have discovered a plot to seize power by radical societies in London: 'the intended insurrection assumed the symbols of the French Revolution; a committee of public safety, consisting of 24, was agreed upon . . . a tri-color flag and cockades were actually prepared; the flag was openly carried and displayed at the first meeting.' Since, however, this meeting at Spa Fields passed off without violence, all that the Committee could do was to call attention to the evidence of the formation of clubs in the provinces, ostensibly dedicated to parliamentary reform but in reality with revolutionary objectives.[14]

These events and the fears they aroused mark the end of the direct impact of the French Revolution upon British internal politics. As a historian of the period has written:

A few years after Waterloo the political weather began to change. The new generation did not share their elders' alarms. The ideas which had inspired the American and French Revolutions became more familiar and less horrifying to people of property. The memory of the Terror and of the War with France began to subside. 1793 was no more effective as a revolutionary bogey to the young men of this decade than 1917 was to those of the 1930s.[15]

It could indeed be said that under the guidance first of Castlereagh and then of Canning, British foreign policy was more concerned with seeing that the Holy Alliance was not used as an excuse for continuous foreign intervention by the Great Powers than with the possible threat from subversion on the French model.

To critical foreigners, in particular the French legitimists, English statesmen appeared recklessly indifferent to such dangers when set against the commercial interests they believed to be at stake. Chateaubriand, now ambassador to a capital where he had once sought refuge, tried to prevent the British government from recognizing the newly proclaimed Latin American Republics: 'Il y a déjà assez d'idées républicaines dans le monde. Augmenter la masse de ces idées, c'est compromettre de plus en plus le sort des monarchies en Europe.'[16] The difference was equally acute over French intervention in Spain itself:

Il y a bien ici, parmi les hommes d'Etat, une certaine crainte vague des passions révolutionnaires qui travaillent l'Espagne; mais cette crainte se tait devant les intérêts particuliers: de telle sorte que si d'un côté la Grande-Bretagne pouvait exclure nos marchandises de la Péninsule, et que de l'autre elle pût reconnaître l'indépendance des colonies espagnoles, elle prendrait facilement son parti sur les événements, et se consolerait des malheurs qui pourraient accabler de nouveau les monarchies continentales.[17]

It was not only Spain's future that was at stake: 'la France serait replongée aux troubles du jacobinisme sous l'inspiration de la jacobinerie espagnole.'[18]

What Chateaubriand failed perhaps to realize was that his interpretation of the Revolution did not now correspond to that which was widely held in Britain. He took the view that a break in the continuity of a dynasty was irreparable. After the Revolution of 1830, he was to write that the fall of Charles X was a consequence of the beheading of Louis XVI just as the fall of James II could be traced to the execution of Charles I.[19] Concessions to the revolutionary spirit would only whet its appetite for more. Such sentiments were not unknown among British statesmen. Wellington was one example: 'Obsessed by the first French Revolution, he was adamant that reform threatened the constitution. He was therefore a reactionary in his revulsion from the liberal movements of Europe and in his affinity with the High Tories at home. The French Revolution, however, simply put a permanent edge on these feelings; it did not create them.'[20]

On the other hand, there was a powerful current of opinion to the effect that it was the obduracy of the French monarchy in resisting all reform and of the French aristocracy in clinging to its privileges that had brought about the Revolution; the lesson to be drawn was all in favour of moderate reform.[21] What had been disastrous was that the transformation of the originally moderate aspirations of the Revolution into the excesses of the Terror had discredited all reforms in Europe and set back the march of progress by two generations. Such was Macaulay's view as expressed in 1844.[22] And earlier, in 1832, he had given voice to the view that the evil of the Revolution 'was temporary, and the good durable'.[23]

Macaulay, fifteen years old at the time of Waterloo, was of a generation whose knowledge of the Revolution was through literature rather than direct experience. The same was true of Disraeli, four years his junior. In his attitude to the Revolution the young Disraeli was, as in so much else, a somewhat ambiguous figure.[24] He collaborated after the Revolution of 1830 with the exiled supporters of Charles X and blamed Whig government for what he saw as its excessive friendliness towards his Orleanist successor.[25] On the other hand, he confessed to some exhilaration in contemplating the continental revolutionary tradition and in the following year began (but did not complete) an epic poem, 'The Revolutionary Epick', exalting the Revolution and its embodiment in Napoleon and claiming that since the American Revolution a new principle had been at work in the world, the principle of 'federalism' or 'democracy' with which the old principle of 'feudalism' was in conflict.[26] This youthful enthusiasm did not survive Disraeli's adoption of the Tory cause, and in 1840, when a war against France seemed possible, he could write that 'since the 1st French revol[uti]on never was Europe more convulsed—the world in general never as much'.[27] By 1848, revolution was not to his taste: 'Have you yet recovered the great catastrophe? Its cause is inexplicable, its consequences an alarming mystery. No judgment and no imagination can fathom its probable results.'[28]

It was indeed the two Revolutions of 1830 and 1848 that made assessments of how far the Revolutionary spirit was alive essential to the working out of British policy. More than one view was possible. For Wellington, 1830 merely confirmed his belief that reform would only lead to revolution and his opposition to the growing movement for parliamentary reform.[29] In Whig circles, enthusiasm for the new turn of events echoed the hopes of 1789. Palmerston greeted the fall of Charles X as heralding the triumph of liberalism everywhere.[30] An immediate question was whether the news would stimulate the reform movement or set it back as the great Revolution itself had ultimately done. At the height of the Reform agitation there was a good deal of revolutionary rhetoric about. But did this represent the real situation in the country? Macaulay's own position was an ambiguous one. Sometimes he argued that British conditions in no way resembled those of France; at other times, he threatened recalcitrant anti-Reform peers with the fate of the French aristocracy.[21] Later, he was to ask why it was that the overthrow of Charles X, a much greater oppressor than Louis XVI, should have been accomplished without the terrible consequences attending upon the latter's fall and was to give as his explanation the fact that France had now enjoyed a period in which the supremacy of the law had become ingrained in the national consciousness.[32]

It has been the consensus among historians that it was the development of Britain's own politics and not the French example that precipitated the Reform crisis and made inevitable the passage of the Act of 1832. As Norman Gash has put it, the bulk of English middle-class opinion and the press 'disliked the actions of the French monarchy, and welcomed the July Revolution; but it would have been an odd reversal of the traditional attitude of Englishmen to have looked across the Channel for their model in political conduct. The parallel which more flatteringly struck the insular British mind was that between the July Revolution and their own Revolution of 1688'.[33] The comparison between 1688 and 1830 was one that came easily also to those liberal Frenchmen like Tocqueville, who studied English history in order to point its moral

to their own countrymen. But discontent with the performance of
the July Monarchy, especially in its foreign relations, made the
comparison an unflattering one to the French.[34]

Foreign policy was equally a question for the Whig government
in England, and presented Palmerston as Foreign Secretary with
something of a dilemma. The legatees of the Foxites were
disappointed. They had held to Fox's own view that Britain's entry
into war with France in 1793 had been part of a reactionary
conspiracy. By participating in the European settlement of 1814–15
the British had helped to enslave the peoples of Europe. They now
expected Palmerston to lead the parliamentary democracies including France against the powers of the Holy Alliance dominated
by Russia. Palmerston however, like his predecessors, did not see
Britain's interests as synonymous with those of France; whatever its
form of government, France remained a permanent enemy.[35]

The proper relations between the two countries with parliamentary institutions continued to preoccupy Frenchmen. After his
return from the United States Tocqueville's attention turned
towards England.[36] In 1835 he was concerned at the view that
France presented to its friends abroad.[37] By 1840, when the
confrontation between Britain and France over Egypt was at its
height, Tocqueville went along with popular feeling in its support
of Thiers.[38] By 1841, he was arguing that an alliance with Britain
was impossible; Britain's interest was to monopolize the industry
and commerce of the world so that no common ground could be
found with any competitor. Nor was there any meeting of the
hearts of the two peoples which could support the closer
association of their governments.[39] Tocqueville the liberal thus
echoes the views of the legitimist Chateaubriand.

What then of the proposition that the two countries, alone
among the Great Powers, had in common free institutions? By now
Tocqueville was denying their similarity. It was France whose
institutions inspired other peoples and thus gave her friends and
enemies. England was in fact an exception to the general movement
towards democracy in the world since her institutions remained
aristocratic. In her external policy, she was guided only by
considerations of self-interest.[40]

By the time that the Revolutions of 1848 broke out, Anglo-
French relations were on the whole quite intimate. The unleashing
of what proved to be a new cycle of political instability thus

affected Britain more obviously than the July Revolution and sensitivity was increased by the still unassauged fears of Chartism —a movement whose demands were certainly democratic in Tocqueville's sense. Queen Victoria, who had developed close personal ties with the Orleanist royal family now seeking refuge in Britain, gave voice to the general reaction of the political world: 'Lord Melbourne will agree with the Queen that the last three weeks have brought back the times of the last century, and we are in the midst of troubles abroad. The Revolution in France is a sad and alarming thing. . . . The state of Paris is very gloomy; the rabble armed—keeping the Government in awe—failures in all directions, and nothing but ruin and misery.'[41] Wellington, still a power in the background as Commander-in-Chief, was understandably alarmed and took large-scale military precautions against the danger of a Chartist uprising. Ireland too needed attention: Young Ireland, the latest avatar of Irish nationalism, wished, he believed, 'to deprive the Queen of her crown! and to establish a republick'.[42]

These fears proved unnecessary in that the measures taken were successful. But the possibility of the new French regime calling into question the whole European settlement remained of great concern.[43] Lamartine's circular dispatch to the French ambassadors abroad seemed vividly to justify such fears.[44] The principles propounded, had they been incorporated in the Treaties of 1814 and 1815, would in Wellington's view have 'had King Louis Philippe interfering in the insurrection in Canada in 1837, and in Ireland in 1839, 1840, 1841, 1842, 1843'. The French government holding such views was not one with which Britain could be associated: 'neither I nor, as I believe, any Englishman could desire to see Her Majesty allied with the French Republic in interference in the internal government of other countries.'[45]

The preoccupation of the French at home, particularly with regard to the attempt of the Paris populace to emulate its predecessors and give the Revolution a tilt to the left, and the subsequent repression, meant that although much of Europe was convulsed by the revolutionary and nationalist upheavals of 1848–9, a direct Anglo-French confrontation was avoided. The effect of the period between 1848 and Louis Napoleon's *coup d'état* of 2 December 1851 was to reinforce all British suspicions about the apparently congenital instability of French politics.

Walter Bagehot, who may be taken as the epitome of the

practical non-ideological ethos of mid-Victorian England, made his original reputation as a journalist with his despatches on the *coup d'état* written at the age of 25.[46] They were to be the prelude to a long and continuous concern with the affairs of France.[47] From the first he was aware of the predominance of memories of the great Revolution in French political thinking and of the break it made with all France's past: 'the first revolution is to the French what the deluge is to the rest of mankind; the whole system then underwent an entire change.'[48]

British attitudes towards the Second Empire were thus inevitably mixed. While circumstances might bring the two governments together, as in the Crimean War and again in the Cobden Treaty on trade in 1860, at other times their relations were tense. But on the whole any element of stability seemed preferable to a renewed bout of revolutionary upheaval. French liberals were depressed that their British counterparts seemed so indifferent to the dictatorial nature of the Emperor's rule. On the other hand, Tocqueville, confirming to himself in his visit of 1857 the reinforced solidity of British institutions, could not deny the primordial importance of the British example for other European countries. It was this sentiment that explains his welcome to the news that the Indian Mutiny had been suppressed: 'L'Angleterre, d'ailleurs, malgré tous ses défauts qui sont grands, est après tout, le seul pays de liberté politique qui soit encore en Europe, et je ne désire point que les amis de la servitude qui nous inondent aient la joie de voir ce dernier foyer foulé aux pieds des sauvages.'[49]

The question for British statecraft was whether Napoleon III could be relied upon to act as the force for stability for which they would have hoped. In 1863 Bagehot was calling attention to the fact that Napoleon saw himself as the heir to the democratic tradition, albeit a democracy transmuted into the rule of one man. By then he had not only re-etablished the glory of his dynasty and added two provinces to the territorial limits of France, but 'created one kingdom, that of Italy, and one Empire, that of Mexico; and if England would have sanctioned or encouraged the enterprise, he would probably have added the Southern American Confederacy to the list of republics and Poland to the list of monarchies'; in addition, in Bagehot's view, he needed to satisfy another master besides the French people, 'the revolutionary party throughout Europe—the democratic element in continental states—the discontented and oppressed Nationalities—those, in a word, who are fond of describing themselves as the adherents and devotees of the "Principles of 1789".[50]

The growth of discontent in France and the endeavour of Napoleon III to move towards some more parliamentary form of government was no doubt flattering to those with a native parliamentary tradition, and French liberals did not hesitate to indulge in some flattery in this respect. French liberals of that generation contrasted France's unhappy history with that of England: French public opinion, unable to make its voice heard through regular institutions, sought to undermine the existing order and in the end produced a revolutionary convulsion, whereas in England the aristocracy had succeeded in recruiting itself from below and the middle class had available to it a considerable share of political power and almost total liberty, resulting in social concord, and a movement towards democracy so regular and benign as hardly to be perceived.[51]

Speaking to a Scottish audience, Prévost-Paradol tried to explain how the fear of revolution of the socialist variety had brought about the acceptance of the autocratic rule of the Emperor:

In those [these?] quiet islands political progress is going on hand-in-hand with the public peace, and order and liberty are supporting each other under the light and sway [*sic*] of a beloved and respected Sovereign. Not so in our distracted land. We live still under the hard law of old times, that hard, unwritten but unshaken law, which recites that man must earn his bread with his sweat, and his liberty with his blood.[52]

It is not to be wondered at that the chief exponent of a fully conservative standpoint in British politics should have made France the focus of much of his attention. There was for Lord Salisbury in respect of France, so his daughter tells us, 'an intimacy to start with, both actual and intellectual. Diplomatically, he was destined to be often in opposition to her; politically, his essentially British temperament distrusted her faith in impractical logic, while her later policy towards religion was necessarily repellent to him. But with her culture and her civilisation his sympathies were very close.'[53] In particular he was fascinated with the French Revolution, on which he collected a remarkable private library.[54] It provided lessons and analogies even for issues remote from France itself. Thus when in 1862 he deplored the commemoration by English non-conformists of the ejected Puritan divine two hundred years earlier, he wrote: 'There must always be Girondins to pave the way for Jacobins; there must always be Presbyterians to open the door for Independents; there must always be sentimental Liberals to smooth the way for hard-headed practical Radicals'.[55]

Salisbury also held the view that one must not make too much of the differences between the institutional development of the two peoples. In reviewing a book advocating greater decentralization for France, he wrote: 'the author does good service in reminding the world that not only are the races which inhabit France and England in great measure of the same stock, but up to a certain point in their history, they both bore in their institutions the same germ of liberty. Accidental causes have determined that the germ should wither in one case and bear fruit in the other; but such accidents constitute no inherent incapacity.'[56] It was the turn taken by the French Revolution during the Terror that was responsible for the divergence in the paths taken by the two countries. The financial imprudence of the Revolutionary government had contributed to its substitution of the state for all other instruments of authority. At the height of the Terror, he noted, a quarter of the entire adult male population were directly the state's employees.[57] Hence above all the subsequent inability of French institutions to develop answers to new demands and the seesaw between oppression and revolution: 'It is interesting to us, who look safely down from the lofty fortresses of liberty, to watch the curious cycle of vicissitudes by which the progress of the contrast is marked'; but Salisbury noted that the current of popular discontent would not forever be controlled, and when it broke its floodgates it would be 'a torrent before which not only privilege and prerogative but all law and order are swept away'.[58] Nearly a decade later Prévost-Paradol was to echo the English Conservative's forebodings: 'la Révolution française a fondé une société, elle cherche encore son gouvernement.'[59]

In such a perspective, English liberals could also express doubts as to the possibility of a peaceful move towards parliamentary government such as Napoleon III appeared to be attempting in the final phase of his rule. The gulf between moderate men and Red Republicans was as deep as ever; yet a defeat for French liberals would be a defeat for liberals everywhere.[60]

The war of 1870, the fall of Napoleon III, and above all the Paris Commune seemed to justify all such forebodings.[61] By September

1870, Bagehot was asking: 'Do the Conditions Requisite for a Stable Government exist in France?'[62] Salisbury's fears were even more acute. Unlike most of his compatriots, who only turned against Germany when the scope of Bismarck's ambitions became apparent, Salisbury was on the French side from the beginning of the war.[63] But this did not prevent him from seeing that it was France's own political weaknesses that had led to her downfall, and these sprang from the French Revolution—'the great modern exemplar and source of the evils'. 'Whatever else Bismarck does,' wrote Salisbury during the siege of Paris, 'I do hope he will burn down the Faubourg St. Antoine and crush out the Paris mob. Their freaks and madnesses have been a curse to Europe for the last eighty years.'[64]

But the setting up of the Paris Commune and its challenge to the legality of the new French Republic was symptomatic of something even more sinister than the renewed internationalization of the revolutionary movement:

The organisation which carried out the Revolution of the 18th of March does not profess to accept the frontiers of nations as the limits of its action. It aspires to be the combination of the workmen of all countries against the employers of all countries. It depreciates patriotism, both as a sentiment belonging to the old order of things, and as tending to hinder the purely class sympathy which is to enable the workman to subdue every other power to his own. . . . The relations which the Commune held at first with the national enemy of the French: the number of foreigners of all nations— Germans, Poles, Italians, Russians, Americans—who appeared among its members and officers: the ostentatious destruction of the Vendôme column, sufficiently show that the fact of the Internationale having made its first public appearance as a revolutionary power in France implies no special connection with the people of France, and certainly no restriction of its activity to that country.

Nor did he spare his mockery for the British apologists for the Commune:

The authorities of St. Pancras, in our own metropolis, probably carry the enthusiasm of vestrydom as high as it has ever risen in the human heart, and they detest the central government with a hatred which will yield to no other upon earth. But their emotions have never reached even to the mildest tint of the heroic.[65]

Bagehot was no less forthright: 'round these sincere though discordant fanatics in the red factions there have gathered the able miscreants and the clever outcasts not of France only, but of the world.'[66]

Bagehot's hope that peasant France would once again conquer the Paris revolutionary mob was to be fulfilled. The progress of the Third Republic to the stability apparently achieved in 1875 was watched by British observers with by now sympathetic interest. Yet even after the coming into effect of the new Constitution doubts remained. Both on the Right and on the Left, the French government had its enemies. But they were enemies not just of the government of the day but of the system itself. What was lacking was an alternative grouping ready to take office without changing the rules: 'If France could ever organise a real parliamentary opposition as powerful and semi-official as ours, we should no longer fear periodic spasms of revolutionary ardour.'[67]

But while the fear of the revolutionary inspiration might persist, the changing balance of power made France, under whatever regime, no longer the threat to stability that it had been. If by 1891, as we have seen, France could be reconciled with Russia, the sword-bearer of the counter-revolution, it was not for British statesmen to be more Tsarist than the Tsar.

By the end of the century in France itself it was possible to proclaim adherence to the ideals of the French Revolution while repudiating its sequel in the Napoleonic era. As the best of all British writers on France put it: 'The grandeur of the Revolution in the eyes of those who had witnessed it, or had received its tradition from actors in it, would not have been apparent without its patriotic aspect and its military glory.'[68] The same author takes up the familiar theme of the follies of the men of 1789 whose sentiments had so appealed to British radicals:

In nobility of principle the moderate men of '89 have no advantage over the Jacobins of '93, and it was the improvident destructiveness of the former and their incapacity to govern which delivered the destinies of France into the hands of the Terrorists; for the anarchy which reigned for ten years was the immediate effect of the precipitate overthrow of the ancient authorities, and the insufficiency and the discord of the new rulers. If France had not been delivered from that anarchy by the indirect means of exterior military conquest, and reorganised by the same instrument, little would have been heard of the grandeur of the French Revolution, though some of the most ecstatic in its praise are those who most deplore the means which made it glorious and fashioned out of its chaos a new France.[69]

Two hundred years after the Revolution and nearly a century since Bodley wrote, the ambiguities and paradoxes are still there.

NOTES

[1] R. H. Ullman, *Britain and the Russian Civil War* (Princeton, 1968), p. 97.

[2] Ibid. 102. In 1922, when arguing for trying to enter into relations with the Soviet government, Lloyd George returned to his theme: 'His position was somewhat similar to that of Mr Pitt who, in the year 1797, had adopted almost precisely the same attitude towards the French Revolution as he was adopting towards the Russian Soviet: that is to say, he hated their doctrines but thought only of establishing peace in Europe' (Cabinet minutes, 27 March 1922, in M. Gilbert, *Winston S. Churchill* (London, 1977), vol. iv; quotation from *Companion*, Part 3, *Documents April 1921–November 1922*, pp. 1832–3). In calling attention to the ideological aspects of the struggle, Churchill was also echoing the position of Burke at the earlier juncture. See Edmund Burke, *Letters on a Regicide Peace*, in *Works* (London, 1812), vols. viii and ix.

[3] On the international aspects of the French Revolution from its outbreak until 1800, see R. R. Palmer, *The Age of the Democratic Revolution: A Political History of Europe and America, 1760–1800* (Princeton, vol. i, 1959; vol. ii, 1964). One may question Professor Palmer's belief that the American Revolution was democratic in the French sense; but his general treatment remains suggestive.

[4] See for example Albert Goodwin, *The Friends of Liberty: The English Democratic Movement in the Age of the French Revolution* (London, 1979).

[5] For the obstacles placed by the Labour movement in the way of action against the Bolshevik regime between 1917 and 1921, and its general attitude towards the Russian Revolution, see Stephen White, *Britain and the Bolshevik Revolution: a Study in the Politics of Diplomacy, 1920–1924* (London, 1979), ch. 2, 'Labour and Soviet Russia'.

[6] For a description of the occasion and its repercussions, see George Kennan, *The Fateful Alliance: France, Russia and the Coming of the First World War* (New York, 1984), ch. 7, 'Cronstadt'. The Revolution in Russia was thus something of a boon to French intellectuals of the Left, and historians of a Marxist bent such as Albert Mathiez could accept the Russian Revolution as fulfilling the latent promise of its French predecessor. Like Lloyd George, French historians of the Left excuse the Terror as a reaction to external circumstances, irrespective of the fact that it reached its height after the containment of the foreign threat. See F. Furet, *Penser la Révolution Française* (Paris, 1979). Terror in Russia also claimed many more victims after 'intervention' than during it.

[7] See the admirable and penetrating discussion of these matters in T. C. W. Blanning, *The Origins of the French Revolutionary Wars* (London, 1986). On the other hand, it must be admitted that some Frenchmen saw Britain's entry into the war as primarily the consequence of hostility to the ideas of the Revolution. Chateaubriand, who spent part of the period in England, was to write many years later that Burke 'en se déclarant contre la Révolution française . . . entraîna son pays dans cette longue voie d'hostilités qui aboutit aux champs de Waterloo. Isolée pendant vingt-deux ans, l'Angleterre défendit sa constitution contre les idées qui l'envahissent aujourd'hui et l'entraînent au sort commun de l'ancienne civilisation' (*Mémoires d'outre-tombe*, ed. M. Levaillant (Paris, 1948), i. 501).

[8] Ian R. Christie, *Stress and Stability in late Eighteenth Century Britain: Reflections on the British Avoidance of Revolution: the Ford Lectures delivered in the University of Oxford, 1983–1984* (Oxford, 1984), p. 158. Cf. David Caute, *The Fellow Travellers: a Postscript to the Enlightenment* (rev. edn., New Haven and London, 1988).

[9] For an analysis and useful documents see A. Cobban, ed., *The Debate on the French Revolution, 1789–1800* (London, 1950).

[10] Goodwin, op. cit. 135.

[11] T. B. Schofield, 'Conservative Political Thought in Britain in response to the French Revolution', *Historical Journal*, 29 (1986), 601–22.

[12] There is a moving fictional treatment of the events of 1798 in Thomas Flanagan, *The Year of the French* (London, 1979).

[13] Marianne Elliott, *Partners in Revolution: The United Irishmen and France* (New Haven, 1982), p. 212.

[14] *Report of the Secret Committee of the House of Commons on the disturbed State of the Country*, 19 Feb. 1817, in A. Aspinall and E. Anthony Smith, eds., *English Historical Documents, 1783–1832* (London, 1959), pp. 325–9 (quotation from p. 327). For an argument that ministerial fears were genuine if ill-founded, see Wendy Hinde, *Castlereagh* (London, 1981).

[15] Michael Brock, *The Great Reform Act* (London, 1973), p. 41.

[16] Despatch of 12 Apr. 1822 in Chateaubriand, op. cit., iii. 94.

[17] Despatch of 28 June 1822, ibid. 116.

[18] Ibid. 188.

[19] Ibid. 673.

[20] Elizabeth Longford, *Wellington: Pillar of State* (London, 1972), p. 416.

[21] Biancamaria Fontana, *Rethinking the Politics of Commercial Society: The Edinburgh Review 1802–1832* (Cambridge, 1985).

[22] Essay on Barère, in Macaulay, *Collected Works* (London, 1907), x. 272–3.

[23] Essay on Mirabeau, ibid. viii. 220.

[24] Paul Smith, 'Disraeli's Politics', *Transactions of the Royal Historical Society*, 5th series, no. 37 (1987), 65–85.

[25] Disraeli collaborated in the anonymous anti-Whig *England and France: or a cure for Ministerial Gallomania* (1832). See Robert Blake, *Disraeli* (London, 1966), p. 85.

[26] Letter to Sara Austen, 1 Dec. 1833, in J. A. W. Gunn *et al.*, eds., *Benjamin Disraeli, Letters* (Toronto, 1982), i. 380.

[27] Letter to Sarah Disraeli, 22 Oct. 1840, ibid. iii. 303.

[28] Letter to Lady Londonderry, May Day (*sic*) 1848, in W. F. Monypenny and G. Buckle, *The Life of Benjamin Disraeli, Earl of Beaconsfield* (London, 1927), i. 992.

[29] 'What has happened is the revolution acted over again by many of the same characters, the use of the same means, the same symbols, and the adoption of nearly the same measures' ('Wellington's Memorandum on British Relations with France', 14 Aug. 1830, in Aspinall and Smith, op. cit. 974).

[30] Kenneth Bourne, *Palmerston: The Early Years, 1784–1841* (London, 1982), p. 314.

[31] Fontana, op. cit. 152–3.

[32] Macaulay, op. cit., viii. 227. Macaulay's optimism about the French was to be called into question by the events of 1848.

[33] Norman Gash, *Mr Secretary Peel* (London, 1961), p. 638. Michael Brock takes broadly the same view.

[34] 'Tu y verrais entre autres des ressemblances bien singulières entre le temps qui a suivi immédiatement la Révolution de 1688 et la nôtre, avec cette différence

capitale cependant que la Révolution de 1688 ayant fait rentrer l'Angleterre dans ses alliances naturelles et dans son véritable rôle extérieur, la figure du pays quant aux étrangers est tout de suite devenue plus grande. Tandis que le contraire est arrivé après 1830 par des raisons opposées' (Tocqueville to Louis de Kergorlay, 25 Oct. 1842, *Œuvres Complètes*, ed. J.-P. Mayer (Paris, 1977), xiii, part 2, 109).

[35] Bourne, op. cit. 332–49.

[36] See Max Beloff, 'Tocqueville et l'Angleterre', in *Alexis de Tocqueville Livre du Centenaire, 1859–1959* (Paris, 1960), pp. 87–100.

[37] Tocqueville to Royer-Collard, 28 Aug. 1835 *Œuvres Complètes* (Paris, 1970), ix. 11.

[38] Tocqueville to Royer-Collard, 15 Aug. 1840, ibid. 90.

[39] Article written in 1841, *Œuvres Complètes*, iii, part 2, 322–5.

[40] Speech in the Chamber, 20 Jan. 1845, ibid. 425–7.

[41] Queen Victoria to Viscount Melbourne, 15 Mar. 1848, *The Letters of Queen Victoria* (London, 1907), ii. 195.

[42] Longford, op. cit. 380.

[43] In writing many years ago about the Revolutions of 1848, I pointed out how the intervening years had made possible the rapid dissemination of ideas not possible in 1789. I may have underestimated the extent of their passage at least from France to England at the earlier period. See Max Beloff, '1848–1948: A Retrospect', in George Woodcock, ed., *A Hundred Years of Revolution, 1848 and After* (London, 1948), pp. 41–59.

[44] A translation of the Lamartine despatch is in Woodcock, op. cit. 186–92.

[45] Letter to Lord John Russell, 11 Mar. 1848, ibid. 250.

[46] 'Letters on the French *Coup d'Etat* of 1851', Jan.–Mar. 1852, in Walter Bagehot, *The Collected Works*, ed. N. St John Stevas (London, 1968), iv. 29–84.

[47] As late as 1876 he was still reflecting on the contribution of the Revolution of 1830 to the fall of Wellington and on the way in which both reformers and anti-reformers had called French experience to their aid. See Bagehot, op. cit., iii. 215–18.

[48] Ibid., iv. 48. On 1848 repeating as farce what in 1789 had been tragedy, see Karl Marx, 'The Eighteenth Brumaire of Louis Napoleon Bonaparte' in Karl Marx and Frederick Engels, *Selected Works* (London, 1950), vol. i. Guizot himself, in his writings after 1848, did not attach importance to the problems that had precipitated the Revolution, but described his fault as having been to underestimate the revolutionary urge. See Douglas Johnson, *Guizot* (London, 1963), p. 260.

[49] Tocqueville to A. de Circourt, 25 Oct. 1857, *Œuvres Complètes* (Paris, 1983), xviii. 424.

[50] Bagehot, 'The Emperor of the French' (*The Economist*, 5 Dec. 1863), in *Collected Works*, iv. 107.

[51] L.-A. Prévost-Paradol, *La France Nouvelle* (Paris, 1868), pp. 44–7.

[52] Prévost-Paradol, *France, Two Lectures* (Edinburgh, 1869), pp. 30–1. What Prévost-Paradol probably said was 'enlightened sway' but this was misheard by the recorder of the lecture.

[53] Gwendolen Cecil, *Life of Robert Marquess of Salisbury* (London, 1921), ii. 32.

[54] Paul Smith, *Lord Salisbury on Politics* (Cambridge, 1972), p. 35. For guidance to Salisbury's writings see also M. Pinto-Duschinsky, *The Political Thought of Lord Salisbury, 1854–1868* (London, 1967).

[55] 'The Bicentenary', *Quarterly Review*, 112 (1862), 255.

[56] Review of Elias Régnault, *La Province: ce qu'elle est et ce qu'elle doit être*, 'French Literature', *Saturday Review*, 12 (1861), 618–19.

[57] Review of the third volume of H. von Sybels, *Geschichte der Revolutionszeit von 1789 bis 1795*, 'German Literature', *Saturday Review* 11 (1861), p. 78. It would

be nice to be able to think of a British statesman of today who could review a work in German on an episode in French history and have the review published in a weekly paper.

[58] 'English Politics and Parties', in *Bentley's Quarterly Review* 1 (1859), 1.

[59] Prévost-Paradol, *La France Nouvelle*, p. 296.

[60] Bagehot, 'The Gravity and Difficulty of Affairs in France' (*The Economist*, 7 Aug. 1869), *Collected Works*, iv. 131–4.

[61] The place of these events in the history of the French revolutionary movement is well set out in J. P. Plamenatz, *The Revolutionary Movement in France, 1815–1871* (London, 1952).

[62] Title of article in *The Economist*, 10 Sept. 1870. See *Collected Works*, viii. 182–6.

[63] For the changing British attitude towards France and Germany see R. Millman, *British Foreign Policy and the Coming of the Franco-Prussian War* (Oxford, 1965), pp. 211 ff.

[64] Quoted by Paul Smith, op. cit. 105.

[65] 'The Commune and the Internationale', *Quarterly Review*, 131 (1871), 550 and 551.

[66] Bagehot, 'The Politics of France as They Should Affect Her Credit' (*The Economist*, 3 June 1871), *Collected Works*, viii. 201.

[67] Bagehot, 'The Opposition in France' (*The Economist*, 19 July 1873), ibid. 226.

[68] J. E. C. Bodley, *France* (London, 1898), i. 98. Not everyone agrees with this assessment of Bodley's book. But I know of no other English-speaking writer who has so thoroughly and successfully immersed himself in French society so as to get the feel of French political life correct. The late Sir Denis Brogan comes nearest. More recent writers have been 'political scientists', compelled to rely on academe and the media—useful, but marginal to the real thing.

[69] Ibid. 99.

Macaulay and the French Revolution

JOHN CLIVE

IN a year such as the present one, it may strike the irreverent that 'productivity' might well be added to liberty, equality, and fraternity as one of the ultimate aims of the French Revolution; that all the struggles, all the agonies, and all the bloodshed took place, in part, so that in subsequent years professors the world over would be able to produce enormous quantities of controversial books and articles. A far less extreme version of this frivolous and possibly untenable thesis does, I believe, apply to Macaulay. He did not really write an inordinate amount on the subject; but what he did write, or utter in his parliamentary speeches, was as much concerned with English as it was with French history and politics. In other words, it could be argued that in the course of the years encompassing the great Reform Bill (1827–35), in which he produced the bulk of those writings and speeches, he took it for granted that the French Revolution supplied a ready-made armoury of helpful warnings, contrasts, and analogies, all of which could be applied to his own country's past, present, and future.

Three authors have dealt with important aspects of my topic: Joseph Hamburger, to whose persistence and ingenuity we owe the publication, almost a century and a half after it was first printed, of the completed portion of Macaulay's projected 'History of France from the Restoration of the Bourbons to the Accession of Louis Philippe', and whose own *Macaulay and the Whig Tradition* treats the historian's political thought as a whole; Hedva Ben-Israel, who puts Macaulay's attitude to the French Revolution into the more general context of what other nineteenth-century English historians had to say about the subject; and John Burrow, who has most recently—and wittily—illuminated Macaulay's particular brand of Whiggism.[1] I shall not try to compete with these writers, but merely wish to indicate a few of the ways in which Macaulay found both relevance and significance in the events of the Revolution, not hesitating to quote him liberally, whenever appropriate. Like many other historians before and after him, he seemed to find the subject especially conducive to vigorous and lively comment.

In one of his early *Edinburgh Review* essays (June 1827) he defended the moderate Canning coalition then in power, and warned of the consequences that would ensue, were it succeeded by an oligarchic Tory faction. The result was bound to be a reactionary regime, which would be followed by 'a revolution, a bloody and unsparing revolution—a revolution which will make the ears of those who hear of it tingle in the remotest countries, and in the remotest times'.[2] A republican sect, as audacious as the French Jacobins, but superior to them in acuteness and resolution, was arising within the middle classes. If diehard Tories came to power, that sect (presumably the Utilitarians) would become leaders of a strong democratic party within the ranks of the educated, would join forces with spinners, grinders, and weavers already chafing in a period of distress and ripe for revolution; and there would then be formed an alliance between the disaffected multitude and a large portion of the middle orders, with every reformer in the country being goaded into becoming a revolutionist.

That sort of alliance was not only anathema to Macaulay himself but, as he well knew, was also the chief and most constant dread of the English upper classes. Now, it conjured up in his mind an analogy with the situation in France in 1773, when Turgot was called to the head of affairs. The reforms he then contemplated would not only have conciliated the people, but would also have saved church, aristocracy, and throne from the commotions that ensued. But a crowd of narrow-minded nobles—the Newcastles and Salisburys of France—would not have it so. Misrule followed, then poverty and disarray; and, finally, the fierce and tumultous roar of a great people, conscious of irresistible strength, maddened by intolerable wrongs, and sick of deferred hopes.[3] Then, at last, concessions were made. But they came too late. It was the end of the old regime. And, even though the Bourbon exiles returned after the defeat of Napoleon, it was a world in which the old boundaries had been obliterated and the old laws forgotten. This was a faithful picture of what had happened in France, and it might well shortly be happening in England. Macaulay expressed the hope that those who now, in the pride of rank and opulence, sneered at what he had (anonymously) written, 'in the bitter sincerity of our hearts', would not one day find themselves thankful 'for a porringer of broth at the door of some Spanish convent', or imploring some Italian money-lender 'to advance another pistole on his George'.[4]

A few years later, in his speeches in favour of the Reform Bill,

Macaulay, now not merely an *Edinburgh* reviewer, but also an ornament of the Whigs in the House of Commons, amplified some of the points he had previously made in his article on the Canning coalition, and continued to emphasize analogies with French events. By that time, of course, the Revolution of 1830 had taken place, Macaulay had travelled to France to see its results for himself, and had noted in his journal that 'the general effect of that great change [produced by the first French Revolution] has been most salutary. A vast and thriving middle class has risen on the ruins of an exclusive and oppressive aristocracy.'[5] In his very first House of Commons speech on reform, the one that was to make him into a famous orator overnight, he adverted to the fact that history was full of revolutions produced by causes similar to those now at work in England: 'A portion of the community which had been of no account expands and becomes strong. It demands a place in the system, suited, not to its former weakness, but to its present power. If this is granted, all is well. If this is refused, then comes the struggle between the young energy of one class and the ancient privileges of another.' Among the historical precedents for such a revolution was the struggle which the French Third Estate had maintained against the aristocracy of birth. Such a struggle could be avoided only if timely concessions were made: 'Reform that you may preserve.'[6]

In his subsequent speeches on reform, he expanded on this theme. While he did not want to admit that the Whigs were reformers mainly from dread of violence—that, as Lord Mahon put it, he was using arguments *ad terrorem*—he maintained in his speech of 5 July 1831 that it was permissible to engage in an 'honourable' appeal to fear. Thus, if reform were now left to the Tories, leery of major concessions, a war between power and opinion would result, one of whose consequences would undoubtedly be that those 'Jacobin mountebanks', whom the Whig bill would at once send back to their native obscurity, would rise into fearful importance. To argue, as some did, that the French aristocracy should have stood firm in 1789, and should not have surrendered its privileges, was entirely mistaken. The error had been, rather, to have waited too long: 'It was because the French aristocracy resisted reform in 1783 that they were unable to resist revolution in 1789. It was because they clung too long to odious exemptions, and distinctions, that they were at last unable to save their lands, their mansions, and their heads. They would not endure Turgot; and they had to endure Robespierre.'[7]

One of those who disagreed with Macaulay's historical analysis was his chief parliamentary opponent in the Reform Bill debates, that unrepentant Tory and formidably learned *Quarterly* reviewer, John Wilson Croker. In September 1831, it was clear that the House of Commons would give a second reading to its revamped Reform Bill and that the sole hope of the Tories for ultimately defeating it lay in the House of Lords. Macaulay now undertook to warn those Tories in the House of Commons who were recommending 'firmness' to the upper house. In his most vivid manner, he conjured up images of stately mansions along the streets of the Faubourg St Germain sinking into decay and portioned out into lodging rooms; of ruined castles in the Loire valley; of an aristocracy 'as splendid, as brave, as proud, as accomplished as Europe ever saw . . . driven forth to exile and beggary . . . to cut wood in the back settlements of America, or to teach French in the schoolrooms of London'. And why had this happened? 'Because they had no sympathy with the people, no discernment of the signs of their time; . . . because they refused all concession till the time had arrived when no concessions would avail'.[8] The British aristocracy, Macaulay concluded, was different. Happily some of them—Talbots, Cavendishes, Howards—were, in fact, among the friends of the people. Thus it was not he who counted himself among those who represented the peerage as a class whose power was necessarily incompatible with the just influence of the people in the state.

His speech was an appeal to the House of Lords to follow the example of the Commons, and to pass the Reform Bill while there was still time for concessions. But Croker disagreed in no uncertain terms with Macaulay's analogy: it was, he said, the French aristocracy's 'deplorable pusillanimity', not its 'high and haughty resistance', that had led to their country's over-throw. A Montmorency and a Noailles, among others, had voted to surrender the French nobility's privileges on the night of 4 August 1789. What had followed? The Montmorencies had gone into exile; and the Noailles had died on the scaffold.[9] The House of Lords, for the moment, seemed to agree with Croker. On 8 October 1831 it rejected the Reform Bill.

As for Macaulay, Hedva Ben-Israel may well have a point when she argues that he gave up the French analogy in the course of the debate of 16 December 1831, 'retreating no doubt under the heavy fire of Croker's factual knowledge'.[10] But, of course, even if she is correct, that is not the way Macaulay himself would have put it; and some of what he actually said in his speech on that day still dealt with France. He raised the whole problem of history in large and small instalments, dramatizing the very issue on which he had differed with his critics:

'The French Revolution,' says one expositor, 'was the effect of concession.' 'Not so,' cries another. 'The French Revolution was produced by the obstinacy of an arbitrary government.' 'If the French nobles,' said the first, 'had refused to sit with the Third Estate, they would never have been driven from their country.' 'They would never have been driven from their country,' answers the other, 'if they had agreed to the reforms proposed by M. Turgot.'[11]

Macaulay went on to say that history in small portions proves anything or nothing, but is full of useful and precious instruction when contemplated in large portions, in terms of the lifetime of great societies. This may indeed have been a way of avoiding arguments about detailed historical problems, a debater's subterfuge. On the other hand, it led him to introduce a historical principle in which he deeply believed (and to which I shall return later in this essay)—the difference between a government and a nation. The history of England, he goes on to assert, is the history of a government constantly giving way before the nation; advancing sometimes peaceably, sometimes after violent struggle. As for France, the government of Louis XVI was much better and milder than that of Louis XIV. Yet Louis XIV was admired, even loved by his people, while Louis XVI died on the scaffold. (In a manner one might anachronistically call Churchillian, Macaulay often refuses to use the word 'guillotine'!) Why the difference between the fate of the two monarchs? 'Because, though the government had made many steps in the career of improvement, it had not advanced so rapidly as the nation.'[12]

Here, then, whatever tactical scholarly retreat in the face of Croker's learning may also have been involved, is a way of looking at history in the *longue haleine*, which served Macaulay at one and the same time as a goad for hastening the passage of the Reform Bill, as well as an explanatory principle for the eventual explosive violence of the French Revolution. His domestic political appeal is still fuelled by fear, but by a fear differently focused: not that aristocratic concessions might come too late, but, rather, that, given continued stubbornness on the part of the House of Lords, the government of England would, by this time, fail to be brought, as it always had been in previous history, into harmony with the English nation at large. It need hardly be added that spinners, grinders, and weavers had not yet earned their right, by education and income, to be considered a part of that nation.

Thus, even in those of his parliamentary speeches in which Macaulay made use most explicitly of the analogy of the French Revolution, in order to press for speedy political action, the comforts and contrasts of English history were never far to seek. And that, of course, is even more true of his *Edinburgh* essays, which provided a more leisurely forum for historical lucubration. Take, for instance, Macaulay's seeming obsession with the errors and misapprehensions of the so-called Plutarchian school of historians, writers including Plutarch himself and his imitators. Those historians and biographers, he asserts in his essay on 'History' (May 1828), while living under the despotic sway of the Roman Empire, took it upon themselves to salute and celebrate the love of liberty and the patriotic feelings to be found in ancient Greece and in the Roman Republic; to pay homage to the heroic, and frequently murderous, exploits of such as Leonidas, Epaminondas, Timoleon, Brutus, and Cato; unaware that the feelings and actions they so greatly admired had sprung from local and occasional causes, and that in almost all the little common-wealths of antiquity, liberty was used as a mere pretext for measures directed against everything that made it valuable. Those measures stifled discussion, corrupted the administration of justice, and (what Macaulay certainly never had the slightest wish to inhibit) discouraged the accumulation of property. The Plutarchians conceived of liberty as monks conceived of love, as cockneys conceived of the happiness and innocence of rural life, as novel-reading sempstresses conceived of Almack's and Grosvenor Square, accomplished Marquesses and handsome Colonels of the guards.[13]

These historians and biographers, so Macaulay maintained in his later essay on 'Mirabeau' (July 1832), were 'men who raved about patriotism without having ever had a country, and eulogised tyrannicide while crouching before tyrants'.[14] The sad truth was that the transactions of the French Revolution took their character in some measure from the pernicious influence of the Plutarchians on the Revolutionaries. True, the greater part of the crimes of the Revolution sprang from the relaxation of law, from popular ignorance, remembrance of past oppression, fear of foreign conquest, rapacity, ambition, and party spirit. 'But many atrocious proceedings must, doubtless, be ascribed to heated imagination, to perverted principle, to a distaste for what was vulgar in morals, and a passion for what was startling and dubious.'[15] And little wonder. For, given their enthusiasm for the Plutarchians, one need hardly be surprised to find what Revolutionary leaders under their influence forgot, in chanting rhapsodies to Athenian democracy, that in Athens there were ten slaves to every one citizen, and decorated their anti-aristocratic invectives with panegyrics on Brutus and Cato, 'two aristocrats, fiercer, prouder, and more exclusive, than any that emigrated with the Count of Artois'.[16]

Unlike Karl Marx, who, later in the nineteenth century, would be found endorsing the Roman parallels employed by the French Revolutionaries because they were aiding the appointed task of bringing about a genuine world-historical event, Macaulay found nothing but harm in what he considered to have constituted a serious misuse of history. But his purpose in reprimanding the French neo-Plutarchians was just as much to exalt the English as to reprimand the French. The English did not *need* Greek and Roman historical parallels to underpin their libertarian tradition. Unlike the French, who unhappily could not look back to a pattern of steady political reform in their own domestic history, and were thus forced to have mistaken recourse to antiquity, England had her Magna Carta, her very own Westminster Hall and Abbey, as well as Habeas Corpus, trial by jury, and the Bill of Rights to look back on; and required neither Capitol, nor Forum, nor the laws of Solon to further her struggles for liberty: 'We think with far less pleasure of Cato tearing out his entrails than of Russell saying, as he turned away from his wife, that the bitterness of death was past. Our liberty is neither Greek nor Roman, but essentially English.'[17] Thus Macaulay combined his attack on the misguided and artificial posturings of the French Revolutionaries with patriotic praise for the authentic, home-grown tradition of liberty in the happy possession of England.

The substance of that tradition, nowadays frequently referred to as 'the Whig interpretation of history', may be sought in almost all of Macaulay's historical works. But it is in *Napoleon and the Restoration of the Bourbons*, written during 1830–1, that one finds him explicitly contrasting the advantages of such a native tradition with the French Revolutionaries' need for classical examples, inalienable rights, and fictional social contracts. The leaders of the popular party at the time of Charles I were content to know that liberty was the lawful birthright of Englishmen. *Their* social contract was not fictional, but still extant on original parchment, with the sealed wax affixed at Runnymede. 'Thus our ancestors carried into rebellion the feeling of legitimacy; and, even in the act of innovating, appealed to ancient prescription.' And so, in the very wildest licence of faction and civil war, they still preserved something of the gravity belonging to ancient and firmly established governments. The Presbyterians overcame the Royalists. But there were no September Massacres. The Independents overcame the Presbyterians. But there was nothing like the vengeance inflicted by the Mountain on the Gironde.[18] It was in this manner that Macaulay made use of the French Revolution, not merely in order to warn, and to instil fear of what might happen if political reform were not granted; but also in order to provide reassurance that, for sound historical reasons, the English way would, even at the worst of times, never be anything like the French way.

The nature and extent of the violence that occurred during the French Revolution were important to Macaulay, quite apart from their unfortunate connection with pernicious and mistaken classical examples. He considered the subject most fully in his essay on Bertrand Barère (April 1844), 'this Jacobin carrion' who had recently been 'enshrined' by a sympathetic biographer in so misleading a fashion that Macaulay declared himself forced (perhaps not exactly against his will) to bring the carrion to the gibbet.[19] And this is indeed what he did, in an essay both lengthy and devastating, which depicted Barère as one of the most unrelievedly treacherous, evil, and wicked characters in all of modern history. My concern here is not so much with Barère as with Macaulay's judgement of the more violent stages of the Revolution.

He approved of the deposition of Louis. Given the European coalition against France, the French had only one alternative in 1792—to deprive the King of his powers as first magistrate, or to submit to foreign dictation. Under the circumstances, one could hardly expect Louis to have brought entire devotion to the national cause. Hereditary monarchy was no doubt a very useful institution in a country like France, 'and masts are very useful parts of a ship. But, if the ship is on her beam-ends, it may be necessary to cut the masts away.' Once the ship has been righted, she can be repaired in port. But, meanwhile, she must be 'hacked with unsparing hand, lest that which, under ordinary circumstances is an essential part of her fabric, should, in her extreme distress, sink to the bottom'.[20]

Moreover, the Girondins deserved considerable praise. For great ends, they had concurred in measures which produced much evil as well as much good; which had, for instance, loosened the foundations of property and law. Now, they thought it their duty 'to prop up what it had recently been their duty to batter'.[21] They had seen atrocious crimes, such as the September Massacres, committed in the name of reason and philanthropy. They wanted the perpetrators of that particular crime to be punished. Admitting that the public danger had been pressing, they denied that it justified violation of those principles of morality on which all society rested. They should have stuck to the principle that the season for revolutionary violence was over, and that the reign of law and order ought now to commence. But they lacked decision. By voting, along with the Mountain, for condemning the King to death, they acted against their own convictions; and, in spite of, or perhaps because of, last-minute efforts for a reprieve, they lost both power and moral credit.

The Mountain, for its part, contained some sincere and public-spirited men. But even the best of them 'were far too unscrupulous as to the means which they employed for the purpose of attaining great ends'.[22] Increasingly dominated by the Jacobins, they helped to engineer the Queen's trial and death as well as the execution of the leading Girondins (Macaulay calls the day of that event the saddest in the sad history of the Revolution) and the reign of terror, with the indiscriminate murder of victims young and old: 'Babies torn from the breast were tossed from pike to pike along the Jacobin ranks. One champion of liberty had his pockets well stuffed with ears. Another swaggered about with the finger of a little child in his hat. A few months had sufficed to degrade France below the level of New Zealand.'[23]

It was absurd to claim that any amount of public danger could justify a system of such terror, even on Machiavellian grounds. Jacobin energy was not, as it had sometimes been called, the energy of great rulers, but merely that of the Malay who maddens himself with opium, draws a knife, and 'runs a-muck' through the streets, slashing to right and left at friends and foes. The policy was by no means original, but one that had always prevailed in savage and half-savage nations. A real statesman might, in 1793, have preserved French independence without shedding a drop of innocent blood or plundering a single warehouse. But demagogues, not statesmen, were now the rulers. They did not know how to govern, only how to run the guillotine. (This time he used the word!) Their administration was a tissue, 'not merely of crimes, but of blunders'.[24] France was saved, not by the Committee of Public Safety, but, rather, by the energy, patriotism, and valour of the French people.

There is no reason to believe that Macaulay was any less aware in 1832 of the violent aspects of the French Revolution than he was in 1844. Yet April 1832 was the date of his essay 'Burleigh and his Times', in which he argued that both the Revolution and the Reformation, similar in many ways, *including* the amount of violence, were in the last resort working for the benefit of mankind. Both were uprisings of human reason against castes, the people against nobles and princes in the one case, the laity against the clergy in the other. Both shook to their foundations all the principles on which society rested. Both led to frightful cruelties— Macaulay compared the Anabaptists to the Jacobins. Both were conflicts not between state and state, but between two factions within society. What irritated Macaulay was that some zealous Protestants of his day (for whom, in any event, he had little sympathy to spare) represented the French Revolution as essentially evil because of the crimes and excesses produced in its cause by the spirit of democracy. He himself had no wish either to underrate or to palliate those same crimes and excesses. But he could not but remember that the early Protestants were as touched by them as Hébert, Cloots, and Marat.[25]

But the Reformation was long past. The volcano had spent its rage, the wide waste produced by its eruption was forgotten. Landmarks that were swept away had been replaced, ruined buildings put up again: 'The lava has covered with a rich incrustation the fields which it once devastated, and after having turned a beautiful and fruitful garden into a desert, has again turned the desert into a still more beautiful and fruitful garden.' The French Revolution, on the other hand, was not yet over. Marks of its ravages were still present. The ashes were still hot. In some directions the fire was still spreading:

Yet experience surely entitles us to believe that this explosion, like that which preceded it, will fertilise the soil which it has devastated. Already, in those parts in which we have suffered most severely, rich cultivation and secure dwellings have begun to appear amidst the waste. The more we read of the history of past ages, the more we observe the signs of our times, the more we feel our hearts filled and swelled up by a good hope for the future destinies of the human race.[26]

It is significant that Macaulay's optimism applies not so much to the Revolution itself as to its later consequences. For one thing, there was the obvious but none the less important fact that the Revolution encompassed such a lengthy series of events, and consisted of so many different phases, that contemporary observers were certainly entitled to change their minds in judging it. Macaulay expressed that view forcefully in two essays, one on Sir James Mackintosh (July 1835), the other on Etienne Dumont's memoirs of Mirabeau (July 1832). The essay on Mackintosh, a prominent Whig lawyer and man of learning and Macaulay's admired mentor, who had died in 1832, was written in the form of a review of his posthumous *History of the Revolution in England in 1688*. But it began with a vigorous defence against charges brought by the editor of that *History*, to the effect that a decade or so after writing his anti-Burkean tract, *Vindiciae Gallicae*, expressing sympathy with the French Revolution (1791), Mackintosh had abandoned those sympathetic views from interested motives.

Macaulay readily admitted that Mackintosh's views on the subject did indeed undergo some change. But had that process not been common, indeed almost universal? How could the French Revolution, or revolution in general, appear in exactly the same light to an observer on the day when the Bastille fell, on the day when the Girondins were executed, on the day when the Directory shipped off its principal opponents to Guiana, and on the day when the legislative body was driven from its hall at the point of the bayonet? The Revolution was a new phenomenon in politics. Previous history could not enable any person to judge with certainty the course that events might follow. Reform of great abuses, about which men rejoiced, was followed by commotion, proscription, confiscation, civil and foreign wars, Revolutionary tribunals, *guillotinades*, *noyades*, *fusillades*, and, finally, a military despotism which threatened the independence of every state in Europe. Anyone who held exactly the same opinion about the Revolution in 1794, 1804, and 1814 (and, for that matter, 1834) would have had to be either a divinely inspired prophet or an obstinate fool. Mackintosh was neither. He was simply a wise and good man, and the change that his views underwent in a more conservative direction was a change that occurred in the mind of almost any wise and good man in Europe. It is in this essay, and in this connection, that Macaulay tells his parable about the traveller who encounters strange fruit, a passage worth quoting in its entirety, both for its substance and its style:

A traveller falls in with a berry which he has never before seen. He tastes it, and finds it sweet and refreshing. He praises it, and resolves to introduce it into his own country. But in a few minutes he is taken violently sick; he is convulsed; he is at the point of death. He of course changes his opinion, pronounces this delicious food a poison, blames his own folly in tasting it, and cautions his friends against it. After a long and violent struggle he recovers, and finds himself much exhausted by his sufferings, but free from some chronic complaints which had been the torment of his life. He then changes his opinion again, and pronounces this fruit a very powerful remedy, which ought to be employed only in extreme cases and with great caution, but which ought not to be absolutely excluded from the Pharmacopoeia. And would it not be the height of absurdity to call such a man fickle and inconsistent, because he had repeatedly altered his judgment? If he had not altered his judgment, would he have been a rational being? It was exactly the same with the French Revolution.[27]

The parable applied to Dumont as much as to Mackintosh. If Mackintosh was a Whig who first opposed Burke, and subsequently changed his mind, Dumont was the translator and disciple of Bentham. His translations had helped to make his master famous throughout Europe, and he could legitimately be expected to have possessed strong democratic sympathies. Now, much to the delight of the Tories, Croker in particular, Dumont revealed in his book on Mirabeau, written in 1799, that he himself then had little respect for the French Revolution and those who had brought it about. But Macaulay pointed out in 1832 what he was to amplify three years later, when he came to write about Mackintosh, that before one could share in either the satisfaction of the Tories or the mortification of the democrats, one ought to recall that 1799 was a time when enthusiasm for the Revolution had abated, and its solid advantages were not yet fully visible. The evils that attend every great change had been severely felt, the benefit was still to come: 'The price—a heavy price—had been paid. The thing purchased had not yet been delivered.'[28] France was then in that state in which violent revolutions almost always leave a nation, when the habit of obedience has been lost, and the spell of prescription has been broken. Government power consisted merely in physical, and not at all in moral force. Madame Roland was by no means alone in deploring those crimes that were being committed in the name of liberty. It was, therefore, wholly understandable that Dumont, though sympathetic to the popular cause, should have gone so far as to maintain that Burke's view of the French Revolution had, on the whole, been justified by events, and had probably helped to save Europe from great disasters.

Had Dumont died in 1799, he would have died, Macaulay wrote, 'to use the new cant word', a decided Conservative; just as the younger Pitt, had he still been alive in 1832, would have died a Reformer. Circumstances shape political attitudes. But had Dumont revised his book in 1829, he in turn would have admitted that the French National Assembly had conferred inestimable benefits on mankind. Like Macaulay himself, he would have realized that the evil was temporary, and the good durable. Yet had Macaulay lived through the Revolution, he could not be sure that, in 1799, he, too, would not have been discouraged and disgusted, and that he would not then have seen in the great victory of the French people only insanity and crime.

What, then, of Macaulay's own views about the ultimate benefits of the French Revolution? As far as he was concerned, revolution in itself was an evil—'an evil, indeed, which ought sometimes to be incurred for the purpose of averting or removing greater evils, but always an evil'.[29] And we have already noted his horror and disgust at the wholesale violence that marked the later stages of the Revolution. Indeed, if in 1789 a wise and good man could have foreseen all the calamaties that lay ahead, 'he would have thought it better to accept those concessions which the King and aristocracy were prepared to offer, and to trust the rest to time and the progress of the human mind, than to make society pass through the agonies and convulsions of an utter dissolution, for the purpose of effecting a complete purification in a few years'. But by 1814 that was no longer a possible choice. The dissolution had occurred. The purification had been accomplished.[30] Dumont's *Mirabeau*, with all its doubts, had failed to convince Macaulay that the French Revolution did not, in the end, prove a great blessing to mankind. Three years later (1835), in the essay on Mackintosh, he employed that same phrase in an even more positive context: 'It is our deliberate opinion that the French Revolution, in spite of all its crimes and follies, was a great blessing to mankind.' But that was not really evident until 1814, the year of the return of the Bourbons. The crucial difference between 1799 and 1814, as he had earlier expounded it in *Napoleon and the Restoration of the Bourbons*, was that by the latter date, legitimacy had crossed over to the side of the Revolution. What the returning ultra-royalists were unable to see was that the Revolution was now no longer a theory, but a fact; not an innovation, but an establishment. It was now those who attacked the Revolution who could be called the real Revolutionaries. In 1799 it was certainly clear that a heavy price had been paid for future benefits, but it was also clear that the thing purchased had not yet been delivered. That is why Macaulay readily understood the negative feelings of Dumont and others at that juncture, and was quick to admit that he might well have shared them. But fifteen years later, things looked different. Writing about the France of 1814, Macaulay had also mentioned the tremendous price that had been paid for the beneficial changes of the Revolution, but had added unhesitatingly that there could by then be no reason for throwing the purchase away.[31]

Both blessing and benefits, 'the purchase', lay in the abolition of those aristocratic privileges and feudal abuses which had oppressed the French people. For the Revolution had been a struggle not so much between nation and King as between two castes, 'the rising up of millions of the oppressed against thousands of oppressors'.[32] The National Assembly deserved scorn for talking at length about the original compact of society, man in a hunting state, and 'other such foolery'. They may have wasted months in quibbling over the words of 'that false and childish declaration of rights on which they professed to found their new constitution'. But what they did to change French society was necessary, and good. Their work of devastation had to be done: 'They had to deal with abuses so horrible and so deeply rooted that the highest political wisdom could scarcely have produced greater good to mankind than was produced by their fierce and senseless temerity'.[33]

The great body of the French people derived real advantages from the abolition of privileges. And, once abolished, those privileges could not be revived: 'The forfeited estates could not be restored; the ancient system of administration could not be reestablished; the church could not again become rich and powerful, without another struggle, at least as terrible as that from the effects of which society was still smarting.'[34] Napoleon was not in power long enough to be able to turn the clock back. Indeed, though his government was not free, he must be given due credit for consolidating the work of the Revolution, and for fortifying the new social system by an alliance with law, order, and religion. The Jacobins had merely demolished the old institutions. Napoleon had erected new institutions on the ruins, and had thus made it impossible to restore the old system without a second demolition.[35]

Such a second demolition had not occurred with the return of the Bourbons. And by the time of Macaulay's visit to France, after the July Revolution of 1830, he was struck by the way in which the original spirit of 1789 had been 'revived with all its original energy, but with an energy moderated by wisdom and humanity'.[36] The Frenchman of 1832 was far better governed than the Frenchman of 1789. The oppressive privileges of a separate caste were gone. Political questions were discussed; political functions were carried out. Louis XVI had made concessions—he went to the scaffold. Charles X established a despotism—not a hair of his head was touched. In spite of the violent manifestations of the Revolutionary period, it had led in the end to the improvement of the rule of law.[37]

All this leads Macaulay, in the essay on Mirabeau (July 1832), once again to turn to England and to what had just become the Reform *Act*. The magnitude of that reform might well be called revolutionary. But the means? Merely an act of parliament, regularly brought in, read, committed, and passed. The force of reason and the forms of law had triumphed. The work of three civil wars had been accomplished by three sessions of parliament. And even during the fiercest extra-parliamentary agitation for reform, there had not been a moment at which any sanguinary act committed against any of the most unpopular men in England would not have filled the country with horror and indignation.[38] That peculiarly English moderation and humanity could be attributed to 150 years of liberty and lawful government. It was no accident that in England government and opinion were so closely connected, since, as we have seen, Macaulay's view of English history postulated a continuous infusion of national sentiment into the composition and workings of government. Thus it was not enough to look at the form of English government at a particular time; it was necessary also to look at the state of the public mind.[39]

In adverting earlier in this essay to Macaulay's principle that government and nation were two separate entities, ideally in a state of continuous yet gradual change and headed in a generally liberal and progressive direction, I promised to return to this point. I do so now because I want to stress that, as Macaulay saw it, it had, in modern times, increasingly become the role of what he called 'the public mind' to serve as a kind of powerful engine that could ensure both the continuity and the greatest possible harmony of the historical process, in which government and nation were always involved.

Take, as an instance, the demand in England for major parliamentary reform. There was a considerable difference between temporary tumults, or irritations, such as, for example, the Gordon Riots, and 'a great, a steady, a long continued movement of the public mind', which could not be stopped like a street riot.[40] Reform was indeed an old question, which had exerted great influence on the English public mind during the previous seventy years. The French Revolution, filling the upper and middle classes with extreme dread of change, and then the Napoleonic wars, had deflected public attention from internal to external politics, thus temporarily postponing the urgency of public demand for reform. 'But the people never lost sight of it.'[41] For Macaulay, both in his *History of England* and in his essays and speeches, public opinion, 'the public mind', was usually the crucial determining factor for great historical changes. And revolutions in opinion, belonging to the class of those 'noiseless revolutions' which Macaulay considered to be of such importance in history, could more often than not be found to underlie the more audible alarms and excursions of great affairs of state.[42]

The French Revolution, too, had been produced by the force of public opinion. No one knew this better than Napoleon, whose chief object as a despotic ruler had been to destroy the spirit which had produced the Revolution and who is said to have remarked that nobody could conceive the difficulties of governing a people who read the *Social Contract* and the *Spirit of Laws*. Too selfish to govern in conformity with the liberal principles of the age, he had set about to bring that spirit into conformity with his despotic maxims of government. He wanted to force political science backwards, so that 'the public mind of Europe' would sink into a 'second childhood'.[43]

Because Napoleon saw that in an age in which opinion was all-powerful, despotism was bound to be founded on falsehood, he tried to stifle freedom of thought, not just within the French Empire, but as it impinged on France from the rest of Europe. And what was the object of his greatest fear and hatred? England, 'the mother of Locke, the nurse of Montesquieu and Voltaire'; England, whose literature, history, and laws had given the first impulse to the spirit which had overthrown the Bourbons. For all he knew, England might again awaken that same spirit in France, and produce another revolution there. Try as he might, it was not easy to keep the French in ignorance on subjects that were freely discussed within a few miles of their coast, by people whom they already considered their political instructors.[44]

Thus Macaulay had a special reason for welcoming, not indeed the grimmer aspects or the more dubious twists and turns, but the originating spirit and the undoubted benefits of the French Revolution. In spite of Napoleon and the return of the Bourbons, it had turned out to be one of those great forward movements of the public mind towards more liberal principles of government and society of which, so he claimed, much of the history of England already consisted. It should not, therefore, be a matter for surprise that the impulse for that movement had, in fact, been English.

It would, of course, be altogether wrong to conclude on this note, to sum up Macaulay's view of the French Revolution as a kind of proprietary pride and pleasure on the grounds that it could be said to have been 'made in England'. That strand exists in his thinking on the subject; but then, so do several others: a genuine loathing of those phases of the Revolution that show violence out of control, an excess which he relates to the extent of misrule that had preceded it; admiration, carefully modulated to leave open a legitimate role for a popularly supported aristocracy in England, for the Revolution's curbing of undue aristocratic privilege and its abolition of feudal abuses; corresponding satisfaction with the increasingly powerful position of the French middle classes, a product of the French Revolution; fear that those Jacobinical and democratic elements let loose by social breakdown and dissolution would gain undue power in the state, and then threaten law and property, whether French, or, by example and extension, English; reinforcement for his patriotic pride in the manner in which England, by her long tradition of timely reforms, had enabled her governance to remain adjusted to the needs of the nation, as determined by the public mind; contempt for French revolutionary antics, whether, amusingly enough, they turned hundreds of Johns and Peters into Scaevolas and Aristogitons,[45] or whether, based on the Plutarchians or other sources containing inauthentic and artificial historical precedents, they entailed more serious consequences, making for bloodshed and violence; in contrast, praise for the English experiential and authentically traditional style of conducting public affairs, with the corollary that authenticity did not exclude the occasional desirability of making innovation more palatable by girding it in the badges and symbols of England's own past.

Can one claim originality for these views? Was Macaulay usually correct in his historical judgements? The answer to both these questions can only be a qualified affirmative. On individual points of contention, other English historians and observers had doubtless anticipated him. Hedva Ben-Israel, for instance, credits him with only one new interpretative idea, when he dares to glorify the very destruction wrought by the National Assembly 'as a vulgar but necessary task'.[46] And even that idea, she comments, owes something perhaps to a cue in Mackintosh. Since, during the years in which he wrote and uttered most of his comments, he was as much the politician as the impartial historian, many of his conclusions are open to question. He did not stop being an English Whig when he wrote about the French Revolution; and in his urge to be constantly comparative (and that urge, I believe, *can* be called original) he at times all too readily fitted events across the Channel into their appointed role in that at least partly mythical account of the ancient English constitution in which he delighted so greatly, or made use of this or that historical example to further the end of his party. One might well, for instance, reserve judgement about the real limits of his anti-aristocratic attitudes, particularly in regard to England.

What makes him still interesting on the subject of the French Revolution is the timing and combination of his observations and insights; his never-failing ability to raise fundamental questions; and, perhaps above all, his inimitable style: forceful, witty, penetrating; full of marvellously varied anecdotes and allusions; and, above all, supremely readable.

NOTES

[1] Joseph Hamburger, ed., Thomas Babington Macaulay, *Napoleon and the Restoration of the Bourbons* (London, 1977); Joseph Hamburger, *Macaulay and the Whig Tradition* (Chicago, 1976); Hedva Ben-Israel, *English Historians on the French Revolution* (Cambridge, 1968); J. W. Burrow, *A Liberal Descent: Victorian Historians and the English Past* (Cambridge, 1981).

[2] 'The Present Administration', *Edinburgh Review*, 46 (1827), 260.

[3] Ibid. 264.

[4] Ibid. 267.

[5] Thomas Babington Macaulay, Journal, Trinity College, Cambridge, Sept. 1830.

[6] *The Complete Works of Lord Macaulay*, 12 vols., Albany Edition (London, 1898), x. 415. (Hereafter referred to as *Works*.)

[7] Macaulay, *Works*, xi. 490–1.

[8] Speech of 20 Sept. 1831, Macaulay, *Works*, xi. 461.

[9] Croker, Speech of 20 Sept. 1831, Hansard, 3rd Series, vii. 315–16.

[10] Ben-Israel, op. cit. 104.

[11] Macaulay, *Works*, xi. 490–1.

[12] Ibid. 492.

[13] Macaulay, 'History' (May 1828), *Works*, vii. 187.

[14] Macaulay, *Works*, viii. 245.

[15] Macaulay, 'History' (May 1828), *Works*, vii. 191.

[16] Macaulay, 'Mirabeau' (July 1832), *Works*, viii. 245.

[17] Ibid. 243; 'History' (May 1828), *Works*, vii. 189; see also Burrow, op. cit., 32–3, 55–8.

[18] Hamburger, ed., Macaulay, *Napoleon*, p. 44.

[19] Macaulay, *Works*, x. 279.

[20] Ibid. 194.

[21] Ibid. 197.

[22] Ibid. 198.

[23] Ibid. 220.

[24] Ibid. 224. The original phrase, 'more than a crime, a blunder', is usually ascribed to Fouché (1804).

[25] Macaulay, *Works*, viii. 189. See Burrow, op. cit. 246–7, for a brilliant discussion of ambivalent Whig views of the Reformation during the nineteenth century, including Macaulay's. He could never forgive the Church of England's association with Divine Right and non-resistance.

[26] Macaulay, 'Burleigh' (April 1832), *Works*, viii. 190.

[27] Macaulay, *Works*, viii. 430–1.

[28] Macaulay, 'Mirabeau', (July 1832), Works, viii. 217.

[29] Hamburger, ed., Macaulay, *Napoleon*, p. 71.

[30] Ibid. 73.

[31] Macaulay, 'Mirabeau' (July 1832), *Works*, viii. 220; 'Mackintosh' (July 1835), *Works*, viii. 431; Hamburger, ed., Macaulay, *Napoleon*, pp. 73–4.

[32] Ibid. 70.

[33] Macaulay, 'Mirabeau' (July 1832), *Works*, viii. 223–4.

[34] Hamburger, ed., Macaulay, *Napoleon*, pp. 59 and 73.

[35] Ibid. 68–9.

[36] Ibid. 62. But see Hamburger, *Macaulay and the Whig Tradition*, p. 44, on the dangers also sensed by Macaulay.

[37] Macaulay, 'Mirabeau' (July 1832), *Works*, viii. 227–8.

[38] Ibid. 229–30.

[39] Speech of 16 Dec. 1831, Macaulay, *Works*, xi. 490–1.

[40] Speech of 5 July 1831, ibid. 443.

[41] Speech of 20 Sept. 1831, ibid. 456–7.

[42] For Macaulay's emphasis on 'the public mind' in his *History of England*, see John Clive, 'Why Read the Great 19-th Century Historians?', *American Scholar*, 48, 1 (1978–9), 37–48.

[43] Hamburger, ed., Macaulay, *Napoleon*, p. 56.

[44] Ibid. 57–8.

[45] Macaulay, 'Barère' (April 1844), *Works*, x. 214.

[46] Ben-Israel, op. cit. 106.

The French Revolution and the Condition of England: Crowds and Power in the Early Victorian Novel

DAVID LODGE

IN the most memorable episode of Mrs Gaskell's novel *North and South* (1855), the heroine, Margaret Hale, gets involved in a violent demonstration. Circumstances have brought her, a genteel southerner, to live in the northern industrial city of Milton, a thinly disguised version of Manchester. There she meets a mill-owner, John Thornton, whose harsh style of management, based on a dogmatic faith in market forces, she finds repellent, though she is impressed by his energy and integrity. Thornton's employees strike when he refuses to consider their claim for an increase in wages. At this juncture Margaret calls on the Thornton house to fetch a water bed for her ailing mother, and, preoccupied with her errand, hardly notices the ominous mood of the crowd gathering around Thornton's mill, which is next to his house. Only when she reaches the door, 'She looked round and heard the first long far-off roll of the tempest; saw the first slow-surging wave of the dark crowd come, with its threatening crest, tumble over and retreat, at the far end of the street . . .'.[1]

Once inside the house, Margaret learns that the striking workers are furious because Thornton has imported cheap Irish labour in their place. Margaret finds herself, willy-nilly, in a siege situation with Thornton and his womenfolk, who manifest varying degrees of courage and panic as they watch, from an upper window, the crowd breaking through the gates of the mill, evidently intent on doing injury to the imported Irish workers. Thornton reveals that he has sent for the military. Margaret, appalled at the prospect of violence, whether by the strikers towards the Irish or by the military towards the strikers, urges Thornton to go out into the courtyard and appeal to the crowd to desist. 'If you have any courage or noble quality in you, go out and speak to them, man to man!' (p. 232). Unable to refuse this challenge to his honour and virility, Thornton goes out into the courtyard and confronts the crowd, watched by Margaret from an open ground-floor window. Her impressions of the crowd are conveyed in such phrases as 'a thousand angry eyes', 'the savage satisfaction of the rolling angry murmur', 'cruel and thoughtless', and 'mad for prey'. Thornton is unable to make himself heard. Seeing some of the demonstrators preparing to throw clogs and stones, Margaret fears that 'in another instant the stormy passions would have passed their bounds, and swept away all barriers of reason' (p. 233.) Impulsively she dashes out into the courtyard and interposes herself between Thornton and the 'angry sea of men'. 'Oh, do not use violence,' she cries to them. 'Do not damage your cause by this violence' (pp. 234–5). Feeling responsible for Thornton's dangerous situation, 'She only thought how she could save him. She threw her arms around him. She made her body into a shield from the fierce people beyond.' Someone throws a stone at Thornton which hits Margaret a glancing blow on the head, drawing blood and rendering her half-unconscious. Appalled and ashamed at this deed, the crowd suddenly loses heart, and rapidly disperses.

As Martin Dodsworth points out in his Introduction to *North and South*, this action is highly charged with sexual significance. To say that 'the whole riot is replete with associations of orgasm' (p. 19) is perhaps overstating the case, but there is no doubt that Margaret's protective gesture is not simply heroic—it also reveals her unacknowledged attraction to Thornton, licensing an intimate physical contact, indistinguishable from an embrace, which would in normal circumstances be unthinkable. Indeed, Margaret is deeply compromised by her public gesture and feels obliged, subsequently, to reject Thornton as a lover in order to demonstrate the purity of her motives. Thus the incident neatly serves a double narrative function: it both reveals the mutual erotic attraction of hero and heroine and retards their union.

To read this episode exclusively in emotional and sexual terms is, however, to diminish and misrepresent *North and South*, which is on one level a novel about industrial relations, about the rights and duties of capital and labour. Margaret belongs by class and emotional allegiance to the side of capital, but she has friends among Thornton's employees, and her position in Milton as a stranger from the genteel south, with a professional and agrarian background, makes her critical and questioning about the supply-and-demand principles upon which Thornton conducts his business. Her gesture of placing herself between Thornton and the workers epitomizes her mediating role in the novel, aiming to neutralize the violence inherent in a conflict-model of industrial relations. Thornton is blamed for provoking his employees at a time of economic depression and great suffering. The corresponding figure on the workers' side is his employee, Nicholas Higgins, an honest and upright man, but stubbornly convinced that only a highly disciplined Union will wring concessions from masters such as Thornton.

One of Higgins's workmates is a man of much weaker moral fibre, called Boucher. With a sick wife and a large family of hungry children, Boucher cannot afford to strike, but obeys the Union out of fear. 'Yo' may be kind hearts, each separate,' he says bitterly to Higgins, 'but once banded together, yo've no more pity for a man than a wild hunger-maddened wolf' (p. 207). When the strike shows no sign of succeeding, the desperate Boucher becomes one of the ringleaders of the riot at Thornton's mill. He is the only one of the rioters Margaret identifies by name. She observes his face in the crowd, 'forlornly desperate and livid with rage' (p. 233). After her intervention and wounding, 'even the most desperate—Boucher himself—drew back, faltered away, scowled and finally went off, muttering curses on the master . . .' (p. 235). Higgins deplores the riot, which brings the strike into disrepute and causes it to collapse, and reproaches Boucher for his part in it. Boucher is arrested, but Thornton does not press charges, on the grounds that his unemployability will be punishment enough, which indeed proves to be the case. Boucher tries unsuccessfully to get work from a mill-owner notorious for refusing to employ Union members. Rejected by the masters as a troublemaker and by his workmates as a class traitor, Boucher commits suicide. Margaret blames Higgins for this tragedy. 'Don't you see how you've made Boucher what he is, by driving him into the Union against his will—without his heart going with it?' Higgins seems to accept the reproach to the extent of dedicating himself to the support of Boucher's widow and children.

Mrs Gaskell's anti-Union bias is very clear in all this. In spite of her respect for working-class leaders such as Higgins, and her sympathy for the sufferings of the workers in times of economic recession, she fears the consequences of their collective action. The spontaneous combination of individuals into a threatening and lawless crowd is causally connected through the Higgins–Boucher subplot to the organized 'combination' of the Trades Union.

Boucher personifies the mindless anarchy and violence that may be released, and cannot be controlled, by working-class militancy. In this respect *North and South* is typical of a group of early Victorian novels which Raymond Williams calls Industrial novels, and which in their own day were sometimes called 'Condition of England' novels. The ones Williams discusses in *Culture and Society* are, in addition to *North and South*, Mrs Gaskell's earlier novel, *Mary Barton* (1848), Disraeli's *Sybil* (1845), Dickens's *Hard Times* (1854), Charles Kingsley's *Alton Locke* (1850), and George Eliot's *Felix Holt* (1866).[2] As Williams notes, the authors' fear of violence, especially violent collective action, dominated their treatment of social and political issues and often warped the narrative and emotional logic of their stories. A turning point in the plots of four of these novels is a riot in which the principal characters are involved in some way. Both Kingsley's and George Eliot's eponymous heroes are implicated in riots which they are trying to control or prevent, and sent to prison in consequence. The climax of *Sybil* finds the heroine caught up in a violent and destructive rebellion of disaffected workers. The two novels which do not have a riot in them are *Mary Barton* (which has an ideologically motivated murder instead) and *Hard Times*. The reason *Hard Times* contains no violent collective action is, I think, because it was partly based on Dickens's journalistic reporting of a prolonged strike of cotton workers in Preston in 1855. According to Humphrey House, Dickens went to Preston 'expecting to find discontent, disorder, and even rioting', and was surprised to find 'that everything was so quiet and the men so well-behaved'.[3] Perhaps he was not only surprised but secretly disappointed, for he betrayed in other novels a kind of horrified fascination with mob violence, notably in the riot scenes of *Barnaby Rudge* (1841), generally taken by modern critics to be his response to the Chartist agitation of the late 1830s, and in his novel about the French Revolution, *A Tale of Two Cities* (1859). Another historical novel with a topical subtext was Charlotte Brontë's *Shirley* (1849), set in the period of the Napoleonic Wars but clearly reflecting, in its treatment of Luddite activity, more recent working-class militancy. In a climactic scene the two heroines of the novel watch the assault of an armed mob on the mill of Robert Moore, whose machines they are intent on wrecking. Moore is a hero in the same mould as Mrs Gaskell's Thornton, convinced that the market must control the economy, even if it means operatives starving and their masters going bankrupt. Like Thornton, he is converted to a more flexible and humane model of industrial relations by the end of the novel. (Moore's enlightenment comes as a result of visiting the Midlands: 'While I was in Birmingham,' he tells Caroline Helstone, 'I looked a little into reality, considered closely, and at their source, the causes of the present troubles of this country . . .' (p. 505).)

I want to come back to that minor character in *North and South* called Boucher. Pronounced 'Bowcher' in Lancashire, it is not such an exotic name for a mill-hand as one might suppose, but it is foregrounded against the name of the other worker who plays a significant part in the story, Higgins. There are 289 Higginses in the 1987 telephone directory for South Manchester, but only twenty Bouchers. Proper names in fiction are of course never neutral: they always signify, if it is only ordinariness. The commonplace 'Higgins' is appropriate to a representative Lancashire workman. The surnames of the hero and heroine, Thornton and Hale, are also perfectly ordinary English names, but they carry fairly obvious symbolic connotations (toughness and prickliness, health and energy) appropriate to the characters. Boucher, however, is neither a common regional name, reinforcing the realistic code in which the novel is written, nor (as long as we pronounce it 'Bowcher') an obviously symbolic one. But as soon as we recognize the derivation of the name from *boucher*, French for 'butcher', and note this character's crucial role in the riot at Thornton's mill, the symbolic force of the name becomes evident, whether Mrs Gaskell consciously intended it or not. It is like a riddle in a Freudian dream-analysis. Butcher—France—riot: the chain of association is short and leads us straight to the French Revolution, the guillotine, and the Terror.

What I hope to show in the remainder of this essay is that the fear of working-class militancy manifested in early and mid-Victorian 'Condition of England' novels, most intensely in their treatment of crowd behaviour, was fuelled and informed by memories and myths of the French Revolution. I say 'memories and myths' because in one sense these novelists were responding to real history and in another they were influenced by and contributing to a highly imaginative, quasi-fictional interpretation of that history.

The French Revolution ushered in the modern political era. It was notable for being a popular uprising which had permanent political effects. Though led for the most part by bourgeois intellectuals, it was driven by the energies of the common people, especially the *sansculottes* of Paris, who took the political initiative at crucial moments—notably the storming of the Bastille in July 1789 which started the Revolution, the march on Versailles in October of the same year which compelled the King to move his court to Paris, and the sack of the Tuileries palace in August 1792 which led to the suspension of the monarchy. Henceforward there was a completely new relationship between crowds and political power in Europe.

I have borrowed the phrase 'crowds and power' from the title of a sociological-cum-anthropological treatise by Elias Canetti,[4] better known perhaps as a novelist, the author of *Auto da Fé*. At the beginning of his book, Canetti expounds an interesting typology of crowds, distinguishing first between the closed crowd and the open crowd. The closed crowd assembles by arrangement in a defined space which limits its numbers—a political rally or religious celebration would be examples. The open crowd appears to gather spontaneously, and seeks voraciously to grow in numbers. It is constituted by a 'discharge' of energy, 'the moment when all who belong to the crowd get rid of their differences and feel equal' (p. 17). The open crowd's tendency to destructiveness, especially of property, is an instinctive rejection of barriers and boundaries, anything which affirms and creates distance between human beings. A closed crowd can become an open crowd—this Canetti designates as an 'eruption', observing that 'since the French Revolution these eruptions have taken on a form which we feel to be modern' (p. 22). There are five emotional types of crowd, classified according to whether their primary motivation is baiting, flight, prohibition, reversal, or feasting. The revolutionary crowd is a reversal crowd—indeed Canetti cites the storming of the Bastille as the classic example of this type. A crowd of striking workers is a prohibition crowd—but as *North and South* demonstrates, not to mention more recent political controversy in Britain over flying pickets, it has always been seen as potentially a reversal crowd.

Obviously there were reversal crowds in history before the French Revolution. Earlier in the eighteenth century, to look no further, there were food riots in France and England in which crowds would compel greedy merchants in times of shortage to sell their produce at low prices. The violent actions of the London mob in the Gordon riots, and in support of Wilkes, aimed to 'reverse' legislation and judicial verdicts. The London mob was, however, to a large extent inspired and manipulated by politicians higher up the social scale, while the food riots were genuinely popular manifestations, but short-lived in their effects. What was unprecedented about the French Revolutionary crowd was that it developed an autonomous will of its own and effected permanent political change.

It also, of course, spilled a great deal of blood. One of the most horrifying episodes of the French Revolution, the September Massacres of 1792, was a manifestation of crowd power, and the support of the *sansculottes* was essential to Robespierre's Reign of Terror. The degeneration of the Revolution of liberty, equality, and fraternity into a bloodbath destroyed its own leaders, alienated sympathetic foreign observers, and bequeathed to posterity the conviction or nagging fear that revolution inevitably produces a tyranny worse than the one it overthrows. The conclusion drawn by thoughtful, more or less progressive, and liberal-minded Victorians, such as the authors of the novels I have mentioned, was that a revolution in England must be avoided by removing the conditions which might provoke it. By representing Chartism and militant industrial action in terms that consciously or unconsciously alluded to the more violent episodes of the French Revolution, they aimed to dissuade the working class from organized political protest, and to frighten their own class into doing something about the Condition of England. This rhetorical strategy, and the idea of the French Revolution which it exploited, derived very largely from the work of Thomas Carlyle.

To give some idea of the authority of Carlyle in the early Victorian period, and the impact of his monumental history of the French Revolution, first published in 1837, a year before the birth of the Chartist movement, one might quote the testimony of Charles Kingsley's autodidact hero, Alton Locke: 'I know no book, always excepting Milton, which at once so quickened and exalted my poetical view of man and his history, as that great prose poem, the single epic of modern days, Thomas Carlyle's *French Revolution*.'[5] The comparison with epic poetry is a conventional literary tribute. *The French Revolution* is in fact much more like a novel, what we would call today a 'non-fiction novel' or the 'New Journalism', that is to say, a narrative which claims to be historically true, but uses techniques developed in prose fiction to tell its story in a vivid and exciting way: scenic construction, shifting points of view, free indirect speech, present tense narration, polyphonic discourse, prolepsis, iterative symbolism, and so on. There is, in fact, no device listed by Tom Wolfe as characteristic of the New Journalism, in his anthology of that name published in 1973, which cannot be found in Carlyle's *The French Revolution*. No wonder it excited and enthused novelists like Kingsley and Charles Dickens—who, according to Carlyle's biographer Froude, carried the book around with him everywhere on its first appearance.[6] Dickens, of course, acknowledged his debt to Carlyle in the preface to *A Tale of Two Cities*, but the historian's influence is almost as palpable in *Barnaby Rudge*.

Carlyle was particularly good at crowd scenes. His description of the storming of the Bastille, the march on Versailles, the storming of the Tuileries, the September Massacres, are wonderfully vivid and exciting. Hilaire Belloc, who took a very different, much more partisan view of the French Revolution, commended Carlyle for comprehending 'one chief fact of the Revolution: the mob. Alone of all European peoples, the French are able to organize themselves from below in large masses, and Paris, which wrought the Revolution, can do it better than the rest of France.'[7] As Belloc observes, Carlyle was the last person one would have expected to acknowledge this fact, because of his own proto-fascist belief in the necessity for strong leaders, but in the writing of *The French Revolution*, mimesis triumphed over ideology:

[So] thoroughly has he got inside his subject, so vitally has he raised it up and made it move of its own life, that in his book you see the French mob doing precisely what he would have told you, had you asked him, no mob could do. . . . [W]hen he stops to comment on them . . . he is often wrong, but when the description begins he becomes right again by a pure instinct for visualising and for making men act in harmony and in consort in his book.[8]

'The French Revolution', says Carlyle early in his book, 'means here the open violent rebellion, and Victory, of disimprisoned Anarchy against corrupt worn-out Authority.'[9] It is 'surely a great Phenomenon: nay, it is a *transcendental* one, overstepping all rules and experience, the crowning phenomenon of our Modern Time . . .'. It is 'the Death-Birth of a world' (i. 171). Carlyle's treatment of the Revolution is, then, frankly apocalyptic, and his message to the ruling class of early Victorian England was: if you want to avoid apocalypse on this side of the English Channel, you'd better get your act together. As he drew towards the close of his long narrative he spelled it out in his own prophetic style:

'[If] the gods of this lower world will sit on their glittering thrones, indolent as Epicurus' gods, with the living Chaos of Ignorance and Hunger weltering uncared-for at their feet, and smooth Parasites preaching, Peace, peace, when there is no peace,' then the dark Chaos, it would seem, will rise;—has risen, and O Heavens! has it not tanned their skins into breeches for itself? [This is a reference to one of the more horrifying atrocities of the Revolution, eerily proleptic of modern horrors, of a tannery at Meudon where the corpses of the guillotined were flayed to make leather.] That there be no second Sansculottism in our earth for a thousand years, let us understand well what the first was; and let Rich and Poor of us go and do *otherwise*. (ii. 382).

The power of the revolutionary mob is very much part of Carlyle's apocalyptic vision:

Perhaps few terrestrial Appearances are better worth considering than mobs. Your mob is a genuine outburst of Nature. . . . Shudder at it; or even shriek over it, if thou must; nevertheless consider it. Such a complex of human Forces and Individualities hurled forth, in their transcendental mood, to act and react, on circumstances and on one another . . . (i. 201).

The mob is both admired and feared here; admired for its energy, feared because of its destructive potential. It is 'a genuine force of Nature'—hence by implication opposed to Culture, which normally regulates human behaviour.

Canetti lists eight common symbols for the crowd, and all but one of them are drawn from the natural world: fire, the sea, rain, rivers, forest, corn, wind, sand, and the heap. In Carlyle and the Victorian novelists the favourite metaphor is the sea. Fire is also frequently invoked, but its metaphoric force is somewhat weakened by the fact that there is also a metonymic or causal connection between crowds and fire: crowds often set fire to things. The overturning of the culture/nature distinction in crowd behaviour, and the mob's compulsion, noted by Canetti, to break down all barriers and boundaries that normally create distance between human beings, are therefore more strikingly conveyed in metaphors of inundation. The mob that surrounds the palace of Versailles, for instance, is described by Carlyle as a 'living deluge' (i. 223). He invites the reader to 'glance now, for a moment, from the royal windows! A roaring sea of human heads, inundating both courts, billowing against all passages: Menadic women, infuriated men, mad with revenge, with love of mischief, love of plunder!' (i. 226). There is a strain of similar imagery in Mrs Gaskell's account, cited earlier, of the rioting strikers in *North and South*: 'the slow-surging wave of the dark crowd', 'the angry sea of men', their 'rolling angry murmur'. The narrator of *Barnaby Rudge* observes that 'a mob is usually a creature of very mysterious existence, particularly in a large city . . . it is as difficult to follow to its various sources as the sea itself, nor does the parallel stop here, for the ocean is not more fickle and uncertain, more terrible when roused, more unreasonable or more cruel'.[10] The description of the storming of the Bastille in *A Tale of Two Cities* is particularly notable for its elaborate use of sea-imagery. For example:

'Come then!' cried Defarge, in a resounding voice. 'Patriots and friends, we are ready! The Bastille!'

With a roar that sounded as if all the breath in France had been shaped into the detested word, the living sea rose, wave on wave, depth on depth, and overflowed the city to that point. Alarm-bells ringing, drums beating, the sea raging and thundering on its new beach, the attack begun. . . . So resistless was the force of the ocean bearing [Defarge] on, that even to draw his breath or turn his head was as impracticable as if he had been struggling with the surf at the South Sea, until he was landed in the outer court-yard of the Bastille.

The sea of black and threatening waters, and of destructive upheaving of wave against wave, whose depths were yet unfathomed and whose forces were yet unknown. The remorseless sea of turbulently swaying shapes, voices of vengeance, and faces hardened in the furnaces of suffering until the touch of pity could make no mark on them.

But, in the ocean of faces where every fierce and furious expression was in vivid life, there were two groups of faces—each seven in number—so fixedly contrasting with the rest, that never did sea roll which bore more memorable wrecks with it. Seven faces of prisoners, suddenly released by the storm that had burst their tomb, were carried high overhead . . .[11]

When Carlyle's *The French Revolution* was first published it was subtitled 'A History of Sansculottism'[12]—an indication that Carlyle saw the new relationship between crowds and power as the key to understanding his subject. It is in this respect that Carlyle differs from that other great British critic of the Revolution, Edmund Burke. In his *Reflections on the Revolution in France* (1790) Burke had written indignantly of the 'band of cruel ruffians and assassins' who burst into Marie Antoinette's bedchamber at Versailles, and of the 'horrid yells, and shrilling screams and frantic dances, and infamous contumelies, and all the unutterable abominations of the furies of hell, in the abused shape of the vilest of women', that accompanied the royal couple on their forced march to Paris.[13] But these are virtually the only remarks Burke makes about the revolutionary crowd; they are asides in an argument that is essentially abstract—constitutional, moral, philosophical—and aimed at the bourgeois professional and intellectual class directing the Revolution and sitting in the National Assembly. (He was, of course, writing before the onset of the Terror.) It was Carlyle who put the crowd, the *sansculottes*, and their behaviour, at the very centre of the Revolutionary phenomenon, to a powerful emotive effect that novelists subsequently harnessed for their own purposes.

Indeed, Carlyle uses the word *sansculottism* as more or less synonymous with revolution throughout his work, and it is very much part of his apocalyptic vision: 'on a sudden, the Earth yawns asunder, and amid Tartarean smoke, and glare of fierce brightness, rises SANSCULOTTISM, many headed, fire-breathing, and asks: What think you of *me*?' (i. 171). The word *sansculottes* means literally 'without knee-breeches', and was originally a derogatory epithet applied by royalists to the working-class radicals, who wore trousers. But Carlyle does not explain this and sometimes seems to invite a literal rather than a metonymic interpretation of the term, especially by using the rather arch variation, 'sansunmentionables'. That is to say, there is in the word *sansculottes* a suggestion of bared buttocks, one of the oldest and most universal human gestures of insult and contempt, which Carlyle seems to invite, or at least does nothing to suppress. Furthermore, in actual fact many of the *sansculottes* did not wear trousers, but skirts. Women played a part of unprecedented importance in the crowds of the French Revolution, notably in the great march on Versailles which was instigated and largely carried through by women.

Carlyle shows himself to be both fascinated and disturbed by this episode in the section of his book that deals with it, entitled 'The Insurrection of Women'. He tries to dismiss it with ridicule and irony: 'how unfrightful it must have been; ludico-terrific, and most unmanageable' (i. 203). He applies mock-heroic epithets to the women—they are 'Menads', 'Amazons', 'Judiths'. He seizes gleefully on the fact that the march on Versailles took place in pouring rain, and summons up an image of the Esplanade 'covered with groups of squalid dripping women' (i. 211). He compares their alternative National Assembly to Erasmus's ape imitating his master shaving. But he cannot deny the effectiveness of the women's intervention, or the fact that it was a turning point in the Revolution.

Dickens was also disturbed by the role of women in the Revolution, and unlike Carlyle did not try to laugh it off. The most ruthless and cruel revolutionaries in *A Tale of Two Cities* are women—Madame Defarge, always ominously knitting, like one of the Fates, and the anonymous bloodthirsty harridan known as 'the Vengeance'. In one of the few episodes in the novel he took directly from Carlyle, the summary execution of the wretched old extortionist Foulon, who had once recommended the hungry people to eat grass, Dickens emphasizes the participation of women, not mentioned by Carlyle:

The men were terrible ... but the women were a sight to chill the boldest. . . . Give us the blood of Foulon, Give us the heart of Foulon, Give us the body and soul of Foulon, Rend Foulon to pieces, and dig him into the ground, that grass may grow from him. With these cries, numbers of the women, lashed into blind frenzy, whirled about, striking and tearing at their own friends until they dropped into a passionate swoon, and were only saved by the men belonging to them from being trampled underfoot. (p. 252)

This passage is heavily suggestive of pagan myth and ritual, especially the cult of Dionysus, whose priestesses, the Bacchae or Menads, would work themselves up into a similar kind of frenzy. The same connotations are carried over to Dickens's description, later in the novel, of the Carmagnole, the wild chanting dance performed in the streets of Paris by *sansculottes* of both sexes at the height of the Revolution: 'They advanced, retreated, struck at one another's hands, clutched at one another's heads, spun round alone, caught one another and spun round in pairs, until many of them dropped. . . . No fight could have been half so terrible as this dance. It was so emphatically a fallen sport—a something, once innocent, delivered over to devilry . . .' (p. 307).

The key to these passages from Carlyle and Dickens is the idea of transgression. The transgression of traditional power relations

between the classes inherent in revolution is associated with transgression of traditional gender roles and codes of social behaviour. It
is as if revolution were a kind of return of the repressed. The
orgiastic energy of pagan ritual, partly repressed by Catholic
Christianity, but allowed a licensed expression in the tradition of
Carnival, further repressed by Protestantism, capitalism, and the
Enlightenment,[14] seems to erupt in a new and deadly serious form
in the revolutionary mob. The carnival crowd is in Canetti's
typology primarily a feasting crowd; but it is also a kind of reversal
crowd. Normal laws and prohibitions are suspended during
Carnival, and according to Bakhtin, 'the primary carnivalistic act is
the mock crowning and subsequent discrowning of the carnival
king',[15] a phrase that seems grimly appropriate to the fate of Louis
XVI in the course of the Revolution—at first invited to preside over
it, subsequently executed by it. The Revolution in Dickens often
seems like a demonic carnival. It is perhaps significant that in *Hard
Times* he put forward a tamed and sentimentalized version of
carnival, a 'closed' rather than an 'open' crowd—Mr Sleary's
circus—as a rather inadequate answer to the alienation of modern
industrialized society.

It is a critical commonplace that there is a contradiction between
the values Dickens's novels explicitly affirm—love, peace, domest-
icity, sociability—and the investment of his most powerful
imaginative energies in the presentation of evil, anarchy, and the
grotesque. Though he deplored the Gordon Riots, he described
them in *Barnaby Rudge* with a verve and gusto that came near to
identification with the mob, as he half-jokingly acknowledged to
Forster when he was writing these scenes: 'I have let all the
prisoners out of Newgate, burnt down Lord Mansfield's and played
the very devil. . . . I feel quite smoky when I am at work'.[16]

The description of the attack on Newgate in *Barnaby Rudge* was
clearly inspired by the storming of the Bastille, and the destruction
of the country house called The Warren earlier in the novel
corresponds loosely to the sack of the Tuileries. To both actions
Dickens imparts a demonic, orgiastic character:

Men who had been into the cellars, and had staved the casks, rushed to and
fro stark mad, setting fire to all they saw—often to the dresses of their own
friends—and kindling the building in so many parts that some had no time
to escape, and were seen, with drooping hands and blackened faces,
hanging senseless on the window-sills to which they had crawled, until they

were sucked and drawn into the burning gulf. The more the fire crackled and raged, the wilder and more cruel the men grew; as though moving in that element they became friends, and changed their earthly nature for qualities that give delight in hell. (pp. 506–7)

Now, now the door was down. Now they came rushing through the jail, calling to each other in the vaulted passages ... whooping and yelling without a moment's rest; and running through the heat and flames as if they were cased in metal. By their legs, their arms, the hair upon their heads, they dragged the prisoners out. Some threw themselves upon the captives as they got towards the door, and tried to file away their irons; some danced about them with a frenzied joy, and rent their clothes, and were ready, as it seemed, to tear them limb from limb. (p. 249)

These descriptions have a nightmarish quality that is peculiar to Dickens. But the storming of the Bastille, the march on Versailles, and the sack of the Tuileries haunted the imaginations of other Victorian novelists, and lie behind such scenes as the attack on Thornton's mill in *North and South* and the assault on Robert Moore's mill in *Shirley*. Perhaps the most blatant representation of English industrial unrest in terms of the French Revolution occurs at the climax of Disraeli's *Sybil*.

The story of this novel concerns an idealistic young Conservative politician, Egremont, who takes an enlightened interest in social problems, especially after meeting Sybil, the beautiful daughter of a Chartist called Walter Gerard. After Parliament's refusal to consider the Chartist petition of 1839 and subsequent civil disturbances ('Terrible news from Birmingham,' one of the characters reports, '... they are encamped in the Bull Ring amid smoking ruins, and breathe nothing but havoc')[17] Gerard throws in his lot with the violent or 'physical force' wing of the Chartist movement, much to Sybil's dismay, and is charged with conspiracy. When he returns home to a triumphant welcome, Sybil is somewhat reassured by the peaceful, orderly demonstration. But certain individuals in the movement are intent on provoking a violent uprising, partly for selfish personal motives. A general strike turns violent when the Hell-cats of Wodgate, who seem to be Black Country metal workers, led by an ignorant demagogue nicknamed 'Bishop Hatton', join the miners of Lancashire: 'The march of Bishop Hatton at the head of the Hell-cats into the mining districts was perhaps the most striking popular movement since the Pilgrimage of Grace. Mounted on a white mule, wall-eyed and of hideous form, the Bishop brandished a huge hammer with which he had announced that he would destroy the enemies of the people' (pp. 357–8). Whereas the miners demonstrate peacefully: 'The Hell-cats and their followers were of a different temper. . . . They destroyed and ravaged; sacked and gutted houses; plundered cellars; . . . burst open doors, broke windows . . . in short, they robbed and rioted' (p. 359). Sybil, who happens to be travelling through the country at the time of these disturbances, is offered the protection of the de Mowbray family of Mowbray Castle. This is an imitation Norman castle built by a Whig peer of ignoble pedigree—just the kind of pseudo-aristocracy Disraeli's Young England group in the Conservative Party most despised. Lady de Mowbray, however, is a genuine aristocrat, who becomes a kind of Marie Antoinette figure when the castle is besieged by the Hell-cats: 'When they perceived the castle, this dreadful band gave a ferocious shout. Lady de Mowbray showed blood; she was composed and courageous. She observed the mob from the window, and reassuring her daughter and Sybil, she said she would go down and speak to them' (p. 386).

There is a resemblance here to the scene in *North and South* with which I began. Both scenes have perhaps a common origin in Carlyle's description of the invasion of the palace of Versailles, and his injunction to the reader to 'glance now, for a moment, from the royal windows'. In such scenes the heroine, and vicariously the reader, is placed in the besieged building, and thus inevitably identifies with the occupants and owners, threatened by the mob.

The Hell-cats invade the castle, break into the cellars, get drunk, and vandalize the luxurious apartments:

[Bands] were parading the gorgeous salons and gazing with wonderment on their decorations and furniture. Some grimy ruffians had thrown themselves with disdainful delight on the satin couches and the state beds: others rifled the cabinets with an idea that they must be full of money, and finding little in their way, had strewn their contents—papers and books, and works of art—over the floors of the apartments: sometimes a band who had escaped from below with booty, came up to consummate their orgies in the magnificence of the dwelling-rooms. (p. 392)

Compare Carlyle's description of

How deluges of frantic Sansculottism roared through all passages of this Tuileries, ruthless in vengeance; how the valets were butchered, hewed down . . . how in the cellars wine bottles were broken, wine-butts were staved-in and drunk; and upwards to the very garrets, all windows tumbled out their precious royal furnitures: and with gold mirrors, velvet curtains, down of ript feather beds, and dead bodies of men, the Tuileries was like no Garden of the Earth (ii. 125).

Eventually, the Hell-cats set fire to the castle, and their leader perishes in the flames: 'the flame that, rising from the keep of Mowbray, announced to startled country that in a short hour the splendid mimicry of Norman rule would cease to exist told also the pitiless fate of the ruthless savage, who, with analogous pretension, had presumed to style himself the Liberator of the People' (pp. 396–7). Sybil is rescued from a fate worse than death by Egremont, and conveniently turns out to be an heiress, so he can marry her without disturbance to the class system. The love story of *Sybil* is its least convincing element. As a socio-political novel of ideas, however, it is lively, thought-provoking, and well-informed. Disraeli drew cleverly on his political experience and on documentary sources such as Parliamentary Blue Books to make his panoramic picture of England convincing. But the climax of his novel, as far as I know, had no factual source or analogue in England. The sack and destruction of Mowbray Castle is a fiction which projects certain well-established images of the French Revolution onto the social and political unrest of England in the late 1830s and early 1840s.

There is one classic English novel which describes the action of a reversal crowd as disciplined, orderly, and responsible, uncontaminated by criminal and anti-social elements, and that was published some years before Carlyle's *The French Revolution*. I refer to the account of the Porteus Riots in Sir Walter Scott's *The Heart of Midlothian* (1818). In 1736, a popular smuggler called Wilson was hanged in Edinburgh before a sympathetic crowd. The officer in charge of the execution, Captain Porteus, over-reacted to the crowd's behaviour and ordered his men to fire on them, killing several innocent people. Porteus was tried and convicted of murder, but at the last moment was granted a royal reprieve from London, to the great indignation of the populace. That night a highly disciplined mob, its ringleaders disguised in women's dress, broke into the Tolbooth, the old prison of Edinburgh, abducted Porteus, and publicly hanged him. Nobody else was harmed, and so punctilious were the ringleaders that they left payment at the ropemaker's shop from which they took the rope to hang their victim. Their work completed, they melted away, and no one was ever successfully convicted for the action.

Scott's narration of this sequence of events is brilliant, and scrupulously fair. By telling the story partly from the point of view of a Scottish minister who is pressganged into acting as chaplain to the condemned man and vigorously protests against the lawlessness of the action, Scott makes clear that he does not approve it; but, at the same time, he makes us understand the provocation and gives the perpetrators full credit for their determination and self-discipline, which contrast favourably with the muddle and panic of the official custodians of law and order. It is a very good example of George Lukács' perceptive insight into Scott's work, that it was ideologically much more progressive than his actual politics. 'It was the French Revolution, the revolutionary wars and the rise and fall of Napoleon,' says Lukács, 'which for the first time made history a *mass experience.*'[18] Through his recreation of episodes of Scottish history Scott intuitively expressed the new self-consciousness and self-assertiveness of the common people in the Revolutionary period, even though he himself was a romantic Tory with aristocratic aspirations.

The Victorian novelists were unable or unwilling to achieve that degree of disinterestedness. The idea of mass experience, mass consciousness, mass behaviour, frightened them, and their fictional representation of crowds in action is invariably negative. The crowd attracts lawless and violent elements in society, and gives them an opportunity to indulge their evil inclinations; it also releases the evil and destructive potential inherent in all of us. The crowd is cruel, fickle, and irrational, liable to be overcome by a collective madness. Of course one finds such a view of the crowd in literature before the Revolutionary period—in the plays of Shakespeare, for instance.[19] But the French Revolution, especially as represented by Carlyle, had given the idea of the power of the crowd a new and nightmarish dimension which, as I have tried to show, powerfully affected the treatment of the Condition of England in the early Victorian novel.

NOTES

[1] Elizabeth Gaskell, *North and South*, ed. Dorothy Collin, with an introduction by Martin Dodsworth (Harmondsworth, 1970), pp. 226–7. All page references to this edition.

[2] Raymond Williams, *Culture and Society* (London, 1958).

[3] Humphrey House, *The Dickens World* (London, 1960), p. 207.

[4] Elias Canetti, *Crowds and Power*, trans. Carol Stewart (London, 1962). All page references to this edition.

[5] Charles Kingsley, *Alton Locke* (London, 1960), p. 94.

[6] J. A. Froude, *Thomas Carlyle* (London, 1884), i, 93. Cited by Kathleen Tillotson in her introduction to *Barnaby Rudge* (Harmondsworth, 1973), p. 22 n.

[7] Hilaire Belloc, introduction to Thomas Carlyle, *The French Revolution* (London, 1906), i, p. xvi.

[8] Ibid. xvi–xvii.

[9] Thomas Carlyle, *The French Revolution*, i. 170.

[10] Charles Dickens, *Barnaby Rudge* (Harmondsworth, 1973), p. 475. All page references to this edition.

[11] Charles Dickens, *A Tale of Two Cities* (Harmondsworth, 1959), pp. 245–6, 249. All page references to this edition.

[12] See George Rudé, *The Crowd in the French Revolution* (Oxford, 1959), p. 4 n.

[13] Edmund Burke, *Reflections on the Revolution in France* (Harmondsworth, 1982), pp. 164–5.

[14] See Peter Stallybrass and Allon White, *The Politics and Poetics of Transgression* (Ithaca, New York, 1986).

[15] Mikhail Bakhtin, *Problems of Dostoevsky's Poetics*, ed. and trans. Caryl Emerson (Manchester, 1984), p. 124.

[16] Quoted by Kathleen Tillotson in her introduction to *Barnaby Rudge*, p. 29.

[17] Benjamin Disraeli, *Sybil; or, The two nations* (Harmondsworth, 1954), p. 271. All page references to this edition.

[18] Georg Lukács, *The Historical Novel*, trans. Hannah and Stanley Mitchell (Harmondsworth, 1969), p. 20.

[19] *Coriolanus*, in which this theme is particularly prominent, is cited and discussed in two of the Condition of England novels: Charlotte Brontë's *Shirley* (Chapter 6) and George Eliot's *Felix Holt* (Chapter 30).

The French Revolution and
the Avant-Garde

IAN SMALL AND JOSEPHINE GUY

On avait encore la fièvre de la Révolution, et on ne trouvait pas mauvais
que l'art marchât parallèlement avec l'esprit publique.

(Champfleury)

Le réalisme est par essence l'art démocratique.

(Gustave Courbet)

The literary artist is of necessity a scholar, and in what he proposes to do
will have in mind, first of all, the scholar and the scholarly conscience.

(Walter Pater)

It is very much more difficult to talk about a thing than to do it. . . .
Anybody can make history. Only a great man can write it. . . . The world is
made by the singer for the dreamer.

(Oscar Wilde)[1]

OVER the past two decades, discussions of the concept and the
history of the nineteenth-century literary and artistic avant-garde
have tended to isolate two traditions: the 'political', in which artists
and writers are seen as using art in the service of ideological
concerns; and the 'stylistic', in which the principal concern of
avant-garde artists is to disrupt or replace accepted formal devices.
Moreover, these two traditions have become translated into
mutually exclusive definitions: artists or writers can be politically
radical or artistically radical, but they cannot be both.[2]

The instrumentality of the French Revolution in the formation of
an avant-garde as a political phenomenon is well known and may
be taken for granted. It is also generally assumed that French
Revolutionary ideas were the necessary precondition for the
appearance of nineteenth-century artistic radicalism, also known as
the 'avant-garde'.[3] However, the interpretation of the particular
nature of the French Revolution's influence upon art and literature—
that is, its role in determining an artistic avant-garde consciousness—
has taken two quite distinct directions, and these two directions in
their turn account for the two critical traditions outlined above. In
the first of these arguments, the influence of the French Revolution
is a *direct* or political one, in that, as in other areas of life, its legacy

was to politicize art. Hence in France the formation of the artistic avant-garde is attributed to the influence of the writing of Henri de Saint-Simon and the tradition of social thought which his work brought about.[4] In that tradition, art and the artist are seen as having primarily a social function. Although Saint-Simon quite naturally distinguished between the specific tasks of artists, scientists, and social administrators, he saw their final functions in the creation of the new post-Revolutionary state having large areas of similarity: artists had a special social role, and hence particular obligations towards the state. For example:

C'est nous, artistes, qui vous servirons d'avant-garde; la puissance des arts est en effet la plus immédiate et la plus rapide. Nous avons des armes de toute espèce: quand nous voulons répandre des idées neuves parmi les hommes, nous les inscrivons sur le marbre ou sur la toile; nous les popularisons par la poésie et le chant. ... [N]ous devons donc exercer toujours l'action la plus vive et la plus décisive; et si aujourd'hui notre rôle paraît nul ou au moins très-secondaire, c'est qu'il manquait aux arts ce qui est essentiel à leur énergie et à leurs succès, une impulsion commune et une idée générale.[5]

Most accounts of the aesthetics of socialist realism trace its ancestry back to statements such as these. In these accounts, avant-garde artists attempt to produce art in which stylistic and formal elements are subservient to the artist's larger social responsibilities. The consequence of this view is to define the avant-garde in a way which gives priority to artists such as Courbet and to writers such as William Morris, both of whom were concerned principally with overtly political rather than aesthetic questions. The logic of the argument, moreover, is to exclude, or at least marginalize, a large group of writers in France and Britain who experimented solely with form: writers such as Gautier and Hopkins, for whom aesthetic innovation was of paramount importance.[6]

On the other hand, the second—and moreover the dominant—view of the avant-garde sees the influence of the French Revolution as *indirect* in that it was brought about by the translation of the Revolutionary metaphor into a cultural or aesthetic form. In this view, the term 'avant-garde' comes to designate a group of artists in the 1870s who transferred the radical Revolutionary critique of social forms into the domain of artistic forms, and hence were concerned with stylistic (or aesthetic) rather than political revolution.

So avant-garde artists, motivated by a Revolutionary consciousness, attempted to adapt or replace aspects of traditional symbols and icons to produce an appropriate *contemporary* iconography or symbolism. The main proponent of this view is Renato Poggioli in *The Theory of the Avant-Garde*; for Poggioli the history of the authentic avant-garde begins with the formal innovations in art in the last quarter of the nineteenth century.[7] In contradistinction to the first view, his account of the avant-garde ignores what others have seen as earlier, politicized avant-garde art, and so he tends to marginalize the achievement and significance of artists and writers such as Courbet and Morris.

The rather debilitating consequences of these categories are demonstrated by the difficulties which art-historians have experienced in locating the place of Courbet within art-history. In her study of the Revolutionary elements of his 'realist' period and of his reactions to events in France in 1848, Linda Nochlin, somewhat reluctantly perhaps, argues that 'despite the undeniably innovating quality of Courbet's achievement, if one were forced to draw the boundary line between the past and the present in the art of the nineteenth century, one would inevitably draw it in 1863 with Manet's *Olympia* or his *Déjeuner sur l'herbe* rather than in 1850 with Courbet's *Burial at Ornans*'.[8] And the reason for her conclusion, given in a later essay, is that the 'standard' definition of the avant-garde artist simply does not easily fit the case of Courbet:

[I]f we take 'avant-garde' out of its quotation marks, we must come to the conclusion that what is generally implied by the term begins with Manet rather than Courbet. For implicit—and perhaps even central—to our understanding of avant-gardism is the concept of alienation—psychic, social, ontological—utterly foreign to Courbet's approach to art and life.[9]

Underlying this taxonomy of artists is the acceptance of definitions of the avant-garde derived from theorists such as Poggioli in which political and artistic radicalism are seen as incompatible. Indeed Nochlin's thesis and conclusions about Courbet pay tribute to the pervasiveness of theories such as Poggioli's, but they also testify to their inadequacy. That inadequacy was made apparent much more recently in the objections raised by Charles Rosen and Henri Zerner to the Realist Exhibition mounted by Gabriel Weisberg for the Cleveland Museum of Art in 1980.[10] Rosen and Zerner accused Weisberg of a revisionism, symptomatic, they claimed, of much contemporary American art-history, which tended to deny both the centrality and efficacy of the avant-garde in art-history. More specifically, they took issue with the relative insignificance assigned to an artist such as Courbet in so comprehensive an exhibition. Such a relegation, they argued, had the effect of erasing the radical qualities which patently distinguished Courbet from contemporaries such as Bonvin. The exhibition's fundamental mistake was to confuse Realism, an avant-garde movement, with the Realistic, a style of representation which favoured verisimilitude. Rosen and Zerner attempted to reassert Courbet's claims to avant-garde status, and their means of so doing are instructive. Most contemporaries of Courbet found his style exemplary; it was his subject matter, and his attitude towards it, which they objected to, for by treating 'le peuple' in a manner and on a scale hitherto reserved for historical subjects, he removed the distinction between the historical and the contemporary, an ideological position which most found unacceptable.[11] In their review of the Cleveland exhibition Rosen and Zerner attempted to reverse these judgements and to assimilate Courbet into a tradition of *stylistic* rather than *political* radicalism: indeed, for them Courbet's closest literary relation was Flaubert, in that both were more concerned with the *means of representation* than with *what was being represented*. In their argument, Courbet's goal—the 'destruction of the old idealizing rhetorical tradition'—was comparable to Flaubert's conception of *Madame Bovary* as 'a book about nothing': both are part of the same avant-garde impetus towards the 'disappearance of the subject' where 'subject' is defined as 'that which prolongs the thoughts of the spectator beyond the representation: the narrative significance, the moral, the meaning'.[12] Rosen and Zerner thus appropriate but invert the argument usually employed to deny avant-garde status to Courbet: what characterizes his art in their view is now not political but stylistic radicalism. The significant point is that even Courbet's defenders do not fundamentally challenge the hegemony of the categories of writers such as Poggioli: they merely relocate the grounds of his radicalism from one category to another, in this case from the political to the formal or aesthetic. None the less, the problem which Nochlin addresses remains: how can an artist as clearly political in his concerns as Courbet be legitimately assimilated into an avant-garde tradition without a complete denial of the politics of his work? Posed in such a way the 'case' of Courbet makes the evaluative aspects of historical or critical definitions of the avant-garde easy to see.

There are severe problems, however, both theoretical and factual, with both these kinds of histories of the avant-garde. For brevity's sake, it must be sufficient to mention two of the central ones. The first has to do with the accuracy of some historical accounts. If the basic historical distinction is between two kinds of artistic avant-garde, the political and the stylistic or aesthetic, then the relationship between the two becomes a vexed one. Why, for example, did one give way to the other? Historical accounts of the formation of the avant-garde rarely seem aware of this question. Even the most sophisticated proponent of this particular history, Donald D. Egbert, suggests only a mechanism, not a reason, for the change. He argues that the aesthetic avant-garde came about because of artists' growing alienation from the 'state as represented by official academies of art under monarchic or bourgeois control'.[13] But this account of the mechanism for the change, whatever its logical merits or otherwise, is factually incorrect. The two kinds of avant-garde, the 'political' and the 'artistic', were contemporaneous, not consecutive. For example, Gautier and Courbet were contemporaries; so, in Britain, were Swinburne, Pater, Morris, and Whistler. It seems reasonable to demand of general historical influences that they should be just that, and not operate selectively. Such shortcomings inevitably lead to suspicions about the fundamental historiography behind observations such as Egbert's. For if the assumption is that the principal legacy of the French Revolution in artistic matters was the transformation of the aesthetic into the political *tout court*, then inevitably every history of the avant-garde will find the disjunction between the stylistic and the political which many commentators have mentioned. The objections to the historical and critical methodologies such as those described above are, simply put, that they determine in advance what is to count as evidence, and hence their arguments become tautologous.[14]

The second objection has to do with nationality. There have been surprisingly few attempts to locate differences between the avant-gardes of different nationalities. Little attention has been paid to the fact that British and French avant-garde literary and artistic movements were quite different in character and orientation. Moreover, respective avant-gardes were not only different from each other, but within themselves embraced a surprising diversity. Here the exception among commentators once more is Egbert, who does indeed notice differences between the British and French avant-gardes, but accounts for them by simply asserting the general thesis that the more dominant the social control is in a country, the more violent are the reactions against it—on the part of both social and artistic radicals. The argument is a fairly familiar one, not in literary history, perhaps, but certainly in the history of social theory; it maintains first that the legacy of the Revolution in France was to politicize artists and secondly that their avant-garde contemporaries in Britain remained broadly unpoliticized. Now this may perhaps be true as a general social principle, but it certainly is not a self-evidently true statement about the relative social controls over artistic production operating in Britain and France in the middle of the nineteenth century, when, it can be argued, British artists and writers endured much more restrictive censorship laws than in France (especially in the theatre), but produced no correspondingly reactive avant-garde. (In fact, there was no theatrical avant-garde of any significance in Britain until well into the twentieth century, and even that was to a large extent derivative of foreign theatrical models.) Certainly there *are* differences between British and French avant-gardes, as the statements which serve as epigraphs to this essay make clear—differences so distinct that on occasion British and French avant-garde polemics seem in virtual contradiction. French avant-garde art concerned itself with aesthetic innovation, *and*, on occasion, with placing itself in the service of large ideological strategies, in which the search for a new iconography, a new poetics, or a new aesthetic was subservient to political ambition. British avant-garde artists and writers, on the other hand, seemed to be concerned *virtually exclusively with style*: they too sought a new iconography and a new poetics—new ways of representation appropriate to their time—but never apparently for any larger or party political ends.

By way of a contrast to the two lines of argument outlined above, a more fruitful approach to the avant-garde, particularly in the way it accounts for national diversity, is to go back to examine what has been taken as axiomatic: the necessity of French Revolutionary ideas for its formation. By the middle of the nineteenth century, the Revolution's legacy was a *problematic myth*, one mediated to artists in different ways depending upon the intellectual climates in which they worked. Thus from 1848 up to the collapse of the Second Republic, for French artists such as Courbet, the incorporation of Revolutionary proletarian and democratic ideals into a contemporary artistic programme was both appropriate and realizable. However, in the mid-nineteenth century, no translation of such ideas to Britain was possible. Britain had been conspicuous in its wholesale intellectual rejection of the *idea* of change: more precisely, and unlike his French counterparts, the historian Henry Buckle had failed to revolutionize British historiography, and French positivist thinkers such as Comte had been criticized and rejected by early advocates and defenders such as John Stuart Mill.[15] As a consequence it was simply not possible for those British artists attempting to liberate art from its submission to conventional bourgeois morality to adopt the same strategies as their French counterparts. It was the simultaneous awareness of the importance of French models—nearly all British avant-garde writers ardently propagandized their French contemporaries[16]—*and a perception of their inappropriateness to a British context* which shaped the diverse nature of avant-garde movements in Britain, and in particular denied the possibility of complete rupture with the past. The recent French past had made such a rupture an actuality and was testimony to the ability of a culture to create new beginnings. So for Courbet, realist art eschewed the traditions of pictorial art enshrined in the Academy. Even Manet's backward glance at Titian in his *Olympia*, while it acknowledged the existence of tradition, signally refused to engage with it, a detachment and ambiguity which puzzled contemporary critics. However, for British artists, working within an intellectual climate informed both by Whiggish gradualism and by theories of evolutionary change, tradition could not be so easily put aside: it could only be reinterpreted and exploited for different ends. Thus, to adapt T. S. Eliot's phrase, one way of describing the history of the British avant-garde is in terms of the relationship, rendered problematic by revolutionary mythology, between tradition and the individual artist.[17] While the avant-gardism of, say, Swinburne or Pater or Morris was very different, and different again from French contemporaries, they were all in the end responding to precisely the same set of circumstances.

The beginnings of an avant-garde consciousness in Britain can be detected in the 1870s, the period when the crisis in the hitherto dominant ideology of political economy made it possible to embrace Revolutionary ideas for the first time. At that moment a small group of writers made a concerted effort to challenge received opinion and defend the controversial and much pilloried Robert Browning. With the publication of *Sordello* in 1840 Browning's early popularity had waned, and between then and the mid-1860s he was the subject of mainly hostile reviews, one of the most vituperative of which came from the pen of the deeply conservative Alfred Austin who, in the *Temple Bar* in 1869, dismissed Browning's work as the 'very incarnation of discordant obscurity'.[18] Browning's linguistic and stylistic innovations—his esoteric vocabulary, unorthodox metre, and non-standard syntax—met with general disapproval. Nonetheless Browning's 'obscurity' found its defenders, particularly at the hands of those consummate stylists, Walter Pater and Algernon Swinburne. Their defence of Browning was to deny that literature could address a homogenous audience, and as a consequence therefore could have little social significance. In this respect, Browning was no random choice: he was a sufficiently controversial figure, but he was also in some ways eminent. Browning, reinterpreted by Swinburne and Pater, became the literary 'stylist' whose qualities of innovation and single-mindedness marked him off from contemporary poets.

Swinburne's and Pater's choice of Browning is important, for the first British avant-garde movement defined itself in relation to a figure who was quite outside their circle. Browning split with Swinburne in 1877.[19] He had virtually no commerce with writers of the Aesthetic movement, for he had no sympathy with its ambitions for art. In this sense, the Browning of Swinburne is almost a cipher, used in the service of an argument with which he did not wholly agree.[20] Moreover, the split with Swinburne is revealing, for it was over the latter's angry condescension towards the Browning Society and its strenuous attempts to achieve for Browning the popularity which he desired.[21] Swinburne's and Pater's tactics with Browning set a pattern for the avant-garde in Britain in the sense that they attempted to appropriate a tradition, or redefine large areas of literary history, for their own purposes (Browning's work, after all, was not new in the 1870s and, born in 1812, neither was he young). Later appropriations would be more ambitious: Leonardo, Plato, Shakespeare would all be appropriated by Pater or Wilde and would be redefined in terms of Aestheticism's views of its own traditions. On the surface, the uses of tradition in

Britain are quite different from, say, Champfleury's placing of Courbet against, but also outside, traditions of French pictorial art. But the fundamental dilemma, the reconciliation of artist with tradition, is similar.

Underneath the claims about the relationship of artist and tradition, though, a set of *political* judgements are in operation. Here it is useful to go back to Browning and examine Swinburne's and Pater's reviews of him. But a short earlier review of the now forgotten Dr Thomas Gordon Hake by his friend and future patient, Dante Gabriel Rossetti, is helpful in that it sets out the issues perfectly.[22] The 'problem' of Hake was also the 'problem' of Browning, though on a miniature scale: the problem of obscurity. For Rossetti, Hake's poetry was a 'remote and reticent medium', sure to alienate him from the 'general reader'. Hake's language was 'too frequently vague to the point of excess', and his use of formal structures, 'preserved at the expense of meaning', were 'baffling involutions . . . of diction'. Rossetti was, however, prepared to overlook shortcomings such as obscurity because of Hake's obvious originality and artistic sincerity, qualities which, Rossetti acknowledged, would be recognized only by the 'fit reader' or a certain select few capable of looking 'past the author's difficulties to the spirit which shines through them'. Hake's stylistic complexity was thus available only to an intellectual and cultural élite. But then, in a surprising twist in his argument, and one worth quoting at length, Rossetti suggests that Hake is within the main traditions of English poetry:

It appears to us then that Dr Hake is, in relation to his own time, as original a poet as one can well conceive possible. He is uninfluenced by any styles or mannerisms of the day to so absolute a degree as to tempt one to believe that the latest English singer he may have even heard of is Wordsworth; while in some respects his ideas and points of view are newer than the newest in vogue; and the external affinity frequently traceable to elder poets only throws this essential independence into startling and at times almost whimsical relief. His style, at its most characteristic pitch, is a combination of extreme homeliness, as of Quarles or Bunyan, with a formality and even occasional courtliness of diction which recall Pope himself in his most artificial flights; while one is frequently reminded of Gray by sustained vigour of declamation. This is leaving out of the question the direct reference to classical models which is perhaps in reality the chief source of what this poet has in common with the 18th century writers.[23]

Literary traditions have here become redefined in order to accommodate elements of the contemporary avant-garde. Equally important are the uses of this tradition, for not only does it sanction originality, it also justifies élitism: this appropriation of a tradition for an élite was one of the hallmarks of the British avant-garde. It determined the avant-garde's deeply conservative, anti-democratic nature (and so inadvertently also guaranteed its ultimate marginality). The contrast with Courbet's conception of an anti-bourgeois art is striking: Courbet's art is for a homogenous audience, 'le peuple'; it proposes the abolition of connoisseurship and a freedom from institutional controls. Yet despite these obvious differences, both the British and the French avant-gardes were deeply concerned with the notion of originality and hence with the artist's relationship with tradition.

Swinburne's comments, in his essay on George Chapman, on the controversy over Browning went further than Rossetti's on Hake.[24] For him, obscurity was to be understood only in relation to a concept of audience. A good or appropriate audience was an educated one, which of necessity would be a minority one. Democratic propagandizing for 'le peuple' as the single audience for a work was, for Swinburne, an advertisement for mediocrity. Swinburne's defence of Browning was based on one simple premiss: those who judged his work to be obscure were merely confessing to their own intellectual inadequacy. Browning was perfectly comprehensible to the like-minded reader, but never to the 'ready reader':

He is something too much the reverse of obscure; he is too brilliant and subtle for the ready reader of a ready writer to follow with any certainty the track of an intelligence which moves with such incessant rapidity. . . . He never thinks but at full speed; and the rate of his thought is to that of another man's as the speed of a railway to that of a waggon.[25]

This line of argument was later expanded by Pater in his essay on Browning in the *Guardian*. Pater achieves a rare moment of directness when he claims that the task of the contemporary literary stylist, in addressing only an élite, will be to preserve tradition in writing. For Pater, Browning's work was unavailable for a general audience, and this was a consequence of his difference from the general run of mankind. In his essay on 'Style', published in the following year, Pater is uncompromisingly conservative; paradoxically, avant-garde writers are preservers of tradition, not destroyers of it:

That living authority which language needs lies, in truth, in its scholars, who recognising always that every language possesses a genius, a very fastidious genius, of its own, expand at once and purify its very elements. . . . And then, as the scholar is nothing without the historic sense, he will be apt to restore not only really obsolete or really worn-out words, but the finer edge of words still in use. . . . A scholar writing for the scholarly, he will of course leave something to the willing intelligence of his reader. . . . To really strenuous minds there is a pleasurable stimulus in the challenge for a continuous effort on their part, to be rewarded by securer and more intimate grasp of the author's sense.[26]

These points are made in the context of a discussion of Flaubert's style. The significance of Flaubert for the British avant-garde is quite different from his significance in France. What is construed in France in terms of realism (and hence of the transparency of language and the objectivity of literary forms) becomes for Pater and the British avant-garde affiliated to a tradition of literary craftsmanship and of a scholarly respect for language in which its care is entrusted to an élite. Flaubert the chronicler of the *mores* of provincial France becomes simply Flaubert the stylist.

But it is with the work of William Morris that the differences between the politics of the French and the British avant-gardes become most clear and that the usual contrasts between the 'political' and the 'stylistic' avant-gardes have to be revised. On the surface, Morris's politics would lead one to suspect that he had no truck with the avant-garde Aestheticism of Swinburne or Pater. And in the case of *News from Nowhere* or *The Dream of John Ball*, which overtly dramatize or document political debates, such an observation is undoubtedly true.[27] But while these works, and his critical lectures on art delivered and published in the 1880s, allow us to talk of his radicalism, it is his attitude to tradition which marks him out as quite different from French radicals. Put simply, there are few distinctions to be made between Morris's uses of tradition (in all the many art-forms which he practised) and those of his contemporaries. Pictorially his work endorsed the revival of medieval iconography envisaged by the other Pre-Raphaelites; in his writing his use of medieval Icelandic sagas, verbal archaisms (such as the use of 'thou' and the verbal form *-eth* for the second person singular in *News from Nowhere*), and medieval narrative techniques in *The Dream of John Ball*, all demonstrate that he shared the deeply conservative attitudes to tradition of his British contemporaries. Overtly his politics are radical, but given the publishing techniques at his disposal, and his reluctance to embrace popular contemporary forms, the styles which he employs are exclusive, even undemocratic, in a way that the early French avant-garde was not. In all this one can see that the effect of French Revolutionary ideology on the formation of the British avant-garde was profoundly conservative.

The legacy of the French Revolution for the formation of the avant-garde *was* political, although the particular form of that politicization differed between countries and within countries. But significantly, the French Revolution made it necessary for all innovative artists to reassess their attitudes towards tradition, and naturally those reassessments took different forms. To conceive of the avant-garde in this way and thus to define it in the loosest sense as the innovative artist's reaction to the French Revolutionary myth, resolves many of the contradictions which have dogged discussions of it. On a general level it answers Rosen's and Zerner's call for a more 'mobile' concept of the avant-garde, for it allows artists such as Courbet, Gautier, Pater, and Morris to be discussed on the same terms, and all to be counted as authentically avant-garde. More specifically, it dissolves the distinctions between the political and the aesthetic avant-gardes; and consequently it invalidates the judgements based upon those distinctions: Morris is no more 'effectively' or 'authentically' avant-garde than, say, Flaubert or Pater. Moreover, such an argument solves the problem of dating the avant-garde, and in particular it disposes of the forty-year-old assumption that British avant-garde movements such as Aestheticism and Decadence were no more than a late and faded flowering of their French predecessors. On the contrary, in the scheme which we have sketched here, those British movements evolved as a reaction to the British cultural and intellectual climate in which they were situated, and they thus possess a uniquely British national character. Finally such a scheme allows us to explain *why*, without any sense of contradiction, certain artistically radical writers would be either right-wing or left-wing in their party politics. To return to the epigraph of this essay, it is clear that the contradictions between French and British avant-garde polemic was only a superficial one, for this polemic was all generated by strategies to address the same fudamental problem which, in an attenuated form, the French Revolution had posed: the relationship between tradition and the individual.

NOTES

[1] Champfleury, *Grandes figures d'hier et d'aujourd'hui* (Paris, 1861), p. 253, cited in Linda Nochlin, *Gustave Courbet: A Study of Style and Society* (New York, 1976); p. 39; Gustave Courbet, in A. Estignard, *Gustave Courbet* (Paris, 1897), pp. 117–18; Walter Pater, *Appreciations*, (London, 1889; Library edn., 1910), p. 9; Oscar Wilde, 'The Critic as Artist', *Intentions* (London, 1891), in *Collected Works*, ed. G. F. Maine (London, 1948), pp. 962 and 964.

[2] The opposition between these two ways of perceiving the avant-garde (and modernist art) probably found its most famous articulation in the debates between Theodor Adorno, Walter Benjamin, and Georg Lukács. The same opposition underlies Peter Bürger's pessimism in his *Theory of the Avant-Garde* (Manchester, 1984).

[3] See, for example, Matei Calinescu, *Faces of Modernity: Avant-Garde, Decadence, Kitsch* (Bloomington, Indiana, 1979). Peter Bürger is an exception here, for his institutional theory of the avant-garde makes *Aestheticism*, rather than the French Revolution, the necessary condition for the avant-garde, since it was that movement which exposed the institutional nature of art (which, Bürger claims, the avant-garde would subsequently attack in its attempts to reintegrate art into life). However, by locating the first avant-garde so late in the nineteenth century, Bürger's theory is unable to account for an artist such as Courbet, who, it could be argued, in his call for a democratic art free from traditional iconography, exhibited an earlier awareness of the institutional nature of art.

[4] See Donald D. Egbert, 'The Idea of the "Avant-Garde" in Art and Politics', *American Historical Review*, 73 (1967), 339–66; and id. *Social Radicalism and The Arts: Western Europe* (London, 1970).

[5] Claude-Henri de Saint-Simon, 'L'Artiste, le savant et l'industriel' in *Œuvres de Claude-Henri de Saint-Simon* (Geneva, 1977), v. 210–11.

[6] Hopkins's work is totally unconcerned with the sort of political questions which obsessed Morris; yet it is so appropriate to considerations of formal innovation that F. R. Leavis chose to discuss him as the forerunner to twentieth-century English modernist poetry.

[7] See Renato Poggioli, *The Theory of the Avant-Garde* (Cambridge, Mass., 1968).

[8] Linda Nochlin, *Gustave Courbet*, p. 227.

[9] Linda Nochlin, 'The Invention of the Avant-Garde in France, 1830–80' in Thomas B. Hess and John Ashberry, eds., *The Avant-Garde, Art News Annual*, 34 (1968), 16.

[10] Charles Rosen and Henri Zerner, *Romanticism and Realism: the Mythology of Nineteenth Century Art* (London, 1984), pp. 133–79; see also Gabriel P. Weisberg, *The Realist Tradition: French Painting and Drawing 1830–1900* (Cleveland, Ohio, 1980).

[11] For the general critical reception of Courbet's 'realist' works, see Meyer Schapiro, 'Courbet and Popular Imagery: An Essay on Realism and Naiveté', *Journal of the Warburg and Courtauld Institutes*, 4 (1940–1), 164–91; Joseph C. Sloane, *French Painting Between the Past and Present* (Princeton, 1973); and for

details of their subversive political content, see T. J. Clark, *Image of the People: Gustave Courbet and the 1848 Revolution* (London, 1973).

¹² Rosen and Zerner, op. cit. 161.

¹³ Egbert, *Social Radicalism*, p. 717.

¹⁴ This point is made by Peter Jones in a suggestive review of Poggioli's *The Theory of the Avant-Garde* in the *British Journal of Aesthetics*, 9 (1969), 84–9. A perfect example of such tautology is John Weightman, *The Concept of the Avant-Garde* (London, 1973), where his definition of the avant-garde—nineteenth-century artists' preoccupation with time, deriving from an evolutionary rather than a cyclical view of time itself—has the unfortunate consequence of defining not only the movement but also what is to be construed as evidence for that movement. Weightman's view is therefore not disprovable, but neither is it provable. Moreover, as Rosen and Zerner inadvertently make clear, behind many definitions of avant-garde radicalism, and to some extent forming them, there lurks a set of implicit evaluations in which the criteria used to describe avant-garde art are identical with those used to identify what is seen as good, lasting, and valuable art: prescriptions masquerading as descriptions.

¹⁵ See T. W. Heyck, *The Transformation of Intellectual Life in Victorian England* (London, 1982), and John Stuart Mill, *Auguste Comte and Positivism* (London, 1865).

¹⁶ A good example of the propagandizing of a French poet concerned with finding a style appropriate to 'modern' sensibilities is Baudelaire. See Patricia Clements, *Baudelaire and the English Tradition* (Princeton, N.J., 1985).

¹⁷ Hilton Kramer, in *The Age of the Avant-Garde* (London, 1974), has also talked about the avant-garde in terms of its paradoxical relationship with tradition but, in contrast to the argument of this essay, he insists upon a dichotomy between 'the partisans of wholesale revolt [which is] . . . an intransigent radicalism . . . that cancels all debts to the past in the pursuit of a new vision' and the 'champions of harmony and tradition . . . mindful, above all, of the continuity of culture and thus committed to the creative revival of its deepest impulses'. The use of pejorative categories is nowhere more apparent than in his observations about 'this division between art as a form of guerrilla warfare and art conceived as an affirmation of a vital tradition' (p. 5).

¹⁸ Alfred Austin, 'The Poetry of the Period', *Temple Bar*, 26 (1869), 316–33.

¹⁹ See Donald Thomas, *Swinburne: The Poet and his World* (London, 1979).

²⁰ The irony is that Browning eschewed the avant-garde critical approbation which would have ensured his marginality, and throughout his career was constantly willing to compromise in order to achieve a wider audience and easier accessibility. See Morse Peckham, 'Thoughts on Editing *Sordello*', *Studies in Browning and his Circle*, 5, 1 (1977), 11–18.

²¹ Despite his gratitude to defenders such as Swinburne, his hopes were for a mass audience and hence his sympathies lay with the objectives of Furnivall's Browning Society and its aim of annotating his work precisely in order to achieve that audience. See William S. Peterson, *Interrogating the Oracle: A History of the London Browning Society* (Athens, Ohio, 1969).

²² D. G. Rossetti, '*Madeleine* with Other Poems and Parables by Thomas Gordon Hake, M. D.', *The Academy* (1 Feb. 1871), 105–07.

²³ Ibid. 107.

²⁴ Algernon Charles Swinburne, *George Chapman* (London, 1875). The comments on Browning are reprinted in *Swinburne as Critic*, ed. Clyde K. Hyder (London, 1972).

²⁵ Ibid. 157.

²⁶ W. H. Pater, *Appreciations*, pp. 15–17. The 'Style' essay first appeared in

1888. Pater's account of Browning appeared in 1887 and was reprinted post-humously in *Essays from the Guardian* in 1901, but there are comments on the poet as early as 1873 in *The Renaissance*. See W. H. Pater, *The Renaissance*, ed. Donald Hill (Berkeley, Ca., 1980), pp. 170–2. Some of the language which Pater uses to characterize Browning's mental clarity and linguistic complexity (particularly the metaphors of light and optics) was taken over by Swinburne in his comments on Browning in 1875—evidence, perhaps, that these artists were working with a common aim.

[27] It is perhaps worth noting that Morris is central to Egbert's argument, in that, in his view, Morris, more than any other writer, embodied radical ideas in his writing. See Egbert, *Social Radicalism and The Arts*, p. 424 ff. For a different view, however, see E. P. Thompson, *William Morris: Romantic to Revolutionary* (London, 1961); Thompson argues that there are profound contradictions between Morris's art and his politics.

The Transfer of Technology Between Britain and France and the French Revolution

JOHN HARRIS

COMPARATIVE views of British and French industrialization have been the subject of a historiographical seesaw in the post-war years, with either end being successively overweighted. From a view which was almost contemptuous of French performance in the eighteenth and much of the nineteenth centuries, and which cast blame on perverse patterns of social stratification, deficient entrepreneurship, antiquated and restrictive institutions, and inefficiencies in capital formation for a failure to 'modernize' and copy the British pattern of intensive capitalization, large-scale industrialization, and progressive technology, the verdict has quite violently changed. Now the French are credited with a more balanced, gradual, and socially humane progression to industrialization, based on a slower shift from agriculture, on intelligent exploitation of the more sophisticated parts of handicraft industry, and the careful fostering of the newer, high-technology industries behind protective tariff barriers. On a slightly different front there are attempts to show that British growth in what was once thought to have been a period of great industrial success was in fact 'slow', particularly in *per capita* terms, while there are opposite attempts to show that, on selected criteria, eighteenth-century France, rather than Britain, might have been the 'first industrial nation'. Both the older and the newer views seem to have some elements of caricature in them. More light might have been generated if the earlier condemnatory school had enquired why other French industries were not so successful as (say) silk or plate glass, or other branches of French eighteenth-century commerce not so successful as the West Indian, rather than indulging in general criticisms of national social structure or entrepreneurship. Those who mark down the British achievement might reflect that it was fortunate that an industrial revolution happened to be generated which withstood the immense extra pressure of increased population, rather than despising the limited increase in *per capita* incomes which occurred.

Even if the French pattern to industrialization was different, how far was her eventual industrial maturity inevitably based on technologies developed by Britain? Perhaps it may be humbly suggested that while it is natural for historians to be prompted by short-term economic trends in their contemporary world to think again about existing verdicts on earlier periods, it is a trifle demeaning (and even likely to provoke some scepticism among a public which the historical profession is striving to convince of its intellectual and educational importance) if they respond to every shift in the modern economic breeze with a major change in the course of historical interpretation.[1]

The most obvious differences between seventeenth-century European industry and that of the leading industrial countries of the present day are in the field of technology, fundamentally a type of qualitative change. Of course technology is not an autonomous factor and to say that the situations in which it stagnates or flourishes are deeply involved with economic, political, social, and educational factors is to state the obvious. The very serious issues which need to be discussed to determine why long-term techno-logical developments take particular forms are largely passed over, though Bertrand Gille and Eugene Ferguson have influenced scholars in France and America; there are too few harvesters for this particular historical vineyard. This paper, however, does not attempt to address these great themes, but simply to look at the technological balance between England and France in the eighteenth century, and how it was affected by the French Revolution.[2]

One of the clearest ways of establishing technological pre-dominance as between one country and another, a predominance which frequently implies a general industrial superiority, is to determine what are the flows of technology between them. This can be seen by the exchange of ideas, whether set down in the form of literary or graphic data, or built into machinery and equipment (where their movement is a practical possibility), or conveyed by the movement of people. The last is all the more important when much technology is of a craft nature and effectively embodied in the physical skills of a craftsman-technologist. Rather more difficult to assess, but worth examining, is the strength of the efforts made by entrepreneurs, the state, or other agencies of either country, to acquire the technologies of the other, and the extremity of the means they will resort to in order to do so. This may be reflected on the other side by the strength of the measures, legal or organizational, which one country takes to prevent the export of technological secrets which it wishes to keep to itself.

While this paper will argue strongly that the major flow was from Britain to France and that a considerable amount of transfer had been effected by the time of the French Revolution, it only does so once some essential qualifications have been established. First, the position of Britain (which generally means England) as a technological creditor country was a relatively new thing. Had one assembled, let us suppose, a group of knowledgeable merchants of the main European trading countries round a table in one of the new coffee houses in the last decades of the seventeenth century, and had they discussed where some of the highest-quality European goods in trade came from, they would have pointed to Sweden for bar iron and copper, Styria for steel, the Aachen area for brass goods, Venice for drinking glasses and mirrors, Germany for hardware and tools, Northern France for fine linen, Italy for silk goods. They might have noted some exceptions for particular types of these goods, or pointed out that some former supremacies were being challenged—as for instance in France's imitation of Italian silk manufacture or plate glass production. Woollens were, of course, made very widely in many countries, and here, in broadcloths and some of the new draperies, England would be allowed to have the edge.

Where England had important technologies apart from woollen cloth manufacture (and even there the foreign influence on the new draperies is evident) the origin was the Continent. In the English iron industry, for instance, the very terms—'finery', 'chafery', 'twyer', and so on—reflected its technical origins in the Walloon part of the Low Countries and its transmission across parts of Northern France to the Wealden districts of Southern England. The English glass industry, too, showed its French origins in part of its vocabulary (for example 'siege', 'punty') and the flat glass it produced was predominantly the 'broad' glass introduced by Lorrainers and 'crown' (or 'Normandy') glass, the variant on the latter's name being sufficient testimony to its provenance. The use of the reverberatory furnace on an industrial scale seems to have come in from Germany. Printing, of course, as well as paper making, with its subsequent improvements, had come in from the Continent. If English coal mines had begun to make remarkable use of, and improve, the railed way, they had probably taken it from Germany.[3] Some early developments in textile machinery, such as the engine loom, the swivel loom, or silk-throwing machinery came from abroad in the late seventeenth and even the early and mid-eighteenth centuries.

While I shall endeavour to show that very significant developments had been happening in England which were about to alter the situation significantly, and to initiate a strong reverse flow of technology towards the Continent, there is plenty of evidence that up to the time of the Glorious Revolution at any rate, England could be regarded as technologically a debtor nation, and that one might be forgiven for supposing that the stocking-frame was the only indisputably English invention of importance which was now enjoying an introduction into Europe.

One can argue that the technological flows had predominantly moved in the other direction as early as the second decade of the eighteenth century, but it would be unreal to expect that among relatively advanced industrial nations there were not both flows and counterflows, and that, on occasion, Britain was not still the technological debtor which she had more commonly been in the past. The point has been well made by Musson and by Robinson. For example, they show that Matthew Boulton, who sometimes played a leading role in trying to prevent the export of British industrial secrets, played an uninhibited contrary role in trying to seduce foreign workmen to his Birmingham works for the top (the jewellery and luxury end) of the 'toy' trade. They included first-class engravers, die-makers, inlayers of precious metals, ormolu craftsmen, and similar experts. These were not perhaps the central technologies for major industrialization, but they were well worth accquiring for the needs of a limited sector.[4]

More important were techniques in which there were some scientific inputs involved (even if the science was not very exact) and particularly those in the development of which chemical knowledge and experiment had some part. Much of the pioneering here was French and involved liquid bleach derived from chlorine, and dyeing methods developed under the influence of such distinguished men as Dufay, Hellot, Macquer, Berthollet, and Chaptal, who had often been funded by government. The long-sought technique of dyeing in 'Turkey red' seems to have been pioneered by French immigrants to the chief new British cotton regions.[5] While it was only developed at the very moment of the Revolution, Le Blanc's artificial soda was a key invention for the whole future of industrial chemistry, despite the insecure base of the science he endeavoured to apply in his inventive achievement. Once industrially developed and proven, it was useful to glass-makers, soapmakers, and cotton finishers. The view that although the key chemical inventions derived from French science, their use and profit accrued overwhelmingly to the British, has been recently challenged and modified.[6]

It is not possible to look at every flow of Continental, and particularly French, technology into Britain, and this paper will confine itself to industrial technology. In passing it is conceded that other branches of technology had close connections with industrial technology; civil engineering, for instance, impinged upon it principally through major transport works: the Canal du Midi, for example, was far in advance of anything in Britain at the time of its building, nor had we anything like the department of Ponts et Chaussées or its Ecole, set up under Trudaine, which was a great and continuing fount of technological education. On the other hand, the French did not achieve a network of canals closely integrated with industry, or wet dock systems to rival those of Liverpool and London; nor did they develop cast iron as a major building material, whether in the iron bridge or the iron-framed building.

But one outstanding French invention was long envied in Britain, that of cast plate glass. Themselves debtors to Venice in the 1680s for the techniques of blown plate glass, the French had gone on to pioneer the casting of glass on a table, a large-scale process demanding heavy investment in buildings and equipment. While both methods continued to be used for decades by the Compagnie des Glaces, their great Saint-Gobain works came to specialize in casting, by which the very large mirrors which became an important architectural feature of eighteenth-century rooms could best be produced. The story of the English acquisition of the process is a complex one, and has been told elsewhere. It is sufficient to say here that there was (not inappropriately!) a virtual mirror-image of what so frequently happened in the opposite direction; a high-level intervention to approach the senior French manager and technologist to get him to head an imitative British manufacture; a search lower down the chain of command and expertise when he would not come; the seduction of workmen from their employers; the attempts of the French workers and managers involved to bargain between rival English employers once they had crossed the Channel; unanticipated problems in getting the process to work technically and commercially once translated to a very different industrial milieu and using a different fuel. The process, which was under continuous development in England from 1773, only became fully viable about 1792.[7]

If the view were tenable that no breakthrough of great technological significance had occurred in England before the cluster of textile inventions in the middle of the eighteenth century, that they *alone* had attracted French emulation by the Revolution, and that because this group of inventions was industrially narrow it was stochastic, so that technological invention could have occurred as easily in France as in Britain, then this paper would be idle.[8] With Rostow I would insist that the British industrial revolution was 'no random walk'.[9] It was not random because, while they had some independent characteristics, the textile inventions were a continuation of a long succession of innovations into which major inventions of strategic importance were linked. It would be wrong to suggest that there was only one British technological stream of any significance, and only one from which the French might wish to drink, but the most important seems to be the creation of what may be called a coal fuel technology. Fundamentally this would re-emphasize a relationship between coal and emergent British technology long ago asserted by John Nef, without accepting his suggestion that the pace of technological change probably declined between the middle of the seventeenth century and the late eighteenth century.[10] This approach would point to the substitution of coal for wood fuel in smith's work, nailmaking, and the general working (as opposed to the primary production) of metals from the late Middle Ages, the introduction of coal into brewing, dyeing, brick making, salt boiling, and a range of similar activities by the sixteenth century. While some adaptation and some skills were involved in these changes of fuel, they were those in which the major problems of using coal did not significantly enter.

For many processes coal was at first unsuited because of contact between the fuel and the material to be worked on, which was harmed by various chemical pollutants in the coal, while products, workers, or workplaces were unacceptably affected by its smoke.[11]

A grate and a simple chimney might be enough to make coal acceptable for domestic use, but more was often required industrially. The glass industry began to use coal about 1612 and it was made compulsory soon after; firebrick and crucible quality must therefore have been important quite early, and towards the end of the century large cones enclosed furnaces and working space alike, and crucibles were often caped or covered. The manufacture of cementation steel, recently developed on the Continent, was introduced in the second decade of the seventeenth century and the process was almost immediately converted to the use of coal in a reverberatory furnace. It became commercially viable towards the middle of the century; a distinctive type of coned furnace was next evolved, and Britain quickly became a leading quality producer. The salt industry expanded not only with coastal sea water as its basis, but with inland brine and rock salt increasingly having access to coal. The construction of improved salt pans from wrought iron plate was a technique valuable to the later steam-engine boiler-maker.

The late 1670s and early 1680s saw some important new departures in coal-using industry. The new flint glass, with its attractive qualities of clarity and suitability for cutting, was invented, interestingly its production being completely dependent on coal-fired furnaces. Soon afterwards the trials were made which enabled copper to be coal-smelted in reverberatory furnaces, and by the early eighteenth century the general smelting of non-ferrous metals had moved to coal. The great British success with non-ferrous metals, even the late eighteenth-century dominance of European and wider markets by British copper, is often forgotten.

The first half of the eighteenth century saw some inventions of cardinal importance. One, the smelting of iron with coal in the form of coke, occurred in 1709, but did not lead to the satisfaction of the main market, that in wrought iron, for several decades; it did, however, lead to the development of skills in casting which were critical for mechanical engineering. One, available from the 1720s, lay in the provision of large iron cylinders for steam engines. The steam engine itself was of course of immense importance in the long term, and Newcomen's machine was fully developed and working by 1712 and possibly earlier. It has correctly been said to be essentially a part of 'the coal-fuel matrix'. It was immediately involved in the draining of coal mines and of non-ferrous mines where coal could be economically supplied to fuel it; hundreds had been built by the mid-century. It constituted the main technological influence in an expansion of the coal industry, which was to lead to 5.2 million tons of coal being raised in 1750 and the almost incredible figure of 15 million tons in 1800. Some of the elementary understanding of physical properties essential for the working of any steam-powered device originated in the European discoveries of the scientific revolution (though we are still unclear about Newcomen's exact relations with science and scientists). There is, however, no evidence that any other country was about to produce a practical or commercial engine.

Before the middle of the century two other developments with a wide industrial importance had taken place. Both relied on coal fuel. The first was the production in 1745 of cheap sulphuric acid by the large-scale lead-chamber process of Roebuck and Garbett; the key nature of cheap sulphuric acid for the existence of a heavy chemicals industry meant that the commercial feasibility of some main French chemical advances was dependent on its availability. Of great importance, too, was the crucible cast-steel process of Huntsman, providing a high-quality homogeneous steel, of particular importance for metal-working tools.

This may seem a long recital of technological events, but it should be clear from it that well before the middle of the eighteenth century there had been a quite remarkable shift in the technological balance, in the creditor–debtor relationship, between Britain and European nations, including France. We must be careful, also, not to stress those British industries where coal was heavily used to the exclusion of others where it was less important. During the early eighteenth century, in a technological flowering which has never been properly described, and for which the sources are now perhaps largely lost to us, the Birmingham hardware district developed new methods for the light-metal industries in rolls, stamps, presses, plating methods, and mechanical polishing.[12] Again, in the seventeenth century England had developed a considerable horological industry in which a central element was the development of tools, both machine tools and hand tools, which made possible the creation of a dispersed industry of specialist watch-part producers.[13] Hardware production and tool production were not, of course, divorced from coal fuel, but they were not using coal on the scale that, say, smelting industries did.

However, the shift to coal fuel had other features which cannot be fully discussed here. It progressed beyond those uses where coal could be substituted for wood fuel with minimal adjustment, to those where major technological change was required and where the creation of new techniques demanded new equipment and new craft skills. New ranges of refractory materials had to be produced and correctly employed. Fireclay had to be found, firebricks and crucibles improved, furnace types evolved. A body of experience had to be built up on the great varieties and qualities of coal and the specific requirements of the different industries and processes for them, on furnace ventilation and control, on methods of stoking and firing, and on methods of making coke. Increasingly it was found that there were some technological similarities in the needs of different industries as they converted to coal, and that it was possible to speed progress by transferring a whole battery of technical devices and specialist skills from industry to industry. In modern terms a high degree of 'spin-off' was being generated. As the advances were achieved empirically and then embodied into the skills of those carrying out the operations, the new technology was transmitted by on-the-job learning, commonly by apprenticeship, just as older skills had been. The highly empirical, non-theoretical basis of these advances meant that it was not only entrepreneurs or managers who thought of improvements; sometimes workers, even apprentices, contributed. The general success of coal-based improvement usefully concentrated energies on a particular technological front; it also generated an optimistic outlook towards industrial experimentation which must have carried over in some degree to industries in which coal was not critical.

All this had consequences when it came to the transfer of technology abroad. The craft basis of the new technology meant that little of it was put into writing, still less into print, and the nation in Europe which was pioneering new industrial methods of strategic importance, and in remarkable numbers, had a minute technological literature. The way to acquire new technology was to acquire men with the right skills.[14] But they had been so long immersed in coal-using industry that its requirements had largely become unconscious assumptions; matters on which they had never hitherto needed to be articulate now had to be explained to foreigners who often thought coal to be an inconvenient if not a repellent fuel, and its qualities mysterious and perverse.

Furthermore, the sophistication of these technologies meant that each consisted of a series of specialist craft skills, all of which had independent importance, so that a technical team had to be identified and attracted to the 'non-initiating' country before the whole productive process of an industry could be transferred. It was not usually possible to find a solitary expert who could alone practise or pass on all the skills of an industry.[15]

We must now examine the extent to which there were transfers or attempted transfers of British technology to France, emphasizing that in the last few pages we have simply been indicating the main reasons for the turnabout in British technological leadership *vis-à-vis* the Continent by the middle of the eighteenth century. Much more was to come: there was the whole of the new textile technology—jenny, water-frame, mule, power loom, carding engine, cylinder printing. In the steam-power context, rotative motion was achieved; the Watt inventions greatly improved the steam engine, and machines such as the cylinder lathe produced better engines. In metallurgy new methods for the conversion of coke pig to wrought iron culminated in Cort's puddling and rolling process, and the cylinder-blowing of iron furnaces. In non-ferrous metals we should not forget the new technology leading to the copper sheathing of ships. Yet this list certainly does not exhaust British technological progress between the mid-century and the years of the Revolution.

As we now concentrate on the process of transfer, one thing to be noted is the timing of France's interest in, and attempts to transfer, British technology. As early as 1709 we have a request to import English tools and other equipment, including files, regarded as necessary for certain Paris trades. Steel is the main factor here, and interest in English steel processes accelerated over the century.[16] About 1718 there was a remarkable episode when John Law attempted to attract a whole series of British industrial processes and the necessary craftsmen to France. Efforts to establish an exemplary watch industry using English methods at Versailles under Henry Sully attracted particular interest, and may have involved up to seventy immigrant workers. There were also attempts to set up iron, glass, woollen, and steel works, mainly in Normandy, and lists survive of the large number of craftsmen recruited for them. This episode has only been superficially studied as yet, but it is clear that it created sufficient alarm in England for the Government to provide a substantial sum to obtain the return of the workers—an effort which, rather surprisingly, largely succeeded—and it was the main stimulus behind legislation to prevent the suborning of workers and their enticement abroad, which made illegal the main aim of contemporary industrial espionage, the recruitment of the key employees who possessed the essential skills.[17]

While it is clear that French interest in British technology began early in the eighteenth century, to endeavour to provide a chronological account of all the French attempts to acquire the technology of many British industries during the century would be very confusing, as it would be necessary to shift to and fro between different industries and a range of technologies. I shall now look at a series of important industries in sequence. First some metallurgical industries, and, to start with, steel.[18]

England, as we have seen, had successfully developed its own cementation steel industry, based on the heating of Swedish wrought iron bars, surrounded by charcoal in closed refractory chests. These were placed in furnaces which were then fired with coal fuel over many days. France, deficient in steel, produced it by a quite different method, in steel forges. The major centre of production, in the Dauphiné, did not make enough steel, or steel of good enough quality, for the more exacting uses. Consequently France continually tried to make steel equal to that of the better European producers. Sometimes Germany, or Austria, which had more closely analogous processes, were the model, but increasingly, as the century wore on, England provided the pattern. As Gille has pointed out, this was an industry, more than any other, to which scientific talents were directed by the state, from Réaumur in the 1720s to a famous group of scientists who were dedicated supporters of the Revolution. But even before Réaumur a number of projectors had vainly offered their services to the state, and the succession continued throughout the century. Apart from the inducements given by the state to technologists, enlightened noble forgemasters such as De Broglie and Buffon encouraged experimentation in steelmaking at their ironworks. From the mid-century the concentration on English processes was increased by the invention of Hunstman's crucible cast steel, of which the superiority was quickly recognized in France.

Gabriel Jars's famous metallurgical visit to England in the 1760s brought back detail on both processes. This detail was still being heavily relied upon during the prodigious efforts through the early stages of the wars of the Revolution to make good France's steel shortage, particularly in the famous 'Avis' of Berthollet, Monge, and Vandermonde to potential French steelmakers. The extensive archival materials of this period continually cite English steel as the main object of imitation, or the standard to equal. This was particularly the case with the vast enterprise (with two million livres capital at peak) of the company headed by Sanche, which flourished briefly in the early and middle 1780s, and offered prizes for those of its workmen whose steel most nearly approached the English standard. Few of those attempting to make English steel managed to assemble all the needful materials and the full team of expert English workers. Michael Alcock, active in France in the 1760s, had formerly had an interest in a Birmingham steelhouse. But he was fundamentally an expert on Birmingham 'toy' products, not a steelmaker, and he probably lacked some of the essential craft knowledge. Furthermore, his efforts to make steel in France were adversely affected by his failure to use Swedish wrought iron as raw material, and by his attempts to substitute wood for coal as fuel. In the 1770s the engineer De Saudray proposed to make crucible steel in France, and to import Newcastle coal for the purpose. But this project was entangled with his importation of machines and English workers for Birmingham 'toy' production, and it is unclear whether he had the right knowledge or the right workers; nor is there any sign that he knew of the essential need for Swedish wrought iron as a material.

The importance of steelmaking of English quality was recognized over a long period. A remarkable policy document from the Bureau of Commerce in 1788[19] equates the acquisition of steelmaking methods of English standard with that of mechanical spinning as the first technological priorities for France. The list of scientists and technologists involved as experimenters, official observers, investigative commissioners for the Academy of Sciences, or even patrons, is very remarkable—Réaumur, Hellot, Jars and his colleague Duhamel, Macquer, Montigny, Buffon, Grignon, De Dietrich, Abeille, Vandermonde, Berthollet, Monge, Mercklein, Rambourg, Hassenfratz, Vauquelin. All the more significant, then, that steel constitutes a classic case of long technological lag between Britain and its French imitators, despite all the talent and money thrown at the problem.

The French attempts to copy the remarkable new coal-based technologies in ironmaking introduced by British inventors and entrepreneurs were examined some years ago by the late W. H. Chaloner,[20] and more recently by Woronoff[21] in his monumental study of the ferrous metal industry of France in the Revolutionary and Napoleonic period. A few topics within this large subject may still profit from closer examination, but the general position is clear and Woronoff's view incontrovertible: Britain was 'la nation pilote, la référence par excellence'.[22] A quick summary will therefore be sufficient.

The new developments in ironmaking at Coalbrookdale in Shropshire, where iron was first smelted with coked coal in 1709, were certainly notified to Hellot, a major scientist working for the French government, by 1738, as was the role of the Coalbrookdale Company in casting iron cylinders for steam engines.[23] However, given the limited success of the coke-iron process before the 1750s, it is not surprising that Jars's famous visit of investigation and espionage of the mid-1760s was the first to be specifically directed to acquiring the process. In the few years between his return to France and his untimely death he made experiments in coke production, searched for suitable coking coal, and was involved in the first French attempt at operating a coke-fired furnace. His identification of the coal of Montcenis as suitable for coking was critical in the later siting of the great Le Creusot works.[24]

After Jars's death in 1769 the next man to try to obtain British expertise on the process was the artillery officer de la Houlière, who was particularly interested in the advantages of coke-iron naval cannon. His visit to England in 1775 has many interesting facets; for present purposes we will merely record that it led to a famous meeting with the celebrated Wilkinson brothers and the recruitment of William Wilkinson to French government service. He was originally commissioned to install his brother's technique of boring iron naval cannon from the solid at the large government foundry at Indret. Subsequently, however, William Wilkinson, together with Wendel, a famous French artillery officer and ironmaster, undertook the great project at Le Creusot which involved several blast furnaces, five steam engines to operate blowing equipment, reverberatory furnaces for remelting pig, and other important features.[25] Calonne, the Controller-General, expected this to have a notable demonstration effect for French industry, exemplifying the remarkable results to be obtained by turning to English coal-fuel technologies, including steam power.[26]

Such hopes were disappointed. Wilkinson, whose co-operation with the French had been affected by his imperiousness and by mutual suspicions, pocketed his large consultancy fees and went home at the point when the critical development stage was taking place at Le Creusot. The Crown had to subsidize pig output and its quality was very poor, while the subsequent collapse of the Ancien Régime and the disruptions of the Revolution were not good for constructive managerial and technological reform.

France was so ill-endowed with copper and tin ores that the application of the British coal-smelting processes developed at the end of the seventeenth century presented little worthwhile economic opportunity. But military-technological demand was imperative, so that when Britain developed the copper sheathing of ships, and then successfully attacked the technical problems which had put the first generation of coppered ships at risk, France felt it had to follow. The ability to stay for long periods in tropical waters uninjured by the ship worm, the improved speed and manœuverability, the reduced time in dockyards (and thus the greater war-readiness of each ship) were advantages for naval vessels which could not be ignored by the Marine. Once the American War of Independence was over, high-powered French military-technical observers, including Wendel, were quickly despatched to St Helens and Holywell to inspect the works of Thomas Williams, the dynamic entrepreneur who had backed the successful technology, while Williams's sales teams demonstrated their cold-rolled bolts and sheathing to suitably impressed experts at French dockyards, who proceeded to order them. Meanwhile, at Romilly, the French set up a great works for producing naval copper, with a large number of English workers (a 'colony', as Arthur Young described it), some of whom remained even after 1793.[27]

The great importance of the Birmingham 'toy' trade in giving the world its first great impetus towards the large-scale production of light engineering has been surprisingly little emphasized, and tends to be buried under the massive and controversial literature on the American development of interchangeable part production in the next century. But the acquisition of the techniques of 'la quincaillerie anglaise', and production 'à l'instar de Birmingham' were great preoccupations of the French commercial administration in the

middle of the eighteenth century.[28] Their interest was much helped
by the almost fortuitous flight to France of the major Birmingham
industrialist, Michael Alcock, in the mid-1750s. His business career
was a very tangled affair, as were the commercial fortunes of the
great privileged works which he began at La Charité-sur-Loire. The
complex detail has been wrestled with in another paper, but there is
no doubt that he successfully introduced the equipment, largely in
light machine tools, which performed the rolling, plating, piercing,
stamping, and pressing, and the mechanical grinding and polishing
involved in the production of buttons, buckles, and a range of other
small metal goods.

The glass industry has already been pointed out as one where
there had been in earlier centuries a notable flow of manufacturing
methods from France to England,[29] and in the important instance
of plate glass there was another significant transfer in the
eighteenth century, that of the casting process. But another element
in glass technology was the use of coal in furnaces. Though this had
begun in England early in the seventeenth century and was
compulsory by 1615, the use of coal did not reach France until the
beginning of the eighteenth century. Even then it was long confined
to bottle manufacture, where colour and quality of glass were not
as critical as in other branches.[30] Nevertheless, it was widely taken
up there when coal was available, (often imported British coal).
Coal was introduced into one stage of blown plate-glass production
by an outstanding contemporary manager, Oury, in the 1740s.[31]
The anxious care which he gave to the operation, and the
difficulties he met with from the scarce and strongly independent
workers capable of using coal, show the problems of domesticating
coal-using processes in a technologically alien environment. Even
more striking is the long struggle of his successor Deslandes, an
even more celebrated and successful manager of the Compagnie des
Glaces, in endeavouring to change the cast-plate production to coal
use, a struggle which went on with varied, but never complete,
success for nearly twenty years, and was finally abandoned. It
gained ennoblement for Deslandes, and inspired a remarkable
paper which he wrote for the Academy of Science on coal use in
glass furnaces, but its success was restricted by Deslandes' failure to
use the covered crucibles of English glassmakers.

Crucibles were an essential element, as was the use of coal as fuel,
in the production of flint glass, the heavy glass with a high lead

content, capable of producing beautifully clear table glasses, decanters, and chandelier lustres, in which its suitability for cutting was important. Remarkable efforts were made, particularly in the 1780s, to obtain this English manufacture for France. At an early stage the manufacture was under the aegis of the house of Orléans, and sited at St Cloud. Despite successful industrial espionage, the suborning of workmen, and the smuggling out of tools, the early progress of the concern was wildly expensive and technically disastrous, sometimes hilariously so. However, the interest of Marie Antoinette in this fine glass led to the involvement of the Crown and the movement of the whole enterprise to form part of the concentration of English-type technology at Le Creusot. The buildings were so lavish that they eventually formed the mansion of the famous Schneider ironmaster family in the nineteenth century. Despite this impressive initial backing, the firm's product was not particularly good.

Perhaps the most celebrated single British gift to world technology in the eighteenth century was the steam engine, and the French, with their lively eye for anything which introduced a new principle, or embodied a scientific element, took a strong interest from an early stage. When the leading member of the company promoting the Newcomen engine introduced it in Paris in the mid-1720s, it was the object of rivalry from spurious French claimants, and anxieties that its excessive efficiency as a pump might dangerously lower the level of the Seine! But it also received a very careful and perceptive examination and report from leading scientists, Réaumur and Donzembray.[32] Possibly too expensive in fuel for work in Paris, the Newcomen engine is next heard of at Fresnes near Anzin; it continued to be important in that coalfield, though until late in the century the engines there all had imported English cylinders.[33] The engine was employed at other coalfields, too, but the poorer French endowment in coal meant that it did not achieve the enormous numbers which were installed at British mines; nor had France the demand for engines at non-ferrous metal-mines which Cornwall provided.

The steam engine was described and depicted in a number of important French works of a scientific or technological nature, possibly more frequently and more thoroughly than in the country of its birth and main development.[34] Immediate interest was shown by the Bureau of Commerce and the Academy of Science when intelligence of the Watt engine was brought to France in the 1770s. Boulton and Watt became involved with Perier, the engineer to the ambitious Paris waterworks scheme, and Watt engines were shipped to France under licence in remarkable circumstances during the American War of Independence.[35] Perier subsequently erected an engine works and built Watt engines (despite Boulton's and Watt's French privilege), and indeed was involved in the industrial espionage which brought the developed design of the double-acting Watt engine to France. Boulton and Watt were brought on an industrial consultancy trip to France by the French government, but they did not, as they were invited to, replace the Machine of Marly by steam power, or invest in the hardware works at La Charité, though they gave an opinion on it.[36] We must not make too much of the failure of Boulton and Watt to export to France. In fact all foreign sales of Watt engines during the patent period were very modest, perhaps fewer than those of the early Newcomen engine in a comparable period.

The relation of French engineers and inventors to the steam engine is a little paradoxical. Cugnot pioneered locomotion, D'Auxiron and D'Abbans made interesting experiments in inland steam navigation, and Perier was fertile in ideas such as the inversion of the engine for supplying drive to ships' paddle wheels or the use of a tubular boiler. But these ideas usually failed to result in immediately practicable application. In some cases the lack of a coal-fuel matrix may have meant that the demand situation in which French inventors and innovators lived did not give sufficient economic encouragement for the best development of their creative ideas. But the lack of the proper technological back-up for the engineering work involved—a back-up which had largely been created in Britain as a concomitant to a coal-fuel technology—was more immediate and more decisive.

Perier, an engineer highly regarded by Watt, and the most successful of the Frenchmen who tried to expand the use of steam power, contrasted his situation when he began operations in France, with that of Watt, 'when he brought to bear his trained intelligence and genius' on the steam engine. Watt had better facilities to do 'what his imagination suggested to him'. He

had the most skilful foundrymen; all the workshops and even the machines indispensable for the making of difficult parts were available to him; I on the other hand in France was deprived of all means of construction, I could find no foundry to cast the cylinders; the construction of reverberatory furnaces which permitted the casting of large parts, the art of casting in sand were unknown; there was no machine to polish the cylinders, no [cylinder] lathe, in short I was obliged to create everything. It is well known that it is only since I set up my workshops that they have begun to make large machines with any precision in France.[37]

Perier clearly did not do full justice to the engineering problems which Watt had to overcome to produce his engine on a commercial basis, but he was right in thinking that their solution would have been virtually impossible in France.

As would be expected, France had taken a great interest in technological progress in British textiles. So much historical attention has been given to this that the emphasis so far in this paper on other industries should be regarded as a necessary corrective, not an attempt to diminish its importance. This interest did not begin only with the celebrated mechanical inventions in the cotton industry from the 1760s. There had been an attempt to introduce English woollen techniques in the Law scheme of 1718–20, though it had not gone very far. While at the beginning of the seventeenth century the finishing section of English textiles lagged behind the best European practice, and we experienced difficulties in trying to sell our cloths abroad in a finished state, by the early decades of the eighteenth century the situation was reversed, and French producers envied the superior English finishes. It was in these areas that John Holker, the Lancashire Jacobite officer, formerly a textile finisher in Manchester, had particular success when he entered the Rouen cotton industry to make cotton velvets about 1750.

Suborning a considerable number of English workers, Holker introduced hot pressing techniques and cylindrical calenders with cast iron cylinders and emphasied the use of hot liquors in dyeing. Getting in touch with influential industrial inspectors and officials of the Bureau of Commerce, he proposed methods of bringing English workers and processes to France, and in 1755 was made Inspector General of Foreign Manufactures, which meant that he continued to suborn workers and obtain new English processes, generally by industrial espionage. He had the enthusiastic administrative and financial support of the Bureau, successively headed by Trudaine and his son Trudaine de Montigny. However, it was with the finishing process that Holker made such a strong initial impression. The importance of finishing techniques in fact extended beyond woollens and cottons and influenced silk, where French superiority would be expected. For the important item of 'watered' silk Holker brought over the English calenderer John Badger, who successfully established the process at Lyons. Holker himself established the manufacture in France of glazed cardboard, a key element in the pressing which gave the glossy English finishes, while his introduction of the lead-chamber process of sulphuric acid production, immediately useful in the bleaching process, was an essential base for the further expansion of the heavy chemical industry.

It is easy to attribute too much to Holker, though it is astonishing that a man who had spent only a few years in one branch of English textile production should have had the general knowledge of the English industrial scene that his papers exhibit. His official position nevertheless meant that he was naturally approached by the other English artisans who had arrived in France, apart from those he brought over himself. Rouen's importance as a textile centre, particularly for cottons, meant that his main centre of operations was a common point of entry for them, while the Bureau of Commerce referred many newly arrived technicians to him, and asked him to advise them or exercise some supervision over them, even those in distant parts of France. One of these, who had first arrived in France about the same time as Holker, was John Kay, who had become disillusioned with the problems of introducing his fly-shuttle invention in England. He was a difficult man to deal with, but the French officials encouraged his initial invention and subsequent ones, such as new methods of producing hand cards for carding. The use of the fly-shuttle died away after an encouraging start, but began to pick up again late in the century.[38]

The main textile innovations of the late eighteenth century moved from England to France in a continuous one-way flow. It was Holker's son who visited the English textile areas in 1771 and brought back Hargreaves's spinning jenny. The speed of its spread fluctuated, workers sometimes fiercely resisted it, and (perhaps because it was not efficiently used) it was accused of lowering yarn quality, but there was much government pressure to spread its use, particularly when the Eden Treaty exposed the French cotton industry to English competition. The expansion of the cotton industry increased the demand for carding, and again it was English workers who strove to introduce carding engines: Hall, Clarke (Lecler), Milne, Garnett, Wright, and Jones.[39]

The Milne and Hull families, both connected with Holker, were instrumental in bringing into France the first machine which involved cotton production in a powered factory, the water-frame (continu); a son-in-law of one of the Milnes, Foxlow, set up the first steam-powered factory at Orléans. Under Calonne the Milnes contracted with the government to run a textile machinery-building business to provide machines for entrepreneurs who wanted to obtain them, while remaining free to enter into cotton-spinning concerns themselves. The even more important mule (or mule-jenny, as the French called it) of Crompton was brought across the Channel by an existing firm, Morgan and Delahaye of Amiens, who had been in the cotton business since the 1760s and employed English workers. They sent two of them, Spencer and Massey, to Lancashire and they successfully returned with a mule and set up a works to make the machines. As with the water-frame, keenness to acquire the machines meant several more or less simultaneous acts of acquisition; Clarke (Lecler), already established in cotton manufacture in France, brought over a 160-spindle mule together with a mechanic, Pickford. The latter contracted with the government to make textile machines and had a long career helping the transfer of technology to France, in part by assisting in industrial espionage.

It is only intended here to emphasize that there was a successful transfer of technology in textile machines and that it was overwhelmingly in one direction, without detailing the spread of the processes in France. We have already noted that in some aspects of industrial chemicals and dyeing, the chlorine-bleaching of Berthollet, the artificial soda of Le Blanc, the art of 'Turkey-red' dyeing, successful French advances were transferred to Britain at the end of the eighteenth and in the first years of the nineteenth centuries. The strength of the opposite movement, however, is made more obvious if we look at calico-printing, where despite the wide distribution of the industry in Switzerland and France, as well as in Britain, many of the main technical innovations were on the British side, the use of lead acetate for fixing some dyes, the successful use of indigo as a dye, printing with large copper plates (embodied in a purpose-built machine by 1760), and finally Bell's famous roller-printing of 1785, just reaching France in the last years of the century.[40]

An indicator of the strength with which one country desires the techniques developed by another is the lengths to which it will go to get them. It was the extent of the schemes of John Law to acquire English skills and workers for France that led, in the Act of 1719, to legislation against industrial espionage by the suborning of workmen; and the French effort to obtain our industrial secrets was an important influence on later eighteenth-century British legislation directed to the same end. Other European countries took part in industrial espionage in Britain and in the suborning of British workers. Austria, Russia, and Prussia were all involved. Sweden was assiduously (and remarkably continuously) active from the late seventeenth century and through the eighteenth, although its area of interest was largely confined to metal production and working, reflecting the bias of its own industry and exports and also the increasingly successful English rivalry with them. By no means all the Swedish intelligence-gathering was covert or amounted to industrial espionage, but some of it did. The range of French investigation of British industry was much wider than the Swedish, though it fluctuated in thoroughness and regularity. A high proportion consisted of deliberate espionage and illegal suborning of workers, but not all possessors of important new technologies were (as we have seen in the instances of the Wilkinsons, Thomas Williams, and sometimes even Boulton and Watt) reluctant to show their new advances to French visitors. A sense of unassailable technical superiority, or a hope of selling or even manufacturing in France, were sometimes motives for openness. Frequently, of course, counter-measures failed: English skilled workers were highly bribable, adventurous, and footloose, and persistent pressure by French spies or their English agents got men, models, machines, drawings, and tools to France. But optimism about the ease of obtaining British technology, of which Dupont de Nemours affords an example, was not wholly justified. Men were needed with the right blend of techniques and managerial ability, who themselves had, or possessed in association with other emigrants, the full range of specialist skills required by a particular industry; men who were not big-headed or dissolute or without self-discipline, men with the adaptability to overcome the cultural shock of a society with a different language, religion, diet, and general lifestyle, as well as a *dirigiste* attitude to industry unknown in their home country. A lack of such qualities in technological immigrants could mean that techniques were not transferred at all, or at a lower standard than in Britain.

Britain's legislation against the export of artisans and machines clearly placed only a limited restraint on French assiduity in obtaining its technology, an assiduity which indicates, perhaps better than anything else, French perceptions of where the technological balance lay between the two countries. But French industrial spies did feel they were running real risks in Britain, though they exaggerated them to increase their credit with the authorities on their return: some French spies and their English agents were caught and were faced with large bails, fines, and imprisonment.[41] Le Turc would certainly have faced these hazards had he been caught in his successful smuggling of machines and operatives to France for the latest advances in knitting technology, and even more for taking mechanized block and pulley manufacture for the French navy.[42] The security at British workshops and factories imposed by the owners, and sometimes directed as much against domestic as against foreign spies, was not always ineffective, and was sometimes ingenious; the sulphuric-acid producer in the home counties who recruited Welsh operatives who spoke only their native tongue was a good example.[43]

The effects on the development of technology are, of course, only one of many influences on the economy which may be credited to, or blamed upon, the French Revolution and the consequent period of warfare down to 1815. In trying to separate them out there is the danger of taking them too abruptly from their context; the intention here is simply to indicate how far the Anglo-French technological balance had shifted between the end of the Ancien Régime and the end of the First Empire.

The situation of cotton is an interesting one. As we have seen, a stream of British textile technologists had, with the backing of the state and of some energetic entrepreneurs, tried to implant in France the new English technology which had appeared between the inventions of the jenny and the mule, and the first powered factories were being set up based on the water-frame. Once the attack of English competition during the brief operation of the Eden treaty had been averted, the progress of the industry, clearly indicated by raw cotton imports, was resumed, and that import was already noticeably greater in the Year IX than it had been in the years 1787–9. The increase was based on the mechanization of

cotton spinning—'l'essor spectaculaire de la filature mécanique'[44]—
and on the establishment of factories aided by increased enforce-
ment of regulations against imports from Britain, not only for
France but for the countries it controlled or dominated. Spindlage
in the Lille, Roubaix, and Turcoing districts, for instance, rose from
32,000 in 1806 to 114,000 in 1808 and 177,000 in 1810. By the
end of the Empire France possessed a million spindles, a massive
and remarkable development even if it was only about a fifth of the
British equivalent. How had the technology apparently spread so
well, caught on so readily? There can be no doubt that a critical
influence, at a period when it was virtually impossible to convey
technology without the personal intermediacy of the skilled worker,
was the surprisingly large number of British textile technologists to
be found in France throughout the war period. While some
returned home after the excesses of the Revolution and the advent
of war, enough remained to advise on, and share in, the critical
developments of textile machine-making and millwrighting. Despite
British legislation against the emigration of artisans, there was a
substantial topping up of numbers in 1802–3, and the swift
declaration of war by Britain in the latter year had the odd effect of
trapping considerable numbers of them in France as 'otages' until
1814. Again, while French recruitment of English workers was very
difficult during actual warfare, it could sometimes be achieved
indirectly through France's Empire or the countries it dominated.

A recent estimate of the 'hostage' numbers between 1803 and
1814 would suggest that upwards of seventy-five British commercial
men were among them, and at least 316 manufacturers and
artisans. Their special influence in textiles can be seen from the 177
British workers in that industry who have been found by a yet
incomplete survey of many archival sources relating to prisoners of
war and civilian detainees. Dating their first arrival is not easy, but
at least twenty-four textile workers came into France during the
short peace. About sixty of the British textile workers present in
France after 1803 are given as 'mécanicien', a testimony to their
importance in building and maintaining the new textile machinery.[45]

In fact, attempts to open the French and some other continental
markets to the competition of British cotton after 1814 were very
short-lived, as British productive efficiency, and the price levels it
could achieve, proved crushing. But this was not the sole problem:
'du point de vue technique un retard de presque vingt ans

persista'.[46] Why should this have been? In a British industry whose pace of technical development (the effect of major new inventions aside) was extremely rapid, the gaps between 1793 and 1802 and 1803 and 1814 were very important. The interval of 1802–3 was so short that the French would have required a combination of near-perfect knowledge of the gaps that needed to be filled, and a near-perfect flow of operatives, machine builders, millwrights, and managers from Britain to fill them. This might have fully brought up the French to the British practice of about 1800; it could not have affected the gap re-opening between 1803 and 1814.

As Saul and Millward put it, 'technological copying was still possible in wartime, although it was difficult, costly and sometimes dangerous, but it was not possible to the degree necessary to maintain [a] narrow gap between the economies, for the narrowness of that gap depended on frequent visits by French manufacturers to those works in Britain where techniques were more advanced'. While there was a considerable exodus of French manufacturers to cast an eye over the British scene in 1802–3, that which followed 1814 was larger and more continuous.[47] Again, in an industry so rapidly expanding as the cotton industry in Britain, the opportunities open to men of talent and innovative mind were great, and most would stay at home to exploit them. It was often some personal limitation in the ability to exploit the situation which drove British technologists to France. Such limitations, ranging from a fondness for the bottle to an exaggerated idea of their own innovative capacity, could create problems for their French employers.

The immense efforts made by the leaders of the Revolution (and those scientists who were among its most ardent supporters) to overcome the dangerous shortage of steel which faced the army and the marine at the outbreak of the Revolutionary war are well known. I have, however, recently tried to show that there is a clear continuity with the less celebrated, but equally serious efforts made in the last years of the Ancien Régime, and that the same technologists were commonly involved. The overblown claims of Revolutionary administrators and savants had little reality as far as the long-term position of the industry was concerned. A good instance is Fourcroy's boast of the Year III that 'steelmaking is become a native manufacture, and this great resource, created by the spirit of the Revolution, and naturalised among our manufactures, will remain as an advantage when the waves of revolution have subsided',[48] which was grotesquely wrong. The early wartime efforts at steelmaking perhaps solved an immediate military supply crisis at great expense and low productive efficiency, but as soon as the success of French arms re-opened the home market to German and other continental steelmakers, the newly created French industry ironically crumbled, and was abandoned to its fate with remarkable cynicism by successive governments. Even the most promising ventures were allowed to collapse, perhaps because it was fairly clear that they had not been able to master the necessary processes completely enough in the brief period of war shortage. Le Normant at Rouen, for instance, had some English workers, but he lacked fireclay of the right quality for crucibles for cast-steel production as well as the workers to make them to an acceptable standard. The 'Avis aux ouvriers en fer' composed by Berthollet, Monge, and Vandermonde and circulated by the Committee of Public Safety, only illustrated, to those who tried to produce steel with its help, the frailty of written instructions as a guide to processes based on manual skills. At the end of the war Arnaud and Saint-Bris condemned the existing quality of French steel in the roundest terms. 'Je ne puis vous dissimuler, . . . [que] la fabrication des aciers fins est très peu avancée en France', wrote the latter to the Consultative Committee on Arts and Manufactures.[49]

One of the most telling indications of French failure to make any impression on the huge technological gap between British and French steelmaking practice is the setting up of a special *Commission pour le Perfectionnement des Aciers* in 1814 under the presidency of a notable scientist, Vauquelin. The British example was clearly overwhelmingly in the minds of its staff, but the rapid political changes of the next year seem to have assisted in its swift demise. Though salvation came in that very year with the arrival of the Birmingham steelmaking family, the Jacksons, and their workers, that salvation was not instant. The Jacksons struggled and demanded increasing government help through the rest of the decade and much of the next, and it was only in the 1830s that technological and commercial success was assured, so that in the steel industry there was a lag of a most remarkable length.

Despite the apparent establishment of coke-iron production at Le Creusot in the mid-1780s, though with Government subsidy, the subsequent story was depressing; already by 1790 it was realized that the iron was not good enough for its intended purpose, the casting of cannon; the works equipment was used for making bronze and charcoal-iron cannon, and the coke-iron which was made was hard to dispose of, even for less demanding purposes. Reviewing the doleful achievement an official in the Year III reflected, 'Can it be possible that these high hopes of prosperity and success were only an illusion?' Le Creusot, rather than continuing to be a mecca of technological pilgrimage, became in fact a 'contre-exemple'.[50] Some experimentation did nevertheless take place in the iron industry, but the only significant improvement was the use of coal in the chafery stage of the old charcoal-iron refining process where the new fuel was readily available. Trials of the reverberatory furnace in the refining of pig made little progress, and neither the stamping and potting process, nor Cort's puddling and rolling process, were established before the Restoration. An interesting example is that of the Wendel family, at the head of British-type innovation in 1789, who, after political disruption and exile, had to restore their ruined businesses during the Consulate and Empire on the basis of the old charcoal-iron methods. Like other progressive ironmasters, they later had to come across the Channel to learn coal-based ironmaking from scratch, at the new level of efficiency the British had developed since 1789.

In steam power, too, there was an almost complete gap in technological take-up from Britain after 1789. Before then everything effective had come from Britain: the Newcomen engine, the basic Watt engine, rotative motion, the later improvements of Watt such as the double acting engine, parallel motion, the application of the governor. With Revolution and war, British input was cut off, the source of innovation was lost, and France was able to add nothing of her own. The single new gain was the Woolf version of the compound engine brought in from Britain during the Peace of Amiens. Otherwise, as Payen puts it, steam engines were made in France in 1815 only to the state of the art as it had been in England in 1789.[51]

Of course the interruption of the Revolution and war was not always so disastrous for transferred technology. In Birmingham hardware, the personal and commercial problems at La Charité may have had the perverse effect of increasing the diffusion of the new technology, as separate concerns were set up around Paris, Lyons, and Roanne by former partners Fresnais and Le Court, and by Alcock's sons. The availability of good coal was significant, but

not so much as for other English-type metal industries. The outcome
was that the new technologies were fairly well diffused in France by
Napoleonic times. If Alcock had not really fulfilled his boast that he
would make Saint-Étienne and La Charité into 'Birminghams in
France as good as that in England',[52] the technologies he brought
over had become well established and there seems to have been no
need for any further topping up from England. The quality of
French manufactures of this kind seems, however, to have been
lower—at least the producers often thought it worthwhile to mark
their goods as English. There were difficulties in the refurbishment
and re-equipment of some works for the production of naval
copper after the Restoration, but so far no evidence has been found
of any need to have a further infusion of British technology into
that branch of metallurgical industry.

Success in adopting British textile processes, if not to a degree
capable of withstanding British competition, was one important
element in introducing France to the methods of large-scale
industrialization. But without gaining the coal-fuel technologies
capable of providing a large iron industry and the heavy engineering
based upon it, without any significant steel industry, without any
large and flexible power source from the steam engine—itself
essential to any significant native coal industry—France could not
have continued to be a major power. Already by 1790 it had been
recognized that France needed to create an 'industrial revolution'[53]
(this first known use of the term has recently been discovered by
François Crouzet) if its influence was not to be overshadowed. To
some historians the excellent recent demonstration of the necessary
economic and technological basis of great-power status seems to
have been revelatory. Did the French willingly accept the superiority
in the great power league conferred on Britain by its economic and
technological superiority? Did they consciously wish, or even
prefer, a slower path to industrialization, or was there some
element of sour grapes in their adverse comments on the social and
environmental price that their neighbour was having to pay for
more rapid industrialization?

There is no doubt of French industrial indebtedness in the
decades that followed 1815. As Pollard has written:

There is no single important industry in any of the major continental
regions that did not have British pioneers as entrepreneurs, mechanics,

machine builders, skilled foremen and workmen, or suppliers of capital (and usually several of these combined) to set them going. Thus in France, British technical aid in modernising the cotton industry ran from 1738 until well into the nineteenth century, and its details would fill a small volume; woollen, flax and jute machinery similarly waited for British initiative, though there were some significant French inventions in these fields. The indebtedness of the main French coalfields, iron works and engineering establishments is even greater, and in engineering in particular, the British furnished not only the trigger, but stayed there to build up the majority of French works in existence in the first phase of industrialisation, which in turn became the instruments for transforming the rest of economy.[55]

The technological lag between England and France had if anything increased by 1814 as compared with the mid-1780s, and there was less optimism about the ease of catching up. As late as the mid-1820s an outstanding American engineer who visited first France and then Britain found that the practice of British civil engineering had more to tell him than the theory readily purveyed in France. Turning to mechanical engineering, he wrote: 'In practical mechanics the French must be at least one hundred years behind the English. It is indeed astonishing that in a country so contiguous to one where all the mechanical arts are brought to the highest perfection their contrivances in everything should still be so rude. Here I can travel in no direction but I come across some fine specimens of [engineering] art.'[56]

NOTES

[1] A useful summary of the debate can be found in R. Aldrich, 'Late-Comer or Early Starter? New views on French Economic History', *Journal of European Economic History*, 16, 1 (1987), 89–100. This follows the debate to 1982, but it continues. Particularly notable recent contributions are R. Cameron, 'A New View of European Industrialisation', *Economic History Review*, 28 (1985), 1–23, and particularly F. Crouzet's revisions of, and discussion of comments upon, his celebrated paper of the 1960s: 'Angleterre et France au XVIIIᶜ siècle: analyse comparée de deux croissances économiques', *Annales E.S.C.* 11, 2 (1966), 254–91. His re-survey is included in his collected papers, *De la Supériorité de l'Angleterre sur la France* (Paris, 1985), pp. 50–89.

[2] This paper reflects some general views, and some case studies, on transfer of technology published over many years: *Industry and Technology in the Eighteenth Century: Britain and France* (Birmingham, 1972); 'Saint-Gobain and Ravenhead' in B. Ratcliffe, ed., *Britain and her World* (Manchester, 1975), pp. 27–70; 'Skills, Coal and British Industry in the Eighteenth Century', *History*, 61, 202 (1976), 167–82 (subsequently referred to as 'Skills, Coal'); 'Attempts to Transfer English Steel Techniques to France in the Eighteenth Century' in S. Marriner, ed., *Business and*

Businessmen (Liverpool, 1978), pp. 199–233 (subsequently 'Steel Transfer'); 'Industrial Espionage in the Eighteenth Century', *Industrial Archaeology Review*, 7 (1985), 127–38 (subsequently 'Industrial Espionage'); 'Michael Alcock and the Transfer of Birmingham Technology to France before the Revolution', *Journal of European Economic History*, 16, 1 (1986), 7–57 (subsequently 'Birmingham Technology Transfer'); 'The Technological Factor in the Transfer of Technology between Great Britain and France in the Eighteenth Century', *Proceedings of the Fourteenth Consortium on Revolutionary France (1984)* (Athens, Georgia, 1986), pp. 59–68; 'The Diffusion of English Metallurgical Methods to France', *French History*, 2, 1 (1988), 22–44 (subsequently 'Diffusion'). Two particularly important contributions on this subject are those of Peter Mathias, 'Skills and the Diffusion of Innovations from Britain in the Eighteenth Century', *Transactions of the Royal Historical Society*, 5th Series, 25 (1975), 93–113, and David Jeremy, 'Damming the Flood: British Government Efforts to Check the Outflow of Technicians and Machinery, 1780–1843', *Business History Review*, 51 (1977), 1–34, though much of the evidence is for a later period.

[3] M. J. T. Lewis, *Early Modern Railways* (London, 1970), pp. 15–18.

[4] 'The International Exchange of Men and Machines', *Business History*, 1 (1958), 3–15; a later version forms ch. vi of A. E. Musson and Eric Robinson, *Science and Technology in the Industrial Revolution* (Manchester, 1969).

[5] Musson and Robinson, op. cit., chs. viii and ix; John J. Beer, 'Eighteenth Century Theories on the Process of Dyeing', *Isis*, 51, 163 (1960), 21–30.

[6] J. G. Smith, *The Origins and Development of the Heavy Chemical Industry in France* (Oxford, 1979), pp. 307–12.

[7] 'Saint-Gobain and Ravenhead', *passim*.

[8] The view of N. F. R. Crafts. See 'Industrial Revolution in England and France: Some Thoughts on the Question "Why was England First?" ', *Economic History Review*, 30, 3 (1977), 438–41.

[9] For an opposing view see W. W. Rostow, 'No Random Walk: A Comment on "Why was England First?" ', ibid. 31, 4 (1978), 610–12.

[10] J. U. Nef, *The Rise of the British Coal Industry* (London, 1932; repr. 1966). See especially vol. i, pt. ii, chs. 2, 3, and 4.

[11] For fuller statements of the argument of the following paragraphs see 'Skills, Coal', pp. 167–71; 'The Rise of Coal Technology', *Scientific American*, 231, 2 (Aug. 1974), 92–7.

[12] The best recent attempt to deal with these developments is M. Rowlands, *Masters and Men in the West Midland Metalware Trades Before the Industrial Revolution* (Manchester, 1975). See especially ch. 7.

[13] David Landes, *Revolution in Time* (Cambridge, Mass., 1983), pp. 230 ff.; T. C. Barker and F. A. Bailey, 'The Seventeenth Century Origins of Watch-Making in South-West Lancashire' in J. R. Harris, ed., *Liverpool and Merseyside* (London, 1969), pp. 1–15; see also Alan Smith's introduction to *A Catalogue of Tools for Clock and Watchmakers by John Wyke of Liverpool* (Charlottesville, 1987).

[14] 'Skills, Coal', pp. 167–71.

[15] Ibid.

[16] Archives Nationales (subsequently AN) F^{12} 63.

[17] This interesting episode is currently being written up. Sources include in particular *State Papers Foreign, France* (78) 167–9; *State Papers Domestic* (35) Geo I. 14, 17, 24, 25, 26, 61, 78; H. Sully, *Règle Artificielle du Temps* ed. Julien Le Roy (Paris, 1737).

[18] For the following paragraphs see 'Steel Transfer', pp. 199 ff.

[19] AN F^{12} 107/8.

[20] W. H. Chaloner, 'Les Frères John et William Wilkinson et leurs rapports avec la métallurgie française' in *Actes du colloque international: le fer à travers les âges* (Nancy, 1956), pp. 285–301. See also his translations of M. de la Houlière, *Report to the French Government on British Methods of Smelting Iron with Coke* (1775), repr. from *Edgar Allen News* (1948–9), pp. 1–50.

[21] D. Woronoff, *L'Industrie sidérurgique en France pendant la Révolution et l'Empire* (Paris, 1984).

[22] Ibid. 315.

[23] AN O¹ 1293.

[24] See Chaloner, op. cit.; 'Diffusion', p. 34.

[25] Ibid.

[26] P. F. de Dietrich, *Description des gîtes de minerai et des bouches à feu de la France* (Paris, 1786), i, avant-propos, p. xiv.

[27] J. R. Harris, 'Copper and Shipping in the Eighteenth Century', *Economic History Review*, 19, 3 (1966), 550–68; 'Diffusion', pp. 36–8. The quick French interest in the English trial of copper sheathing in 1763 can be seen in Archives Etrangères, Corr. Politique Angleterre, 458: Choiseul to Blosset, 30 Sept. 1764.

[28] For this paragraph see 'Birmingham Technology Transfer', pp. 7 ff.

[29] Eleanor S. Godfrey, *The Development of English Glassmaking, 1560–1640* (Oxford, 1975). See especially ch. II.

[30] Warren L. Scoville, *Capitalism and French Glassmaking 1640–1789* (Berkeley, 1950), pp. 11–14.

[31] For the transfer of plate-glass technologies and the employment of coal see 'Saint-Gobain and Ravenhead', *passim*.

[32] A. Smith, 'The Newcomen Engine at Passy, France, in 1725: a Transfer of Technology which did not take place', *Transactions of the Newcomen Society*, 50 (1978–9), 205–17.

[33] For the Fresnes engine see A. Stowers, 'The Development of the Atmospheric Steam Engine after Newcomen's Death in 1729', *Transactions of the Newcomen Society*, 35 (1962–3), 88.

[34] L. T. C. Rolt and J. Allen, *The Steam Engine of Thomas Newcomen* (Buxton, 1977), pp. 70 ff.

[35] W. H. Chaloner, 'Hazards of Trade with France in Time of War, 1776–1783', *Business History*, 4 (1964), 79–92.

[36] 'Birmingham Technology Transfer', pp. 48–9; 'Industrial Espionage', pp. 132 and 138.

[37] J. C. Perier, *Sur les machines à vapeur* (Paris, 1810), pp. 11–12.

[38] A. Rémond, *John Holker, manufacturier et grand fonctionnaire en France au XVIIIᵉ siècle* (Paris, 1946), pp. 48 ff.; 'Industrial Espionage', pp. 130–1, 134, 138; J. G. Smith, op. cit. 7 ff.

[39] For the introduction of English textile machinery into France see C. Ballot, *L'Introduction du machinisme dans l'industrie française* (Paris, 1923) (the second chapter, 'Le Coton' (pp. 41 ff.), is still valuable); X. Linant de Bellefonds, *Les Techniciens anglais dans l'industrie française au XVIIIᵉ siècle* (Paris, 1971; Sorbonne thesis) (the fifth chapter, L'Introduction des mécaniques anglaises', is also useful). Normandy and Rouen are emphasized in J. Vidalenc, 'Quelques remarques sur le rôle des Anglais dans la révolution industrielle en France, particulièrement en Normandie, de 1750 à 1850', *Annales de Normandie*, 8, 1 (1938), 273–90. Some additional details on the Milnes are given by Robert Glen, 'The Milnes of Stockport and the Export of English Technology during the Early Industrial Revolution', *Cheshire History*, 3 (1979), 15–21. See also AN F¹² 1338, 1340.

[40] S. D. Chapman and S. Chassagne, *European Textile Printers in the Eighteenth Century* (London, 1981), pp. 11 ff.

[41] For French industrial espionage in general, and legislation and counter-measures against it, see 'Industrial Espionage', pp. 128 ff.

[42] A great deal of material on Le Turc is now being examined, particularly AN F^{12} 677c.

[43] G. Jars, *Voyages métallurgiques* (Paris, 1791), iii. 309–11.

[44] F. Crouzet, *De la Supériorité de l'Angleterre sur la France* (Paris, 1985), p. 290. For the view that the technological gap may have been greater in 1815 than in 1789 see p. 328.

[45] See Margaret Audin, *British Hostages in Napoleonic France. The Evidence: With Particular Reference to Manufacturers and Artisans* (Birmingham, 1987; M.Soc.Sci. thesis).

[46] F. Crouzet, op. cit. 293; René Sédillot, *Le Coût de la Révolution française* (Paris, 1987), pp. 184–6.

[47] A. Milward and S. B. Saul, *The Economic Development of Continental Europe* (London, 1975), i. 271.

[48] 'Steel Transfer', p. 220.

[49] Ibid. 220 ff. for this and the following paragraph.

[50] Woronoff, op. cit. 315.

[51] Payen, op. cit. 176.

[52] AN F^{12} 1315 A.

[53] Affaires Etrangères, Mémoires et Documents, Angleterre, 136.

[54] Paul Kennedy, *The Rise and Fall of the Great Powers, Economic Change and Military Conflict from 1500 to 2000* (London, 1988).

[55] S. Pollard, *Peaceful Conquest* (Oxford, 1981), p. 145.

[56] D. H. Stapleton, *The Transfer of Early Industrial Technologies to America* (Philadelphia, 1987), p. 133.

Man's Second Disobedience:
a Vindication of Burke

ROGER SCRUTON

> They who had fed their childhood upon dreams,
> The play-fellows of fancy, who had made
> All powers of swiftness, subtilty, and strength
> Their ministers . . .
> Did . . . find helpers to their hearts' desire,
> And stuff at hand, plastic as they could wish,—
> Were called upon to exercise their skill,
> Not in Utopia,—subterranean fields,—
> Or some secreted island, Heaven knows where!
> But in the very world, which is the world
> Of all of us,—the place where, in the end,
> We find our happiness, or not at all!
> (Wordsworth, *The Prelude*, xi. 125–44)

OF all the great events in modern history, few have been so assiduously moralized as the French Revolution. It was a revolution conducted, so to speak, in the mirror of its own approval, obsessively recording its daily progress, and bequeathing to posterity not only its new concept of virtue and its new species of crime, but also a new language through which both crime and virtue could be meditated. Even now the Revolution is often considered in its own self-image: as a single vast occurrence, a transformation in the order of things, whose effects were felt throughout society, and whose causality lies deeper than the will of individual men. There are historians who protest against that monolithic conception—Richard Cobb, for example, who unceasingly reminds us of the waywardness, indifference, and mute *attentisme* of the provinces during the Revolutionary years.[1] Not the least among the Revolution's legacies, however, is the rooted belief—which no patient Cobbery has yet managed to eradicate— that 1789 marked the entry onto the stage of history of new forces, new political conceptions, and new forms of deed.

I am not a historian. Nevertheless, it seems to me that the French Revolution—however it was caused, however it ended, and whatever it produced—enshrines a process which does have precisely the unity which the Revolutionists proclaimed. I have in mind the events which we describe in retrospect as Jacobinism, and which marked the birth of the 'revolutionary consciousness'. Whatever the causes of the Jacobin power—catastrophe, conspiracy, or cock-up (to mention the three most plausible theories of history)—its meaning, for conservatives at least, is of a total and perhaps unprecedented change, not merely in the conduct of politics, but also in the aims and aspirations of mankind. Nor is this reaction peculiarly English. Even if nothing else in Taine deserves our credulity, he should be given credit at least for this: that he identified in the Revolution a force that was new to the world of politics, and which also demands our moral judgement.[2] In what follows, however, I shall draw little from Taine, and much more from two earlier conservatives: Burke, from whose astonishingly prescient essay[3] the theory of modern conservatism derives; and Tocqueville, recognized on all sides as the wisest, if not the truest, commentator on those great events.[4] I also owe a debt to François Furet, whose *Penser la Révolution Française* takes a step in the direction that I too shall travel.[5]

Reaction to the Revolution has had two connected aspects: an attitude to the events themselves, and a further attitude to their representation. It is part of the genius of Burke and Tocqueville to have recognized (as neither Michelet nor Taine nor even Carlyle seemed to recognize) the extent to which events in the Revolution became responsive to their own interpretation—the extent to which the *self-consciousness* of Revolution became the principal agent of social and political change. The meaning of revolutions is, I believe, to be found exactly here: in the consciousness which guides and inspires them and which, arising out of unbelief, fills the vacuum of man's longing with a belief in collective man. The Revolution involved a war against religion: an attempt to re-create the world as a world uncreated. The modern conservative cannot fail to see in it, therefore, a fatal anticipation of that other and more terrible Revolution which modelled itself, not on the events of 1789, but on a canonical representation of those events, and on a general theory of history in which revolution is described as the primary—indeed the only—form of real social change.

As with that later Revolution, the French Revolution has found constant sympathy in the hearts of liberal and progressive thinkers.

However wedded to the ancient politics of compromise, however appalled by what they deem to be 'temporary excesses' and fanatical *jusqu' auboutisme*, the believers in progress and enlightenment have on the whole seen the Revolution as a positive contribution to their cause. To the good Buckle it seemed as though only mental decay could explain Burke's revulsion towards the events of 1789.[6] While acknowledging the vileness of much that was done thereafter, Buckle, like Michelet, Tawney, and many a like-minded spirit, counted the ultimate cost as less than the vast initial benefit. In vain did Tocqueville argue that the progress, such as it was, had already occurred (a point made powerfully also by Burke); in vain did he point out that the anger unleashed against the aristocrats did not cause, but on the contrary, was caused by the steady erosion of their power;[7] in vain did he show that the ancient habits of oppression had all but vanished, and that the Revolution arose less from a struggle against absolute power than from the *absence* of power in that very central place which had been so foolishly prepared for it. All those wise observations, along with the profound psychological analysis of the new forces which had been swept into the central vacuum, made little impact on the progressive historians of the nineteenth century, just as similar truths about Tsarist Russia have been overlooked by the countless well-meaning commentators for whom the October Revolution was a step in the right direction, a leap forward into the modern world that had been for too long, and too cruelly, delayed.

It is fair to say, however, that the tide has now turned against progressivism. In a striking work, René Sédillot summarizes the results of recent scholarship, and argues that *le bilan final*—two million dead and the almost complete cancellation of every civil liberty being only parts of it—is offset by no discernible long-term advantage, either to France or to mankind.[8] How accurate Sédillot's assessment is I do not know; in what follows it is not so much the measurable destruction as the spiritual condition of revolution which will engage my attention. More important in assessing that condition is the theory of the Revolution which has done the most to inspire it: the theory of Marx, or at least of the Marxists. According to this theory, 1789 was a 'bourgeois' revolution, a transition from 'feudal' to 'capitalist' relations of production, which toppled the 'superstructure' of politics and law, and also the ideology which had inhabited it. Many versions have been assumed or justified—by Jaurès, Mathiez, Lefebvre, and their followers. Its traces survive even in the sophisticated *jeux d'esprit* of Michel Foucault, and in what Alfred Cobban calls the 'myth' of the French Revolution.[9] The relative paucity of Marx's own references to the events of 1789 suggests that he may have glimpsed the glaring truth about them—namely, that they provide a paradigm refutation, rather than a confirming instance, of his theory of historical change. The withering away of the feudal order had occurred long before the Revolution, and had involved the overthrow neither of the prevailing system of politics nor of the law which sustained it. By the time of the Revolution the remaining vestiges of feudalism were irksome ties and privileges which bore little relation to the real economic life of the nation and were an object of resentment for that very reason. Whatever the ultimate causes of the Revolution, it is absurd to suppose that intellectual changes were not first among them: changes in what Marxists call the 'ruling ideology'. I do not mean only the writings of the *philosophes*, or the literary activity that surrounded them and which the authorities tried feebly to suppress. (Feebly, by modern standards, at any rate, and feebly, too, by the standards of the Revolutionaries.) I mean also the incredible burgeoning of intellectual curiosity in eighteenth-century France: the local academies and literary societies;[10] the journals, libraries, and museums; the 'cabinets de lecture'; the movement for a secular education which had already led, in 1762, to the fatal (if to some extent understandable) suppression of the Jesuits; the pamphleteering, the atheistical diatribes; and the admiration for America and the American Revolution, fuelled by a Benjamin Franklin who was to become, in Daniel Mornet's words, 'l'homme le plus à la mode de Paris' during the years 1777–84.[11] And from the *political* changes initiated by this intellectual transformation there emerged a profound *economic* change: a change not towards capitalism but away from it, not in the direction of market relations and the wage contract but in the direction of price-control, rationing, and the re-infoedation of the worker. (The very same causality—from ideological frenzy to economic stasis—can be witnessed in all the revolutions inspired by Marx.) If the Marxist theory means anything, then this is exactly the sequence of events that must conclusively refute it, and no Ptolemaic system of epicycles, no 'relative autonomy', 'uneven development', or 'determination in the last instance' could possibly recommend the theory to anyone who looked impartially at the facts of eighteenth-century France.

Why, then, has the French Revolution been so often seized upon by Marxists as providing their paradigm of historical change? The question goes to the heart of my subject-matter. The French Revolution—or at least, that central episode upon which revolutionaries focus their attention—was the work of intellectuals, a manifestation of what Tocqueville called 'la politique littéraire'.[12] The Revolutionary consciousness lives by abstract ideas, and regards people as the material upon which to conduct its intellectual experiments. The charm of the Marxist theory is in describing revolutionary transformation as *inevitable*, and as originating wholly outside the realm of ideas: the experiment therefore is certain to succeed, and the human cost is down to history itself. Hence Marxism both sanctions the politics of ideas and at the same time excuses everything done in the name of it. It washes clean the guilty conscience in the same flood of ideas that first instilled its guilt. And, by excusing the Jacobins, Marxism covertly proposes them as an example. (Thus for Lenin, the revolutionary is 'the Jacobin indissolubly tied to the organization of the proletariat, which has become conscious of its interests as a class'.)[13]

Tocqueville justly remarks, and with some amazement, that 'parmi les passions qui sont nées de cette révolution, la première allumée et la dernière éteinte a été la passion irréligieuse'.[14] He goes so far as to suggest that the Revolution was animated by a 'génie antichrétien' although it was a 'génie' which expressed itself with a monkish zeal, being less the child of Voltaire's tolerant deism than the re-creation, in modern dress, of the attitudes pilloried in *Mahomet*. It is this anti-religious zealotry which provides the first important clue to the Revolutionary mentality.

The Revolutionists had been schooled in the sceptical attitudes of Burke's 'literary cabal'.[15] Many of them also saw in religion a bastion of ancient privileges and an unwelcome instrument of conciliation between the estates. However, the hatred unleashed against the Church at the very outset of the Revolution transcended anything that might be inferred from those two currents of opinion. Like the hatred towards the nobility, it was fed less on present injustices and corruption than on myths and stories: it was, in Burke's words, a 'work of art', like the 'anti-bourgeois' propaganda of subsequent revolutions. The hatred of the Church should be seen, I believe, as the hatred of a new priesthood for the old. The Church was less an obstacle to the work of Revolution than a rival in its quest for the possession of men's souls. It was Sieyès, himself an unbelieving clergyman, who first announced the Revolution's astonishing claims over the human subject: 'The nation is prior to everything. It is the source of everything. Its will is always legal. . . . The manner in which a nation exercises its will does not matter; the point is that it does exercise it; any procedure is adequate, and its will is always the supreme law.'[16]

As Alfred Cobban rightly says, such ideas do not belong to the Enlightenment (which had, at least in its intellectual aspect, stood for limited government and individual right), but to a new order of political thinking.[17] Claims previously made only in God's name (and certainly never in the name of a king) have been transferred to, and imposed upon, the human world.

The first act of the Revolutionary Assembly was therefore to expropriate from the Church its lands, liens, and revenues. This property had not always been wisely used. Nevertheless there can be no question that it was a greater public benefit in the Church's hands than in the hands of the Assembly, which used it merely as security for its own escalating debt, and ruined in a few years the savings of centuries. Furthermore, the church property contained much that had been given in perpetuity. The Assembly saw no obstacle in this fact, counting the will of the dead as nothing beside the pressure of its own self-made emergency.

The transfer of church property was no more than a first step: but it is a sure indication that the spirit of Jacobinism was triumphant long before the Jacobins took power. The Republic was now firmly set on the path which led towards its new religion. The ecclesiastical orders were to be dissolved and the loyalty of Catholic priests demanded: the 'non-juring' priest was to go in fear of his life, precisely because he recognized that the oath demanded of him was incompatible with his greater oath to God. Before the practice of the Christian religion had been entirely forbidden in the name of Reason, the Revolution began to introduce its own religious ceremonies—the Federations, described in ridiculous and glowing terms by Michelet as occasions where 'man fraternized in the presence of God'.[18] And as the new Republic began to make itself, in this way, into the principal object of piety and the master of religious ceremonies, it conceived the ambition to transfer to itself all the functions of the Church. These functions—marriage, baptism, moral instruction, the provision of societies and ceremonies—were removed from the priesthood, not so as to return them to society, where they had arisen and where the Church itself had captured them, but so as to bestow them on the state, as episodes in its own mystical legitimacy. It is to the French Revolution that we owe the new kind of 'civil marriage',[19] the civil holidays, the civil ceremonies, and, in due course, the partial expropriation from the family of its children. The motive was twofold: sacrilege, and reconsecration. The Revolution sought first to rid the bonds between people of their ancient sanctity, and therefore installed in the place of the Canon Law of marriage its 'Laws of Marriage and Divorce', calculated to undo as many marriages as were solemnized. (The Soviet code on 'family and marriage', introduced on 18 September 1918, had precisely the same intention.) At the same time the Revolution sought to involve the state, as a mystical presence, in all the deepest human ties and aspirations, and so to attach their fund of pious feeling to itself.[20] Robespierre's Festival of the Supreme Being—in which, when all was revealed, the Supreme Being was seen to be mystically identical with the Revolution itself—was no eccentricity of an isolated fanatic. It was the culmination of a movement which expressed itself throughout the war against the Church. The advance of the Revolution saw not the abolition of the feudal order (which had long since disappeared), but a re-infoedation of the people, with the State as universal lord. Christianity had to be replaced with a creed more suited to this new obedience, a creed which did not insist so embarrassingly on the fact that the individual is answerable for his soul to God alone, and is the property of no earthly master—not even of the state.

What was this new creed which jostled aside the ancient claims of Christianity? Here we find one of the most interesting features of the revolutionary mentality—a feature to be observed as clearly in modern Leninism, in Maoism, and in the campus credos of the 60s. The system of belief, while it has the same ability to absorb refutations and demonize opponents as traditional religion, is almost entirely devoid of content. Its goals and ideals are specified in terms so vague and sloganizing as to possess no real authority beyond that which must inevitably accrue to them in the course of battle. All that is certain—though this alone is sufficient—is that the world is full of obstacles to their realization, and that these obstacles must be destroyed by every means to hand. Of course, there was a philosophy—or, if you like, a theology—which the likes of Robespierre would summon to their aid when posing as men of principle. (In using the word 'posing' I do not mean to imply that they were not themselves taken in by their posture: on the contrary, the revolutionary mentality involves a constant process of 'self-captivation'.) The important fact, however, is the total lack of curiosity shown by the Jacobins as to what the People or the Nation might actually consist in, or as to how Liberty, Equality, and Fraternity might actually be achieved. This absence of curiosity, which was in no way shared by the American Founding Fathers, is a permanent characteristic of the revolutionary consciousness. It can be seen in Marx, in his impoverished and impatient descriptions of the 'full communism' towards which history is tending. And it is even more evident in the writings of Lenin, in which the blocks of wooden language are constantly shifted so as to conceal the goal of communism from view.

In his attacks[21] on the 'prissy' Robespierre, the humourless Saint-Just, and the cranky puritanism of the Terrorists, Richard Cobb therefore seems to me to miss precisely what is most interesting about these people, and most decisive in determining the character of their government: namely, that they in fact have *no* principles, *no* absolute restraints, and recognize no moral obstacles. Their doctrine proposes the goal of popular sovereignty. But it is a goal so vaguely described, so inherently made in the image of its own perpetual postponement, as to argue that doctrine had, for them, some other purpose than to guide, limit, and cast judgement on their actions. Its purpose was not to forbid but to permit, not to judge but to exonerate, not to limit conduct but to enlarge it to the full extent of their moral exorbitance. Like the doctrine of 'full communism', it had no other meaning than to license destruction of existing things: it was not so much a system of belief as a system of unbelief, a means to the delegitimization of rival powers, and to the undoing of true commitments.

The decisive feature of the revolutionary credo, therefore, is its provision of a criterion of legitimacy that no actual institution can ever pass. Rousseau recognized that he had provided such a criterion in *Le Contrat Social* and at one point begged his reader's patience, saying that the apparent contradiction in his argument was no more than apparent.[22] He never troubled, however, to correct the appearance—nor could he have done so, for here, uniquely in Rousseau, appearance is reality, and the flow of slick deception is interrupted by the truth. All revolutionary ideologies are alike in this respect: 'direct democracy', 'social contract', 'the classless society', 'full communism'—all are names for the illegitimacy of actual things, rather than descriptions of a real alternative. The same is true, I would suggest, of the 'Rights of Man', at least as understood by the French Revolutionaries. Having made its Declaration, the Assembly at once went on to reject a proposal that the Duties of Man and of the Citizen should also be included. The Assembly did not wish to hear of duty and obedience; it sought for an instrument of rebellion, a doctrine that would undermine authority, not one that would restrain and discipline its own powers. Those who sever the demand for rights in so brusque a fashion from the burden of duties have, it seems to me, no desire to establish the institutions that will translate this metaphysical abstraction into a real social truth. The patient work of politics has already been set aside, and the word 'right' occurs on their lips not as a clearly defined goal but as a slogan, whose purpose is to carry forward the work of war.

The same is also true of the words 'the People', which Hannah Arendt has described as 'the key words for every understanding of the French Revolution'.[23] For Arendt the term is saturated by the downward-directed compassion of the semi-privileged towards 'le peuple toujours malheureux', as Robespierre described (and made) them. In fact, however, that connotation was no more than the necessary sentimentality of power. 'The People', like 'The Rights of Man', functioned as an instrument of de-legitimization. It is easy to show of any institution that it is *not* identical with 'the people': impossible to demonstrate that it *is*. One after another the old instruments of law and compromise must fall before the hatchet of this potent word. It was to obtain no use more precise than in the phrase 'the enemy of the people', which licensed the elimination of anyone who stood in the Revolution's way.

Of course, there is a positive *image* attached to such words as 'people' (and the more recent 'proletariat'), and this image is immensely important to the self-consciousness of revolution. The revolutionary lays claim to a *constituency*: but this constituency is removed from the real world by his very assumption of the right to speak for it. Thus any member of the working class who speaks out against the revolutionary communist becomes a class 'traitor'. As Lukács put it, one must never mistake 'the actual, psychological state of consciousness of proletarians for the class consciousness of the proletariat'.[24] Only the Party (the priesthood of revolutionaries) can tell you what the proletariat is thinking. Similarly only the Jacobins had access to the mind of the 'people', whose protesting members thereby merely 'betrayed' their collectivized identity, and ceased effectively to exist. The critics of the Jacobins therefore conveyed themselves to the guillotine as surely as the kulaks offered themselves to the firing squad. Something similar can be witnessed, too, in modern feminism, which pretends to speak for all women, and which turns in fury on the actual woman who, by failing to be a feminist, 'betrays' her sex. In all such cases the alleged constituency has been removed entirely from the real world: it has become something discarnate, a spirit-force whose reality exists only in the moment of its conjuration. In Furet's words, 'le "peuple" n'est pas une donnée, ou un concept, qui renvoie à la société empirique. C'est la légitimité de la Révolution, et comme sa définition même: tout pouvoir, toute politique tourne désormais autour de ce principe constituant et pourtant impossible à incarner'.[25]

Nothing positive, then, is offered in these sloganizing words by way of a belief or commitment. Indeed, the Revolution ensures that there *can* be no independent truth of the matter, as to what the rights of man or the will of the people consist in. All procedures which might be used to determine these things are no sooner instituted than destroyed. Decree follows decree in such profusion as to cancel the certainty of law; the constitution is so vague and abstract, and so detached from any procedure for its invocation, as to serve as the flag on the masthead of the ship of state, rather than the hand at the wheel. Soon the citizen comes to recognize that he has no means of knowing, in advance of the drift of power, what the crucial terms refer to. They gain application only after the event, and if he then discovers that the enemy of the people was not Jacques, Marie, or Hubert but himself, this too has no justification, and is further proof of the innocence, the other-worldly blameless-ness, of power. The terms of the doctrine become warnings, which fill up the place of moral duty with the more pliable material of fear. The parallel with modern revolutionary ideology is remarkable. The function of ideology in the Marxist state is not that people should believe it.[26] On the contrary, the function is to make belief irrelevant, to rid the world of rational discussion in all areas where the Party has staked a claim, and where it is rash for the ordinary citizen to venture. These are the areas in which opposition takes root, and by issuing its ideology, the Party provides a guide to conduct—but a guide so vague that only by doing nothing can you improve your chances of survival.

The effect of revolutionary ideology is to introduce a kind of incurable nihilism into the social order, to infect all public processes with the sense that they are without justification, and to be understood merely as the passing drift of power. It therefore acts so as to negate the process of politics—the process which has the conciliation of rival interests as its meaning and its goal. By proclaiming a purely abstract 'Liberty', the Revolution facilitated the destruction of the qualified and partial liberties which come through the work of compromise. By offering abstract Right, it legitimized the destruction of law, and so made the concrete rights of citizenship impossible to claim. By proclaiming the sovereignty of the abstract People, it was able to remove power, privilege, and property from every association of actual human beings.

With the ideological destruction of politics comes also a new form of language, in which power is decked out in glowing euphemisms, while its enemies are demonized in readiness for their 'liquidation'. Here too there is an interesting parallel between the French and the Russian Revolutions. Within a very short time the Assembly is talking to itself in a kind of Newspeak: those opposed to its measures are conspirators and heretics, or else the personal apex of obscure impersonal forces which surround the innocent fount of power: the clergy, the emigration, the counter-revolution. In place of individuals and their decisions we find a strenuous contest of energies: 'progress' against 'reaction', 'liberty' against 'despotism', the Revolution against the Old Regime; to which we can now add socialism against capitalism, bourgeoisie against proletariat, fraternal relations against imperialism. This 'pan-dynamisme', as Françoise Thom has called it,[27] is a quasi-syntactical feature of revolutionary language, by which it drives the idea of personality from the description of power. In the debates of the Jacobin club the members of the Gironde appear not as persons, but as manifestations of a force—'le girondisme'—just as the opponents of our modern revolutionaries are but the visible sign of 'opportunism', 'deviationism', 'bourgeois revisionism', 'infantile leftism', and the rest. (Interestingly, Lenin explicitly compares 'opportunism' to the 'girondisme' which had so exasperated his Jacobin predecessors.)[28] The individual critic becomes 'an enemy of the people', whose rights are automatically cancelled by the 'people' from which they were originally derived—in just the same way as the privileges of the 'anti-socialist' are inevitably cancelled by his opposition to the 'socialism' which is the source of all available goods.

This is not the place to attempt a survey of the *langue de bois* of the French Revolution. A few examples may, however, help to show the workings of a mental process remarkably similar to that so chillingly satirized by Orwell, and so familiar to anyone who enters either a communist country or a British sociology department. In Aulard's collection of documents from the Jacobin Club[29] we find opponents described as 'scélérats ligués avec l'étranger'; as 'un ramas de factieux et d'intrigants'; as 'un peuple de fripons d'étrangers, de contre-révolutionnaires hypocrites qui se placent entre le peuple français et ses représentants'; or simply as 'ceux qui se groupent pour arrêter la marche de la révolution'. By contrast the 'comité de surveillance' is a 'sentinelle de la liberté'; interrogation a 'scrutin épuratoire'; and of course soldiers have long since ceased to be soldiers and attained the dignity of 'défenseurs de la Patrie'. The language recognizes only 'patriotes' and 'suspects'; and proceeds with the same dichotomizing logic that has been persuasively analysed by Petr Fidelius, in his study of the editorials of *Rudé Právo*.[30] While the Jacobin club was perfecting the new mode of discourse, the public was being conscripted into the use of it. People were no longer to address each other as Monsieur or Madame, but only as *citoyen* or *citoyenne*: a word which was, in time, to acquire the same inverted comma use that now attaches to 'comrade' in every communist country. (See Flaubert's *L'Éducation sentimentale*.) The ancient names of streets and communes were discarded, as were the names of the calendar. It is as though the revolutionists sought to destroy not opposition only, but the language through which opposition could be focussed.[31] Here is an example of the process, contained in a submission of 12 November 1793 to the National Convention from a zealous representative in Cahors:

J'ai trouvé ce département fanatisé, royalisé, girondisé, l'esprit public tué, un petit noyau de patriotes molestés, n'osant qu'à peine s'avouer montagnards; j'ai tout défanatisé, tout républicanisé, tout montagnardisé, tout ranimé, tout régénéré. Sociétés populaires épurées, administrations, tribunaux, municipalités purifiées, comités de surveillance créés; aristo-crates, royalistes, fanatiques, girondins reclus; muscadins mis en réquisi-tion, monopoleurs, egoïstes, richards, indifférents, sangsues du peuple pressurés . . .[32]

As with its Marxist successor, such Newspeak also permits a novel kind of duplicity, in which words are used to mean both of two opposing things, and so emptied of all sense besides that conferred on them by power. Robespierre and Marat's discovery of the 'despotism of liberty' is but the extreme example of a process of semantic dissolution, prefigured in Rousseau's notorious 'forced to be free', which can be seen in all the revolutionary terms: liberty, equality, fraternity, people, republic—all are robbed of their sense, melted down, and reforged in a single weapon.

The destruction of language is part of a larger and more interesting destruction, of discourse as such. By 'discourse' I mean all those spontaneous exchanges through which people meet each other on terms, and reconcile their varied interests. The world of the revolutionary is one in which the other is either wholly *with* you, or wholly *against* you. Since he is Other, and therefore not transparently known, you can never assume the total identity of interests which would place him securely on your side. It follows that opposition cannot be *met*: it is not the object of negotiation, and can be the beneficiary of no agreement. Opposition is to be destroyed, '*épuré*', 'liquidated'. As Saint-Just said in 1794, 'a Republic is constituted by the total destruction of that which is opposed to it'.[33] But this 'total destruction' (like all the 'total' ambitions of revolution) cannot be guaranteed. The result is, therefore, a universal suspicion of others and of the world. The revolutionary enters a world which has already secretly betrayed him, and from the very beginning he must expend his energies in rooting out the source of this betrayal—the 'enemy forces' which, in his pan-dynamic vision, are everywhere pulsing behind the illusory social calm. It is no accident that the Revolutionary Assembly established its 'Committee of Inquiry' into conspiracies (which was eventually to become the Committee of General Security) within months of obtaining power. The reign of suspicion was already installed, just as soon as the Tiers Etat—spurred on by the *trente voix*, but by no means controlled by them—forsook the path of compromise. The idea of betrayal was thereafter uppermost in its thoughts, growing until it had absorbed the whole of the Revolutionists' attentions. By 25 January 1792 Robespierre was speaking in the following terms: '[I]ls vous trahiront avec art, avec modération, avec patriotisme; ils vous trahiront lentement, constitutionnellement, commes ils ont fait jusqu'ici; ils vaincront même, s'il le faut, pour vous trahir avec plus de succès.'[34] 'Ils vous trahiront constutionnellement': there speaks the authentic voice of revolution. For the revolutionary, all forms of constitutional government, all forms of parliament in which the outcome cannot be determined in advance by himself, are really forms of betrayal, for the very reason that they grant a voice and an influence to opposition.

We should not be surprised, therefore, at the extraordinary structure of central and peripheral committees which evolved during the course of the Revolution. Cochin has shown how a network of extra-governmental institutions was established in Brittany in the years prior to 1789, and how a kind of 'dictatorship from above' was already exercised over 'Patriots' long before the formation of the National Assembly.[35] Cochin pictures the *comités de correspondance particulière* as establishing a power 'machine' which was already geared for the subversion of the political process, and we should not ignore the resemblance of this 'machine' to the 'parallel structures' of modern revolutionary societies. The resemblance becomes yet more striking after the Revolution. More and more power is taken from the constitutional bodies and vested in committees, whose answerability to the Convention becomes increasingly a matter of form. The 'Central Committee of General Defence' was already in existence by 1792 (before the Terror), and the Committee of Public Safety emerged as the central, *secret* offshoot of this body. This latter committee was empowered to appoint its own *commissaires*, so enforcing its will throughout the country and instituting a system of control remarkably similar to Lenin's democratic centralism, with the clubs making decisions which were then imposed upon the municipalities. By this time power was exercised wholly *outside* the Constitution, as it is in the Leninist state. The process culminated in the famous law of 14 Frimaire an II (4 December 1793), officially a measure for the reform of local government, but in fact ensuring the abolition of local government and the destruction of all institutions through which some degree of representation might be granted or achieved. All authorities and officials were placed by this law under the immediate control of the Committee of Public Safety (except for the police, which remained with the Committee of General Security). Henceforth government would be conducted in secret, and imposed by a network of 'transmission belts' (to use Lenin's idiom) on local activists obedient to the central command.

Those facts are well enough known. What is not always admitted, however, is that, far from being aberrations, they are the correct expression of the revolutionary mentality. Suspicion, betrayal, a sense of universal enmity; measures which 'have not yet gone far enough'; contempt for compromise, and a demonization of opponents—all these are implicit in the revolutionary ideology, and require just the kind of government by conspiracy that has everywhere been the consequence of revolution. The power which acts 'in the name of the people' moves in a mysterious way. Those who exercise it do so in secret, without impeachment or compromise, and with nothing but a doctrine to establish their claim. Someone, they suspect, somewhere, disagrees with them and is therefore betraying them—for disagreement has treachery as its only outlet. The revolutionaries resort to ever more drastic measures in order to destroy this 'traitor'. Nevertheless, despite their efforts, despite their virtue, the enemy (who is, in truth, a projection of their own incurable fear of him) returns constantly to haunt them. At last they confront him: their very measures give reality to the monster of their dreams. But, by a wondrous alchemy, he comes before them in the guise of their own ideal. It is the people who must bear the revolutionary's insolence, and it is the people who finally rise against him in despair. (Hence Robespierre's need to distinguish the 'true' (imagined) from the 'false' (real) people; and hence Lukács's distinction between the mere proletarians themselves and the 'class consciousness' which is their 'truth', and to which only the party priesthood has access.) The only question, therefore, is whether the revolutionary can organize his network quickly enough, and efficiently enough, to prevent the people from combining against him. La Vendée was a near thing: later revolutionaries, while approving the method of genocide initiated by their French predecessors, have taken more precautions.[36] Not wishing to resort to terror in a moment of crisis, they have resorted to terror at the outset, and made it the normal condition of their liberated state.

When we come to consider the Terror, therefore, we should bear in mind that this event has recurred in later and more perfect instances. As with later terrors, that of the Jacobins has its ranks of 'progressive' apologists, arguing with Mathiez that the violence came from below, out of the just grievances of the *sansculottes*,[37] or with Greer that it was a reaction to people who genuinely wished to destroy the Revolution and must therefore expect what they got.[38] Others have referred (in terms later used to excuse the Soviet terror, and still used to excuse the poor Sandinistas in Nicaragua) to the 'emergency' caused by enemy 'encirclement'. None of these excuses should mislead us: the real question is, who created the Revolution's enemies, and how? If I pillage your house, murder your wife, rape your daughter, and torture your son, then of course I have to resort to 'emergency measures' if I am still to enjoy your co-operation in these domestic reforms.

Burke wrote his great essay in 1790: everything that I have described he had already noticed. As yet the King had not been executed, the Jacobins had not staged their *coup d'état*, the public rejoicings were still believable. But the spirit of the Terror existed already; it remained only to transcribe it in legal form. Consider the Law of 4 December 1792—a law which was frequently to be cited in the Revolutionary Tribunals. 'Whoever proposes to establish', it decrees, 'any power detrimental to the sovereignty of the people shall be punished by death.' Not 'tries', but 'proposes'; not 'illegal', 'unconstitutional', or 'seditious', but 'detrimental to the sovereignty of the people'; not 'fine' or 'imprisonment', but 'death'. And the whole thing is worded in such a way that no *mens rea* is required. It is no excuse that I did not *intend* my proposal to be 'detrimental to the sovereignty of the people'. Indeed, I could hardly know how to intend or to avoid such a thing, since only my accusers have the authority to define it. And on their definition hangs my life. There is embodied in the very form of such a law the abrogation of natural justice which was to conclude in the Terror. Moreover, the Law is the perfect expression of the Revolutionary doctrine, as I have described it. It permits everything to power, and allows nothing to its victim. Those interested should compare its wording with the sections of communist codes dealing with subversion, sedition, and 'damaging the interests of the state at home and abroad'. They will see that we are not dealing here with some judicial accident, but with the Revolutionary mentality itself.

Of course, one must not overlook the relative mildness of the French Terror. Even at its height it never managed more than three or four thousand executions a month, and the total—including the *noyades* and similar atrocities—scarcely amounts to a day's work for a modern revolutionary. All the same, it is a sobering thought that the French prisons contained 400,000 people between 1793 and 1794: in appalling conditions which ensured the death of vast numbers of them. (The Bastille had disgorged precisely seven inmates when it was stormed four years before.) It is also a sobering fact that most of those held or executed were either political offenders, captured by the same vague language as that used in the Law of 4 December 1792, or else ordinary people accused of the equally arbitrary 'economic' crimes. Nor were the victims united by any 'class interest' or 'émigré attachment': 84 per cent of those executed belonged to the Third Estate, and by far the largest group among the sufferers was that of the working class.[39]

Rather than dwell on the actual cost of the Terror, however, it is more instructive to examine the new form of 'justice' which it inaugurated. We have already seen one instance of it. But it it is by no means the most astonishing. Like other revolutions, that of France had recourse to retroactive legislation—even when the decree involved a penalty of death.[40] For it regarded law neither as a means for the resolution of social conflict, nor as an instrument of justice, but solely as a way of legitimizing its own insolent dealings. Like the doctrine of 'the People', the 'law' of the French Republic was a self-conferred title of approval, which the patriots pinned to their breasts with all the illusory dignity of a Brezhnev awarding one more medal to himself. Absurd crimes were invented, and given their Newspeak titles: *incivisme*, 'fraternizing with the emigration', 'making proposals detrimental to the sovereignty of the people', etc. A new class of offenders was discovered: the émigrés, strictly comparable in their liturgical function and ultimate fate to the kulaks of Stalin. The laws dealing with these monsters filled two huge volumes, and were so worded as to place on the accused the obligation to prove that he was *not* an émigré, and also so tortuously elaborated as to make this burden impossible to discharge.[41] Trials were frequently conducted by military commissions, and without right of appeal; eventually, after the Law of 22 Prairial (10 June 1794), there ceased to be any real distinction between crime and the suspicion of it, and the gap between accusation and guilt was finally closed.

The destruction of law in the name of legality is also, I suggest, a natural consequence of the revolutionary mentality. Lacking the spirit of compromise, the revolutionary also lacks the sense of law which springs from it. Law, for him, is a command, an edict, a pursuit of 'war by other means', to parody Clausewitz. It is not what it is for the man with *Rechtsgefühl*: a *procedure*, whose truth and justice lie hidden elusively within it, beyond the reach of any peremptory command.[42] Certain features of legal procedure are necessary for justice: the judge must be independent, the accused must have a right to defend himself, the law must be certain, knowable, and not retroactive; and the record must be kept. No such matters have the slightest significance for the revolutionary, and all were abolished by the Revolutionary Tribunals. Indeed the modern revolutionary goes one stage further, dismissing the law and the judiciary altogether, as parts of the 'ideological state apparatus' whose function is to maintain the dominion of the ruling class.[43] Foucault (who, for all his protests, remained a naïve revolutionary to the end) repeats the worn-out Marxian cliché in stunning form: 'the revolution can only take place via the radical elimination of the judicial apparatus, and anything which could introduce the penal apparatus, anything which could reintroduce its ideology and enable this ideology to surrepitiously creep back into popular practices, must be banished'.[44] (And how typical of the revolutionary, to see the heart of the law, not in its procedure, but in its *ideology*!) The French Revolution, Foucault adds, was a 'rebellion against the judiciary', and such, he implies, is the character of honest revolution everywhere.

Tocqueville remarked that there is the greatest difference between a 'revolution' (such as that of 1688, or that which founded the United States of America) through which law and adjudication continue undisturbed and which has the maintenance of law as one of its objects, and a revolution (such as the French) in which legal continuity is cast aside as an obstacle and an irrelevance.[45] As the example of Foucault shows, the distinction will never be significant to the revolutionary. Armed with his Rousseauist doctrines of popular sovereignty, or his Marxist ideas of power and ideology, the revolutionary can delegitimize any existing institution, and find quite imperceivable the distinction between a law aimed at justice, and a law aimed at power. His own power is sustained by the promise to abolish it; he is therefore impatient with all institutions which use existing powers, in order not to abolish but to limit them. That is the thought process which leads to the revolutionary courts. Lenin announced, as one of the ultimate benefits of communism, the 'withering away of law' which was to follow when class conflict had ceased. As a step in this direction he established a new form of procedure, based on the court-martial, but with the added refinement that the rules were not fully knowable in advance of the verdict. The judge can give the verdict only when he is sure that the Party will accept it. In the Soviet court the prosecutor, himself a servant of the Party, can effectively dictate the outcome of a trial (and will do so if the Party has an interest). The model for this Potemkin justice was provided by the Revolutionary Tribunal. And it is now the dominant system of legal procedure in all political trials, not only in the Soviet Empire, China, Vietnam, Laos and Cambodia, Cuba and Nicaragua, but also in Syria, Iran and Iraq, and much of modern Africa.

The decisive features of the Revolutionary Tribunal were these: first, the vagueness of the crimes that it was appointed to try. This pattern has been followed in modern revolutionary systems, where all crimes against the state are couched in terms so wide as to permit the entrapment of anyone required, and where there is no authoritative record that enables the citizen to improve his understanding. Under revolutionary justice you are tried, in the end, not for what you do but for what you are: émigré or kulak, Jew or anti-socialist, enemy of the people or running dog of capitalism—in each case crime is not an action, but a state of being.

Secondly, the procurator had effective charge of the proceedings and was under no discipline (in relation to evidence, precedent, or procedure) that would compel him to deviate from his pre-determined course. Thirdly, the accused was (after the Law of 22 Prairial) denied the right to counsel, and could therefore put up no defence. Finally, judges and juries were both chosen for their political reliability—a reliability which could in any case be assumed, once the penalties of rebellion were known.

The Paris Tribunal was a crude first attempt, and the Potemkin façade is now far better constructed. Those accused by the revolutionary state today have the right to employ a counsel, provided that he acts as a loyal servant of the Party and does not obstruct the smooth working of the trial. In recent political trials in Czechoslovakia certain lawyers made the mistake of actually *defending* their clients: Josef Daniš in the VONS trial, and Jan Čarnogurský in a related trial of Charter signatories. Both found themselves in the dock beside their clients, and condemned to the same penalty as they. The permission to employ a defence counsel is, in other words, a Potemkin permission, just as the procedure imposed on the prosecutor is a Potemkin procedure, which can be set aside whenever the Party requires. Of course, terror has dwindled to the state of 'graveyard stillness' which is the Potemkin equivalent of peace. Nevertheless, the structure of revolutionary justice remains, causing a universal caution, a habit of avoidance, whose main effect is to make the law irrelevant to daily life: a puppet show whose squeaks and growls have long since lost their audience. If Poles, for example, are the least litigious of people, it is not because they have no quarrels with their neighbours: on the contrary. It is rather that you have to be a fool or a party member to take your quarrel to law. The effect of revolutionary justice is therefore to marginalize the law, to rid civil life of the law's moderating influence, and to force all conflicts underground, where they usefully contribute to the fragmentation of the society upon which the totalitarian order depends.

The marginalizing of law is one aspect of the new style of revolutionary politics. There is an immense difference between parliamentary government on the old model, in which the nobility always occupied the important offices, and the modern forms of constitutional democracy, in which government, like every other profession, has become a *carrière ouverte aux talents*. But there is a far greater difference between both those political systems and the government installed by revolution. Revolutionary government does not exist to balance interests and reconcile powers; its office is not that of counsel, nor does it construe its authority in judicial terms—as a final court of appeal in civil conflict. It exists for a purpose, and its legitimacy depends upon hurrying ever onwards towards a vague but imperative goal. Politics ceases to be a part of life, and becomes the whole of it. The philosophy which promises the end of politics, makes politics into the sole human end. Government can be limited neither in its sphere of application nor in its powers, while legitimacy is henceforth self-bestowed by doctrine, rather than acquired by habitual usage. Revolutionary government inevitably moves in a totalitarian direction, absorbing subsidiary social powers, and conscripting the population to its ill-considered purposes. Moreover, because the goal is always receding, the regime must manufacture a conspiracy of enemies, at home and abroad, who are acting so as to thwart its designs. To maintain the state of emergency, a spectacle must be provided: show-trials, executions, dawn arrests and denunciations; propaganda, ceremonies, military parades; and of course the threat, constantly made and often executed, of internal and external war.

A philosophical observation will perhaps clarify those remarks. The task of the French Revolution was to remake the social order, in conformity with a 'social contract', to forge a society which was explicitly consented to by all its citizens. All individuals would henceforth be dissolved in a 'general will' whose movements would express their unqualified and unmediated participation: thus would 'the People' be born. In order to produce this 'society consented to', the Revolution set about destroying the very process of consent. Traditional society, while not the *object* of consent, is nevertheless the *product* of consent, arising 'by an invisible hand' from the countless negotiations, agreements, votes, and compromises that compose the unforced life of association. Philosophers of the 'social contract' attempt to translate this consensual order into an order consented to: to make the results of our contracts into the first object of them. But this is precisely to suppose that we could understand the outcome of social interaction before we had engaged in it: that we could agree *now* on a social order that arises from choices that we cannot *now* envisage.

Because of its goal-directed nature, revolutionary politics declares itself to be uniquely rational, even the rule of Reason itself. But collective rationality arises as a solution to what the game-theorists calls a 'co-ordination problem'. It comes about not because people have a common goal and work out a policy for achieving it, but because they are able to *adjust* their goals, and so create the flexible system of negotiation without which no man is able to respond reasonably or kindly to his fellows. The point has been expressed in many ways—in the Austrian theory of the market, in Burke's defence of prejudice and tradition, in Oakeshott's attack on 'Rationalism in politics'. Only its deep emotional need to ignore all criticism has enabled the revolutionary mentality to remain unaffected by this, the core argument of modern conservatism.

The new goal-directed politics licensed three moves in a totalitarian direction—moves which constituted a triumph for abstract Reason over concrete reasonableness. First came the attempt to absorb civil society into the state. I have already touched on this in the matter of the civil ceremonies. Equally important was the attempt to regulate relations between people, by replacing the consensual process of manners with a species of 'social decree', imposing forms of address and customs on the people in the interests of ideological conformity. In proceeding against the Church, the Assembly also made it quite clear that it recognized the rights of *no* autonomous institutions, and subsequently (18 August 1792) decreed accordingly: 'a state that is truly free ought not to suffer within its bosom any corporation, not even such as, being dedicated to public instruction, have merited well of the *Patrie*.' (Note the Newspeak.) The Republic thereafter permitted partnerships—associations for gain—but dreaded those unselfish people who sought to unite for some religious, charitable, literary, or scientific purpose. In fairness to the Revolutionists, it should be said that private charities had suffered considerably in the last days of the Ancien Régime.[46] But they had suffered from that very same disrespect for free association and corporate personality which reached its culmination in the decree of 18 August 1792.

Revolutionary governments have since gone through the same cycle of 'moral expropriations' as the French Revolutionists, nationalizing all institutions, from universities and churches down to chess clubs, orchestras, and *besedy*. (The special case of Poland is the exception which proves the rule.) Everywhere you observe the collapse of institutional life—especially in the countryside of central Europe, once so rich in autonomous associations and local loyalties. Not only have charities been expropriated and their funds diverted in defiance of trust; charities themselves have been outlawed. The process began after the Russian Revolution, with the confiscation of all church property, the imprisonment, torture, or murder of the more active members of the clergy, and the forbidding of any kind of social work on the part of those in Holy Orders.[47] When the first of the great famines arrived in 1921, the Church established a relief committee; but it was at once decreed illegal and dissolved. A civilian committee to provide homes for the millions of orphans created by famine and civil war was also dissolved, and replaced by another organization, under direct command of the Cheka, which had its own uses for homeless children. It is true that the Bolsheviks did, at one point, permit a group of private citizens to form an 'All Russian Famine Relief Committee'. But the function of this committee was to attract funds from the West (and from the United States in particular). Once the donations had arrived, the Committee was arrested, its organization dissolved, and its funds appropriated for the use of the Party.

Since that time there have been, so far as I know, few legal charities in communist countries, other than those organized (under great difficulties and constant risk of expropriation) by the Catholic Church in Poland, and by the Protestant Churches in East Germany. Of course there are illegal charities—mutual support groups, 'flying universities', and so on. Certain good citizens of Hungary, for example, have recently combined to relieve the sufferings of the poor (of whom there are increasingly many, in a country whose Potemkin economy has yet to be understood by Western observers); but they have been compelled to meet, raise funds, and distribute relief in secret, and in constant fear of reprisals. Moreover, the holdings of such charities, lacking the protection of the law, are at the mercy of those who control them. The whole concept of 'beneficial ownership' has been expelled from public life.

That the French Revolution did not proceed so far is less important than the fact that it moved in this direction at all—that it began to use the machinery of the state in order to destroy the institution-building impulse which is the foundation of society. Perhaps it did not need Hegel to demonstrate to us that State and Civil Society are distinct 'moments' in the life of a body politic; perhaps it did not need Solidarity to remind us of the catastrophe that ensues, when the distinction between them (between *władza* and *społeczeństwo*) is abolished. But defenders of the French Revolution often fail to see that the suspicion of civil society lies in the very spirit of revolution and in the 'politics of goals' which it imposes.

The second totalitarian consequence of the new politics was the tendency towards ownership of the individual by the state. As Tocqueville astutely points out[48] this tendency is present in those statist conceptions of reform that preceded the Revolution and did so much to make it possible. But it took on a new character and a new impetus with the events of 1789. Besides all that we have already touched on, concerning the administration of justice; besides the system of internal passports, price controls, compulsory loans, and laws against association; besides the interdiction exerted over the publication, expression, and even possession of opinions 'detrimental' to the 'People'; besides the attempt to extinguish the national religion of France, and to expropriate its moral functions— besides all this, there arose two new and momentous changes in the relation between the individual and the state: the system of compulsory education, and the *levée en masse*. The first of these was brought to fruition only by Napoleon; the second of them made Napoleon possible.

It proved impossible, in the event, to carry through the educational programmes: private schools were permitted to re-open, when it was discovered that no other means existed to ensure the goal of universal instruction. Neutrally described, such a goal can hardly be disapproved of. And from Lenin to the Sandinistas it has been a vital part of revolutionary propaganda to devote itself to campaigns of education (which increasingly turn, however, into campaigns of 're-education' of the kind which can last for a lifetime). Nevertheless, the value that we attach to education should not blind us to the startling fact that the educational level of the French declined during the Revolutionary period.[49] Nor should it cause us to excuse the extraordinary presumption of a sovereign power that obliges us to educate our children, and obliges them to attend schools of its own devising. The new role of the state in our lives is given a further, and chilling twist by Saint-Just, in educational proposals which he did not live to carry through:

The child, the citizen, belong to the *Patrie*.

Communal instruction is necessary.

Children belong to their mother until the age of five, if she clothes and feeds them. After that, to the Republic, until they die.[50]

What Saint-Just here makes explicit in his words is elsewhere implicit in the acts and projects of the Revolutionists. The revolutionary's advocacy of education conceals another and vaster design: to lay hold of the infant soul, and mould it according to his own requirements.

Universal military conscription is at one level merely an extrapolation to the maximum of a practice already familiar in post-Renaissance monarchies. However, the *levée en masse* expresses a wholly new attitude to the condition of citizenship. The entire nation was now to be flung at its 'enemies' (whose enmity was caused, not by the French nation, but, at least in part, by the belligerent policies of its leaders). Any able-bodied man could be called up, at any time and for any cause. It was not only to war that the French population was conscripted: the Revolutionary Armies were given extensive policing functions and maintained as a permanently mobilized vehicle for the execution of Revolutionary commands. The Revolutionary Armies, the *commissaires* and *sociétés populaires* together provided a foretaste of the system which was to reach perfection in the *komsomol*. For the first time in history we encounter a society *conscripted for peace*, in which the conditions of peace and war have become effectively indistinguishable. The whole of France lived under a kind of martial law, in which the citizens subjected also served in the army which subjected them. It is true, as the Revolutionaries declared, that each stage in their reforms introduced new liberties: but they were liberties for the government, to exert over the citizen rights of ownership that had seldom been known in Christian Europe and had never been asserted so extensively. Once again, we have a remarkable foretaste of the pattern to come.

This brings us to the third totalitarian tendency in the politics of goals: the destruction of the economy, and the elimination from public life of the habit of responsible accounting. The expropriation of the church lands set the pattern for what was to follow. These resources, husbanded over centuries, were squandered almost at once, used first as security for increasingly inflated *assignats*, and finally sold off in the attempt to finance the projects, the bureaucracies, and the wars of Revolution. The *assignat* provided a foretaste of the 'soft currencies' of modern revolutionary states: pieces of paper whose meaning is a dishonoured promise, and whose ultimate purpose is not to facilitate economic transactions, but to exploit them to the limit of their taxable surplus. The rouble and the zloty, like the chits issued under the 'trucking system', are ways not only of paying the labourer for his hours of work, but also of extracting more labour from him through a tax on his subsequent transactions. The same was true of the *assignats*, which were an open mortgage of the entire public capital, including the human capital which was the principal part of it.

By the winter of 1793–4 the economic cost of the Revolution was apparent to everyone: price controls and rationing, queues and black markets, and that slow rotting away of honesty which is the inevitable consequence of an arrangement in which private property is only spasmodically respected, and in which too much is owned by the state. Of course things did not go so far in this direction as they were taken by Lenin and his successors. The idea of an economy *entirely* owned and run by the state had yet to seize the imagination of the power-hungry intellectual. Nevertheless, the decree against *accaparement* (26 July 1793), which dealt out terrible punishments for hoarding, provides an interesting anticipation of the famine-inducing measures of more recent revolutions;[51] while the forced loan of September 1793, combined with the 'General Maximum', were as near as the Revolutionaries—with the means at their disposal—could come to exerting their will over the entire national economy. The result was a destruction of free trade, a re-infoedation of the citizen, and a subversion of the habits of accounting.

This public *gaspillage* is a striking instance of what follows when the dead and the unborn are disenfranchised, as they are by every revolution. Far from being a sentimental indulgence, an irrational break on the use of present funds, the respect for the dead, and for the will of the dead, is part of prudent husbandry. The recognition that goods are held in trust from past to future generations and that rights of ownership are conditional on responsible accounting, is the true source of social saving. The habit of saving is a form of piety, and the destruction of this habit by revolutionary governments lies at the heart of their economic failure, and of their need to live by spoliation.

This brings me to a final interesting parallel between the French and the Russian Revolutions. The Revolution was founded on a principle of 'de-legitimization': no government was to be legitimate unless it conformed to the principle of popular sovereignty. That this was an implied declaration of war on France's neighbours was made clear in a decree of November 1792, offering assistance to all peoples who 'rise against their governments'. The threat was carried into reality in February 1793, with the declaration of war against England. Peace and stability were re-established in Europe only after Wellington's victory at Waterloo: by that time the international order had been entirely discomposed, and untold suffering inflicted on the peoples of Europe.

Leninism, being founded, like the French Revolution, in a universalist ideology, regards no national boundary as legitimate, and declares itself on the side of 'liberation' everywhere. Both states illustrate the need felt by revolutionary governments to impose on their neighbours, and to fill the world with protestations of Potemkin friendship. (For the Revolutionary, Potemkin friendship is far more valuable than real friendship, since real friendship is freely given, whereas Potemkin friendship is controlled.) The dictated friendship which now binds the states of Eastern and Central Europe derives, like the friendship dictated by the Revolutionists to the people of Holland, from the ideology of revolution: from the thinking which removes legitimacy from all actual institutions in the name of an unattainable ideal. The ideology which excuses the monopoly of power therefore also justifies, and indeed requires, its unlimited expansion.

Given these similarities, we may well ask why the French Revolution failed to achieve the sempiternal quality which is so striking a feature of its successor. The explanation, I venture to suggest, lies not in the ends of the Revolutionaries, but in the deficient means available for their realization. Power came too quickly to the Jacobins, and its seizure was not preceded by that patient work of organization to which Lenin devoted so much of his energy. Their 'party-mindedness' was a fragile and fissiparous thing, which did not survive their own personal downfall. The Communist Party was built slowly, first on a foundation of loyalty and discipline, and then on a clear principle of rational self-interest. Once the Bolsheviks took power the party member was to obey the one above him, and control the one below, for the reason that only through the Party could there be privilege or power. The first work of the Party was therefore to destroy all forms of advantage that were not provided by itself. This is the secret of communist longevity. Once in power, the entire ruling élite can be destroyed without damage to the structure, and without the rank-and-file acting upon any principle besides that of 'endarkened self-interest'. The Party is sustained not by plans (which are merely liturgical fictions), but by the very invisible hand which Adam Smith had discerned in the market economy.

Furthermore, the Revolutionaries did not fully grasp the value of front organizations, or of the network of Potemkin institutions which play such an important part in dispelling truth from its central place in social discourse, and putting power and ideology in its place. The success of revolutionary government, and its transition to the stable point of 'graveyard stillness', depend upon the ability to produce a public habit of mendacity. Falsehood must become a way of life; as Havel puts it, people must learn 'to live within the lie'.[52] The Revolutionists went some way in this direction. But they did not surround themselves with the necessary mask (the *manto*, as the Sandinistas call it), and worked always in the knowledge—fatal to their project—that the truth was still perceivable. In the communist state, with its Potemkin courts, Potemkin churches, Potemkin schools, universities and academies, with its Potemkin patriots such as Jaruzelski, and its true patriots such as Walesa, Havel, and Sakharov presented to the people as Potemkin traitors, we find the ideal of revolutionary order: a state in which the question of legitimacy cannot be answered in the negative, for the reason that, lacking a forum, a voice, and a language, it cannot be raised.

The Revolutionists' comparative failure was not entirely their fault. They lacked the technological resources available to their successors: in particular they lacked the complete control over the means of communication, and the technology of surveillance, which have enabled their successors to act rapidly at a distance and to impose their will without delay wherever force is needed. Human progress has overcome the Revolutionists' disability, and there is no longer any reason why a revolution, once successfully established, should thereafter lose power.

I have tried to defend Burke's conservative reaction to the French Revolution; but I am conscious that I have done no more than to identify one spiritual current within that great event. I am conscious, too, that I have said nothing to describe its meaning, and that until I do so, all talk of a conservative 'reaction' must be premature. In conclusion, therefore, I shall offer an interpretation of the revolutionary consciousness, which will, I hope, explain precisely why Burke and his successors have found it so abhorrent.

The actions which have occupied my attention involved a formidable concentration of religious energy. But this energy was not turned towards the transcendental. On the contrary, the Revolution placed its gods on earth, and described them in 'the language of man': liberty, equality, fraternity. Yet what do these idols amount to? The pursuit of them was to destroy every imperfect human value—freedom, justice, and fellowship—which they might otherwise have sanctified. Moreover, they were to threaten not only the religious and moral, but also the aesthetic values of our civilization, mobilizing people behind one of the greatest acts of organized vandalism in the history of mankind.

These abstractions stepped down into the world of men from the sphere of metaphysics and laid waste the patient work of centuries, finding nothing in the merely empirical world that could match their own geometrical perfection. At the same time, the Revolutionaries began to adore their idols, not in spite of, but because of the fact that they filled the world with terror. 'Liberty', since it denoted no achievable goal, came to refer to the purely *negative* principle that all powers on earth are powers of usurpation, and can therefore be destroyed. Likewise, 'equality' referred to no achievable order: it meant neither justice, nor law, nor that 'respect for persons' which was set before us by Kant. It too had a negative application: it was a weapon against privilege, a denial of distinction, and an inspiration to the eye and hand of envy.

Worst of the idols, however, was the third: fraternity. This most potent of abstractions has been the source of socialist dreams from the Revolution to the present day. The General Will of Rousseau, the 'People' of Robespierre, the 'phalanstery' of Fourier, the commune of Marx, the *fascio* of the Italian anarchists, the *groupe en fusion* of Sartre: all express the same contradictory idea, of a free society without institutions, in which people spontaneously group together in life-affirming globules, and from which the dead shell of law, procedure, custom, and authority has fallen away. The aim is for a 'society without obedience', indeed, for a 'unity in disobedience', where conflict, competition, domination, and subservience are all unknown. Each version of the dream is as unreal as the last, and none more unreal than that which has dominated radical socialism in our time—the dream of the great alliance, the 'historic bloc', as Gramsci described it, which brings worker and intellectual together in defiance of established power. Contemplating, Pygmalion-like, the worker of his fantasy, our modern revolutionary is stirred by a passionate love: love for himself, as the architect of this noble

vision. The heroic worker combines in his protean personality the
contradictory attributes of self-affirming liberty and class solidarity;
he is at once the proud individual, answerable to himself alone, and
the submissive unit, joined to his companions in the universal
sympathy of the 'mass'. As with Robespierre's *peuple*, which
can not be *toujours malheureux* and the object of compassion, and
at the same time sovereign and without the need for a condescending
love, so too with the industrial worker. The proletarian of the
Leninist must mirror the striving individualism of the alienated
intellectual; but at the same time he must display the complete
social immersion, the 'class solidarity', from which the intellectual
feels himself so tragically sundered. The worker of the future, like
the 'People' of Robespierre, must be completely free, and at the
same time bound by the consoling solidarity of the oppressed. The
contradictory nature of the idol is the immediate result of its having
stepped from the transcendental into the empirical realm. And yet
the idol is worshipped as such, in full consciousness of its
impossibility. This transcendental unity of the 'people', this
unmediated, un-negotiated bond in which intellectual and worker
are mystically united and dissolved, flesh of each other's flesh, is
described precisely by Sartre as 'a concrete totalization continually
de-totalized, contradictory and problematic, never closed back on
itself, never completed, yet nevertheless one single experience'.[54]
And in pursuit of this acknowledged contradiction men such as
Sartre are prepared to pull down all actual institutions, all actual
relations between people, all that is merely negotiated, compromised,
and half-convinced. As with the Revolutionists, the *real* reference to
the transcendental, which is there in the humble forms of ordinary
love, is cancelled, on behalf of an earthly idol whose sole reality is
to destroy human relations, by measuring them against a standard
which they cannot attain.

We are confronted by an astonishing fact—one that we should
treat with all due solemnity, since it touches on the meaning of our
lives. Liberty, equality, and fraternity become the objects of
religious zeal only to destroy freedom, justice, and fellowship. Their
earthly reality is precisely Nothing, and the spirit of nihilism blows
through them with a force that is all the more mysterious in that we
the worshippers provide it.

Let us return for a moment to the religion against which the
Revolutionaries rebelled, and the fundamental doctrine which the

deists and humanists had already cast aside as unfit for human Reason. God, says the Christian, has three natures, and we come to Him by three separate paths: when we worship Him as transcendental law-giver; when we encounter Him incarnate; and when the Holy Spirit moves in and around us in its work of peace. To express the thought in other, and more mitigated, terms: our worship is owed to something that is not of this world, and whose law-giving capacity is inseparable from its transcendence. But this does not mean that the world is *bereft* of God, or that we can find Him nowhere in our experience. On the contrary, sanctity comes to us in two modalities; and not to respond to its imperative is to live incompletely and meaninglessly.

The first modality lies in the incarnate person: the animal in whom the light of reason shines, and who looks at us from eyes which tell of freedom. Only now and then—in love, hatred, and desire—does the reality of this incarnation overwhelm and trouble us.[55] But the underlying sense of it is there in all respect, and all affection. It is this which forbids us to treat another's life and freedom as expendable, or to weigh his survival in the balance of our own individual profit. Our calculations stop short at the threshold of the other, precisely because his flesh is sanctified. The first effect of the revolutionary mentality is to undo this experience of the sacred. Once the idols have been brought to earth, individual freedom, and the flesh which harbours it, become *property*. They can be placed in the balance of calculation, and discarded 'for the public good'. Revolution leads to murder, for the simple reason that it rids the world of the experience upon which the refusal to murder depends.

The second modality of the sacred lies in counsel, association, and institution-building. In countless ways men combine in a spirit of conciliation, willing to renounce even their dearest ambitions for the sake of agreement with their fellows. In the true council, men are prepared to accept a corporate decision which corresponds with nothing that they previously desired, for the reason that the council itself is vested with authority. The spirit of co-operation may issue in decisions which coincide with the will of no participant: and this corporate will in turn implies a corporate liability, and a corporate right and wrong. In such circumstances the law speaks sometimes of a trust, sometimes of a corporate person, sometimes of an 'unincorporated association'—and through each concept endeavours to give reality to a will, and a responsibility, that attaches to no individual man. It thereby glosses a deeper moral concept, known to Quakers as 'the sense of the meeting' and to the rest of us as 'we'.

This 'we' bears a countenance: it has authority, right, responsibility, and freedom. We gladly submit to it, and embody its personality in offices, insignia, and ceremonies. For modern man, of course, the ceremonial aspect of membership is more muted than it was—certainly more muted than in the guilds immortalized in *Die Meistersinger* (the only great drama which has a corporate person as its central character). Nevertheless, the ceremony of membership exists, and especially in that haven of free association which is the United States of America. People *celebrate* their membership, just as adolescents celebrated once their transition to the adult world. In such ways, the spirit of counsel surrounds and transforms our lives, enriches the individual and offers him not only an experience of community, but a sense of public validity. From our respect for the 'small platoon', far greater emotions rise in us: our sense of duty is spread more widely than the circle which inspired it, to embrace other places and other times. We come at last to respect the dead and the unborn; and this is the experience upon which free and stable government is founded.

The process of politics thrives, I suggest, only where the claims and duties of the corporation are recognized. The most striking fact about the revolutionary is that, bowing to the idol of a 'General Will' or some other abstract 'fraternity' which knows no mediation, no negotiation, and no half-heartedness, he finds himself at once suspicious of real associations. With the advent of revolution the true work of institution-building comes to an end; so too does charity; so too does every other form of combination which lies outside the 'People's' or the Party's control. There results a society devoid of counsel, in which (as Cochin recognized)[56] decisions have all the impersonality of a machine. In this respect too, revolution turns against the world: it leads to the destruction of corporate persons, just as it leads to the murder of individuals, since it has abolished the experience of sanctity which conditions our respect for them.

To put the point in a nutshell: the revolutionary transfers his worship to the world, and so destroys the two experiences of God that are actually contained in it. It is part of the 'génie du

Christianisme' to have summarized these experiences in the doctrines of the incarnate God and the Holy Spirit. And it is a further instance of its *génie* to have recognized the existence of the Spirit as a person, and so to have founded a personal and independent church. But the language of Christianity is not imposed on us. In more secular idiom: the experience of authority (and therefore the impulse to obedience) comes to us in three related forms: the authority of the moral law, whose foundation is transcendental; the authority of incarnate freedom; and the authority of counsel. If I use the Christian language it is because it identifies more accurately the points at which our lives are consecrated, and which call forth the revolutionary sacrilege.

Moreover, in judging the revolutions of Europe, it is to the religion of Europe that we should turn. The revolution is, I believe, a supreme act of Christian disobedience. Rather than worship a transcendental God, the revolutionary brings Him to earth, and reshapes Him in the form of an ideal community. At once the two other forms of obedience are cancelled, and God's face in the world is overcast and imperceivable. The worship of the idol becomes a worship of nothing—but it is a potent nothingness, which threatens everything real. It is the very same nothingness which, captured in a handkerchief, caused Othello to destroy the sacred thing which God had given him—and all for Nothing. As to what, or who, this Nothing consists in, the question answers itself.

(*The author is grateful to the Social Philosophy and Policy Center of Bowling Green State University, Ohio, for the leisure necessary to work on this paper.*)

NOTES

[1] Richard Cobb's views have been marvellously and meanderingly expressed in a variety of works, of which *The Police and the People: French Popular Protest 1789–1820* (London, 1970) and *Les Armées révolutionnaires, instruments de la Terreur dans les départements* (2 vols., Paris and the Hague, 1961 and 1963) have been particularly influential. More important, from the interpretative point of view, however, are the essays in *Reactions to the French Revolution* (London, 1972) and *A Second Identity* (London, 1969).

[2] Hippolyte Taine, *Les Origines de la France contemporaine* (Paris, 1875). The relevant parts were translated by John Durand as *The French Revolution* (New York, 1878; repr. Gloucester, Mass., 1962).

[3] Edmund Burke, *Reflections on the Revolution in France*, in *Works*, vol. 3 (Boston, Mass., Little, Brown and Co., 1865).

[4] Alexis de Tocqueville, *L'Ancien régime et la Révolution* (Paris, 1877).

[5] François Furet, *Penser la Révolution française* (Paris, 1978; rev. ed. 1983).

[6] Henry Thomas Buckle, *History of Civilization in England* (London, 1861), i. 425–33: a passage written with the author's usual verve and conviction.

[7] The point here is again also made by Burke, and is reaffirmed in a different context by Hannah Arendt who, taking her cue from Tocqueville, argues that antisemitism reached its climax in Europe when Jews had lost their influence and power. See *The Origins of Totalitarianism* (New York, 1969), p. 4. Much more important, however, is Burke's observation: that the revolutionary hates something which he himself *constructs*, something which is a 'work of art' more than a reality (op. cit. 415). Real power in the hands of the aristocrats would be as much an obstacle to revolutionary emotions as would real power in the hands of the mythologized 'bourgeoisie' of more recent revolutions.

[8] René Sédillot, *Le Coût de la Révolution française* (Paris, 1987).

[9] Alfred Cobban, 'The Myth of the French Revolution' in *Aspects of the French Revolution* (New York, 1968), pp. 90–111. See also Colin Lucas, 'Nobles, Bourgeois and the Origins of the French Revolution', *Past and Present*, 60 (Aug. 1973), repr. in Douglas Johnson, ed., *French Society and the Revolution* (Cambridge, 1976).

[10] See the monumental study by Augustin Cochin, *Les Sociétés de pensée et la Révolution en Bretagne* (Paris, 1925).

[11] Daniel Mornet, *Les Origines intellectuelles de la Révolution française (1715–1787)* (Paris, 1944), p. 393.

[12] Tocqueville, op. cit. 208 and 303.

[13] V. I. Lenin, 'One Step Forward, Two Steps Back', in *Selected Works* (Moscow, 1963) p. 387. I have amended the translation. Lenin goes on interestingly to identify 'opportunism' with 'Girondism', and, in blocks of soulless Newspeak, to offer precisely the parallel between the two Revolutions that I wish to develop. Elsewhere Lenin compares the Bolsheviks with 'the Jacobins of 1793'. See 'Enemies of the People', *Pravda* (June 1917), in R. C. Tucker, ed., *The Lenin Anthology* (New York, 1975), p. 305.

[14] Tocqueville, op. cit. 7.

[15] Burke, op. cit., especially pp. 347 ff.

[16] L'abbé Sieyès, *Qu'est-ce que le Tiers Etat?* (Paris, 1789), translated as E. Sieyès, *What is the Third Estate?*, trans. M. Blondel, ed. S. E. Finer, introduction by Peter Campbell (London, 1963), pp. 124, 128.

[17] Cobban, 'The Enlightenment and the French Revolution' in *Aspects of the French Revolution*, p. 24.

[18] Jules Michelet, *History of the French Revolution*, trans. Charles Cocks (Chicago, 1967), p. 444. Michelet's book is one of the first examples of a literary genre which became standard after the Russian Revolution: a panegyric, written half in Newspeak, half in a fairy-tale pastiche, in which deeds of heroism and fantastic protestations of commitment forge in unison the 'new society'.

[19] 'Civil Marriage' is as old as Roman Law, and probably already existed before the Twelve Tables; nevertheless it was not designed as a replacement for the sacred ceremonies, but only as a supplement, to cure deficiencies and confer legitimacy, in the absence of *confarreatio*. See Theodor Mommsen, *The History of Rome*, trans. W. P. Dickson (New York, 1868), i. 129–30.

[20] See Jean Robiquet, *Daily Life in the French Revolution*, trans. James Kirkup (London, 1964), ch. 9.

[21] See, for example, *Reactions to the French Revolution*, pp. 5 f. and 128.

[22] J.-J. Rousseau, *Le Contrat Social*, book 2, ch. 4, note.

[23] Hannah Arendt, *On Revolution* (New York, 1963), p. 69.

[24] Georg Lukács, *History and Class Consciousness, Studies in Marxist Dialectics*, trans. R. Livingstone (London 1971), p. 74.

[25] Furet, *Penser la Révolution française*, p. 76. Things have improved on the Left since the discovery that animals too are an oppressed class. Being dumb by nature, no animal can 'betray' the cause of his own liberation, not even those animals whose lives depend upon our eating them.

[26] This point has been brought home by a number of writers, Kolakowski, Havel, and Zinoviev perhaps being the most important.

[27] Françoise Thom, *La Langue de bois* (Paris, 1987).

[28] See n. 13 above.

[29] F.-A. Aulard, *La Société des Jacobins, recueil de documents* (Paris, 1897).

[30] Petr Fidelius (pseud.), *Jazyk a moc* ('Language and Power') (Munich, 1983). Fidelius's book has been translated by Erika Abrams as *L'Esprit post-totalitaire*, (Paris, 1985). See also the same author's 'Totalitarian Language', *Salisbury Review*, 2, 2 (1984), 33–5.

[31] But see further the analysis of Newspeak in Thom, op. cit.

[32] Quoted in James Logan Godfrey, 'Revolutionary Justice', *The James Sprunt Studies in History and Political Science*, xxxiii, 71.

[33] Speech of 8 Ventôse (26 Feb. 1894), to be found in Buchez and Roux, *Histoire parlementaire de la Révolution française* (Paris 1834–1838), xxxi, 300 (my translation).

[34] Speech of 25 Jan. 1792 to the Jacobins. Maximilien Robespierre, *Œuvres* (Paris, n.d.), iii. 142, 'Troisième discours de Maximilien Robespierre sur la guerre'.

[35] Cochin, op. cit., vol. i.

[36] That the Revolutionary armies aimed to commit, and partly succeeded in committing, genocide against the rebellious people of La Vendée is clear from research summarized in Sédillot, op. cit. 24 f.

[37] Albert Mathiez, *La Vie chère et le mouvement social sous la Terreur* (Paris, 1927).

[38] Donald Greer, *The Incidence of the Terror during the French Revolution* (Cambridge, Mass., 1935).

[39] Ibid. 96 f.

[40] As in the decree of 16 Dec. 1793.

[41] Paul Mautouchet, *Le Gouvernement révolutionnaire* (Paris, 1912), pp. 158–71.

[42] See my '*Rechtsgefühl* and the Rule of Law' in J. C. Nyíri and Barry Smith, eds., *Practical Knowledge: Outline of a Theory of Traditions and Skills* (London, 1988), pp. 61–89.

[43] Louis Althusser, *Lenin and Philosophy and Other Essays*, trans. Ben Brewster (London, 1971), p. 131. See my *Thinkers of the New Left* (London, 1985), ch. 9.

[44] Michel Foucault, *Power/Knowledge: Selected Interviews and Other Writings 1972–77*, ed. Colin Gordon (Brighton, 1980), p. 16.

[45] Tocqueville, op. cit. 296–7. Tocqueville adds that, in the French Revolution, it was not the process of justice, but the administrative *apparatus* that remained intact.

[46] Tocqueville, op. cit. 280–1.

[47] See Timothy Ware, *The Orthodox Church* (Harmondsworth, 1963).

[48] Tocqueville, op. cit. 101–5.

[49] Sédillot, op cit. 89–93.

[50] Saint-Just's education system is discussed in Robiquet, op. cit. 83. Precisely similar proposals were put forward in the Soviet Union in 1918, with Zlata Lilina, director of education in Petrograd, demanding the 'nationalization' of all children. See Mikhail Heller and Aleksandr M. Nekrich, *Utopia in Power* (New York, 1986), p. 61.

[51] See Robert Conquest, *The Harvest of Sorrow* (Oxford, 1986), and Myron Dolot, *Execution by Hunger* (New York, 1985).

[52] Václav Havel, 'The Power of the Powerless' in *Václav Havel, Or Living in Truth*, ed. Jan Vladislav (London, 1987), p. 45.

[53] That this judgement is deserved is conclusively shown by Sédillot, op. cit. 117–47. And that the Revolution required the desecration of so many lovely things says something important about both the sacred and the beautiful.

[54] J.-P. Sartre, *Between Existentialism and Marxism*, trans. J. Matthews (London, 1974; reissued 1983), p. 109. I discuss Sartre's revolutionary mentality in *Thinkers of the New Left*, ch. 15.

[55] I have described this process in *Sexual Desire* (London, 1986).

[56] Cochin, op. cit., i. 17–18.

A Note on Hungary

The Hungarian Government has recently made an effort to legalize some charitable activities. SZETA, the charity referred to on p. 209, has now been officially recognized.

NOTES ON CONTRIBUTORS
AND EDITORS

LORD BELOFF, F.B.A., F.R.Hist.Soc., was formerly Gladstone Professor of Government and Public Administration in the University of Oxford; he is now Emeritus Professor and Emeritus Fellow of All Souls College. His books include *The Foreign Policy of Soviet Russia: 1929–1941, The Age of Absolutism: 1660–1815, Imperial Sunset,* and *Wars and Warfare.* His edition of the *Federalist* was published in 1948, with a revised edition in 1988. He was the British editor of the multi-volume work, published in Milan between 1960 and 1967, *L'Europe du XIXᵉ et XXᵉ siècle.* He holds an honorary doctorate from the University of Aix-Marseille III.

JOHN CLIVE received his Ph.D. in history from Harvard in 1952, and, except for four years at the University of Chicago (1960–4), has been teaching there since. He became William R. Kenan, Jr. Professor of History and Literature in 1978. His *Scotch Reviewers,* a history of the early years of the *Edinburgh Review,* appeared in 1957. In 1973 he published *Macaulay: The Shaping of the Historian,* which won the National Book Award in History in 1974 and the Robert Livingston Schuyler Prize of the American Historical Association in 1976. In 1989 Alfred A. Knopf will publish a selection of his historiographical essays, under the title *Not By Fact Alone: Essays on the Writing and Reading of History.*

CERI CROSSLEY is Senior Lecturer in French at the University of Birmingham. He is the author of *Edgar Quinet (1803–1875): A Study in Romantic Thought,* of *Alfred de Musset: 'Lorenzaccio',* and of articles on intellectual history and comparative literature. In 1988 he and Ian Small published a collection of essays by various hands entitled *Studies in Anglo-French Cultural Relations.*

CLIVE EMSLEY is Reader in History at the Open University. He was educated at the University of York and at Peterhouse, Cambridge. He has been Visiting Professor at the University of Paris VIII (Saint-Denis/ Vincennes) and at the University of Calgary, Canada. His initial research was concerned with the machinery and maintenance of public order in England during the period of the French Revolution; he is now chiefly concerned with questions of crime and policing in England and France since the late eighteenth century. His publications include *British Society and the French Wars: 1792–1815, Policing and its Context: 1750–1870,* and *Crime and Society in England: 1750–1900.*

JOSEPHINE GUY is a doctoral student in the English Department in the University of Birmingham. Her research is into the sociology of literary movements in the last half of the nineteenth century.

JOHN HARRIS is Professor of Economic History in the University of Birmingham. He has written widely on economic and technological relations between Britain and France in the eighteenth and nineteenth centuries.

DAVID LODGE is Honorary Professor of Modern English Literature in the University of Birmingham, where he taught from 1960 to 1987. He is now a full-time writer. His critical publications include *Language of Fiction* (1966), *The Modes of Modern Writing* (1977), and *Working with Structuralism* (1981). He is also the author of several novels, including *Changing Places* (1975), *Small World* (1984), and, most recently, *Nice Work* (1988).

BRIAN RIGBY is Lecturer in French at the University of Warwick. He was educated at New College, Oxford, where he read French and German and did postgraduate work in comparative literature in French and English. His main research area is the study of the intellectual and cultural links between France and England in the late eighteenth and early nineteenth centuries. He has published on such figures as Volney, Stendhal, Hazlitt, Constant, and Hugo. He also works in the field of modern French cultural studies, in which he has published on intellectuals, and popular and mass culture.

ROGER SCRUTON is Professor of Aesthetics at Birkbeck College in the University of London. He was educated at High Wycombe Royal Grammar School and Jesus College, Cambridge. He is a member of the Inner Temple and editor of the *Salisbury Review*. He has published widely on philosophy, literature, and the arts. His books include *Art and Imagination*, *The Aesthetics of Architecture*, *The Meaning of Conservatism*, *Fortnight's Anger*, *A Dictionary of Political Thought*, *Sexual Desire*, and *A Land Held Hostage: Lebanon and the West*. He is currently finishing a book of stories.

IAN SMALL is Senior Lecturer in English at the University of Birmingham. His previous publications include *The Aesthetes* and editions of Walter Pater's *Marius The Epicurean* and Oscar Wilde's society dramas.

GEORGE WOODCOCK is Emeritus Professor in the University of British Columbia. He was editor of *Now* in London from 1940 to 1947. He returned to his native Canada in 1949 and taught English at the University of Washington and English and Asian Studies at the University of British Columbia. He edited *Canadian Literature*, which he founded, from 1959 to 1977. His many books include *Anarchism*, *The Crystal Spirit: A Study of George Orwell*, *Gandhi*, *Faces of India*, *The British in the Far East*,

Who Killed the British Empire?, *Thomas Merton: Monk and Poet*, *William Godwin*, and *Pierre-Joseph Proudhon*. This year he will be publishing *A Social History of Canada* and *Caves in the Desert*, an account of travels in China.